Paradox and Representation

Nakagami Kenji, 1986.
Photographed by Noriko Shibuya.

Paradox and Representation

*Silenced Voices in the
Narratives of
Nakagami Kenji*

MACHIKO ISHIKAWA

CORNELL EAST ASIA SERIES
an imprint of
Cornell University Press
Ithaca and London

This publication was made possible by a generous subvention from the Surugadai University.

First published 2020 by Cornell University Press

Library of Congress Cataloging-in-Publication Data
Names: Ishikawa, Machiko, 1978– author.
Title: Paradox and representation : silenced voices in the narratives of Nakagami Kenji / Machiko Ishikawa.
Description: Ithaca, New York : East Asia Program, Cornell University, [2019] | Series: Cornell East Asia series ; number 198 | Includes bibliographical references and index. |
Identifiers: LCCN 2019053226 (print) | LCCN 2019053227 (ebook) | ISBN 9781501751943 (hardcover) | ISBN 9781501751950 (ebook) | ISBN 9781501751967 (pdf)
Subjects: LCSH: Nakagami, Kenji—Criticism and interpretation. | Buraku people in literature.
Classification: LCC PL857.A3683 Z65 2019 (print) | LCC PL857.A3683 (ebook) | DDC 895.63/5—dc23
LC record available at https://lccn.loc.gov/2019053226
LC ebook record available at https://lccn.loc.gov/2019053227

Cover: Photographs by Kōndo Manabu
Cover design: Matsuda Yōichi

Number 198 in the Cornell East Asia Series

Contents

Acknowledgments

I have many people to thank for the publication of this book. Barbara Hartley, my doctoral supervisor, had a strong and inspirational belief in the importance of my work and managed to help me make something positive from difficult times. Pam Allen first introduced me to the work of Gayatri Chakravorty Spivak. I thank Mai Shaikhanuar-Cota, Managing Editor of Cornell East Asia Series, for her great support through this publication process. In Australia, I had ongoing support from staff at the University of Tasmania, especially Hashimoto Yōji and Suganuma Katsuhiko, who were always available for guidance and advice. Tomoko Aoyama, Maria Flutsch, and Mats Karlsson provided incisive advice and feedback on my work; Mayumi Shinozaki provided invaluable assistance during my research time at the National Library of Australia. Aneita McGregor was unstinting in her generosity in the process of proofreading this book. I received ongoing assistance from people in Japan. Kiwa Kyō, Nakagami Nori, Karatani Kōjin, Tsujimoto Yūichi, Matsumoto Iwao, Takazawa Shūji, and Morimoto Yūji honored me during my research in Shingū by sharing their thoughts and memories of Nakagami Kenji. Watanabe Naomi kindly acted as my supervisor during my research at Waseda University as a Japan Foundation Fellow. It was this opportunity and the generosity of the Japan Foundation that permitted me to conduct in-depth research in Japan into my thesis topic. Shimamura Teru and Shimamura Yukie extended hospitality to myself and my daughter during our stay in Sangenjaya. Kobayashi Fukuko of Waseda University and Hidaka Shōji and Murai Mayako of Kanagawa University permitted me to attend workshops that they conducted. Kuribayashi Tsuyoshi and Kuribayashi Michiko, Konishi Yōko, and Nakamori Tsuneo warmly welcomed my visit to the 2014 Fire Festival in Shingū. Osaka Eiko, Jenny Scott, Kawasaki Yōko, Nishino Ryōta, Okada Tōru, and Maruyama Tetsurō generously gave their time in Tokyo. Shibuya Noriko kindly provided one of her photos of Nakagami to be found on page ii of this book. I also thank Matsuda Yōichi for his work on the artistic design of this book and Kondō Manabu whose photograph is on the book's front cover. My thanks also go to members of Ishinokai—Ishii Yasushirō, Kamijō Satoshi, Satō Yasutomo and Satō Megumi, Suzuki Kaori, Matsumoto Kai, Hori Maiko, Arakawa Kazushige—and the scholars who support our activities—Gōda Hideyuki, Tamura Satoko, and Anne McKnight. Each shared a passion for literature during meetings at Nihon University and at Buoy in Shinjuku's Golden Gai. Others who offered great support include Donald, Mikako, Mei, Mia, Motoko, Steve, Emerald, Masa, Angela, Kiyomi, Hitomi, Lina, Terry, Sally, Alex, Rie, Grant, Aaron, Hide, and Craig. I thank my parents, Iwata Shigeru and Iwata Reiko; my uncle and aunt, Fujii Tagiru and Fujii Yūko; and my brother Kōichi and his family. They have always believed in me and wished for my success. I owe my deepest gratitude to my daughter, Mimori, for her limitless patience and love. Without the assistance of all the people mentioned here, this book would never have been completed.

Above all, I give my deepest thanks to Nakagami Kenji, whose narratives have graced my life.

References

Part of chapter 1 includes a largely edited version of a discussion published as "Exclusionism and the Burakumin: Literary Movement, Legislative Countermeasures and the Sayama Incident," *Cultural and Social Division in Contemporary Japan: Rethinking Discourses of Inclusion and Exclusion* (2019): 165–83.

Part of chapter 2 includes a largely reworked version of a discussion published as an online article entitled "Writing the Sense of Loss in the Inner Self: A Narrative of Nakagami Kenji and Nagayama Norio in Late 1960s Tokyo," *Proceedings of the 18th Conference of the Japanese Studies Association of Australia* (2014).

The first section of chapter 3 includes a largely edited version of a discussion published as "Nakagami Kenji's 'Writing Back to the Centre' through the Subaltern Narrative: Reading the Hidden Outcast Voice in 'Misaki' and Karekinada," *New Voice* 5 (2011): 1–24

The first section of chapter 5 is a reworked version of material that appeared as "Reading Nakagami Kenji's Subaltern Burakumin Narratives through the Perspective of the Omina (Old Woman)," *Japan Studies Association Journal* 11 (2013): 158–78.

Matters of Technical Presentation

According to convention in Japan and Korea, names are presented with surname first and given name after. Exceptions are made in the case of writers who have written and published in English, such as Yumiko Iida. After the first reference, I refer to writers in the manner that is the common practice in the literature. While this is generally by using the family name, in some cases a writer is conventionally known in Japanese literary discourse by her or his given name. Shimazaki Tōson, for example, is referred to as Tōson.

Multiple brief quotations from the same source within a single paragraph are cited at the point of final reference within the paragraph. Modified words or expressions within a quote appear in square brackets. All translations of Japanese-language material are my own, unless otherwise cited. I note modifications of existing published English translations.

Introduction

This book provides a reading of selected works by Nakagami Kenji (1946–1992) to investigate how he represented the voices of the *mukoku*, the socially silenced, in Japan. Born in 1946 in Kasuga, a precinct in the city of Shingū in Wakayama prefecture, Nakagami was the only Burakumin or Japanese "outcaste"[1] writer to win the prestigious Akutagawa Literary Prize, and the first postwar-born writer to do so.[2] Set across a vast forest far south of Kyoto on the eastern coast of the Kii Peninsula at the mouth of the Kumano River, Shingū is the largest center in the region known as Kishū Kumano, an area that encompasses Wakayama prefecture and sections of Mie prefecture.[3] Nakagami's birthplace, Kasuga, was one of Shingū's *hisabetsu buraku* (Burakumin districts; literally, discriminated communities/hamlets). Accordingly, his narratives often depict the otherness of Kishu Kumano, long regarded as *komoriku* (hidden country) on the periphery of Japan. Although many of Nakagami's narratives undoubtedly feature accounts of life in the *hisabetsu buraku*, he had the broader objective of depicting various kinds of people—including ethnic minorities, illegitimate children, migrant workers, dis-

---

1. The term *outcaste* is commonly used in English-language scholarship for Burakumin, or Buraku people. It is not used in Japanese discourse. The term should not be associated with the better-known Indian *Dalit*. For further detail, see Amos 2011, 29–32.

2. In 2019, the population of Shingū was approximately 29,000. See city of Shingū official website (*Wakayama ken Shingū shi*), https://www.city.shingu.lg.jp /forms/top/top.aspx/ (accessed March 19, 2019).

3. The Kii Peninsula (which is also called by its traditional name, Kishū) consists of Wakayama prefecture, Mie prefecture, and Nara prefecture.

abled people, traumatized people, the aged, and sex workers—who
have been oppressed by the exclusionary systems of hegemonic
thought and the social structures created by these systems in Japan.
To Nakagami, these systems deny the principle and the lived experience of "difference."

What does it mean to read the literature of Nakagami Kenji?
Some are drawn to the legends of wandering Kumano nobles that
are frequently described in Nakagami's narratives. Many recognize
the cyclic repetition of both Japanese and Western ancient myths,
and the Freudian psychoanalytic metanarrative, that runs through
the saga of the son's desire to violate taboos such as patricide, fratricide, and incest. Some literary circles admire how Nakagami's
1976 prize-winning narrative, "Misaki" ("The Cape"), brought new
vitality to the traditional Japanese literary world, while others emphasize the writer's role as the last novelist to emerge from that
tradition. For those interested in Burakumin issues, reading Nakagami is to read the experience of this outcaste community. There
are also readers who are enthralled by the vigor of the rhythm and
"pulse"[4] that echoes from the depths of Nakagami's language, lik-
ening reading his texts to listening to a John Coltrane jazz performance[5] or an Anton Bruckner symphony.[6] The brief obituary for
Nakagami published in *Time* magazine in August 1992 stated that
"Nakagami Kenji, died aged 46, is a novelist known for his star-
tlingly sensual prose about Japan's social outcaste."[7] I agree with
that statement wholeheartedly, as did literary critic Asada Akira (b.
1957) who said that this was the obituary that gave the most "fitting
account" of Nakagami and his contribution as a novelist.[8]

It is now more than a quarter of a century since Nakagami died
from kidney cancer. At that time, I was a college student in Japan
and I recall that few Nakagami works could be found on the shelves

---

4. Nakazawa 1995, 1.

5. Ono 1985, 80–83.

6. Karatani and Kawamura 1996, 160–61.

7. Obituary of Nakagami in *Time* (August 1992), cited in Asada 1996, 23.

8. Asada 1996, 23.

of bookstores in suburban Nagoya, where I lived. According to critic and Nakagami's longtime friend Karatani Kōjin (b. 1941), this was also the case in bookshops in Tokyo and even in the public library in Shingū, the writer's hometown.[9] Certainly Nakagami's books have never enjoyed the popularity of the works of Murakami Haruki (b. 1949), for example. As a student, I found Nakagami's material quite difficult to read. Although his language did not always permit an inexperienced reader to indulge in the pleasures of his narrative world, the greeting given by the Burakumin women who featured in his narratives, "Ine, tsurai nē" (Things are hard, aren't they, sister?),[10] embedded itself in my heart. I often felt those words were my own during the more than two decades that passed since I first read Nakagami, so I decided to read his work once again. As the quote indicates, and as will become apparent in the second half of the book, the women's voices in Nakagami's narratives left a powerful impression. While Nakagami is often read as a masculinist writer, with significant critical attention given to his male characters, I wish to expand this interpretation by profiling the voices of a number of previously overlooked women in his texts.

Following Nakagami's death, Karatani, with fellow scholars Asada, Yomota Inuhiko, and Watanabe Naomi, compiled the writer's material into the fifteen-volume *Nakagami Kenji zenshū* (The complete works of Nakagami Kenji, 1995–1996; abbreviated as NKZ). At the same time, these four were instrumental in organizing and hosting a series of round-table discussions in literary journals, popular magazines, conferences, and symposiums. Particularly significant was their participation in the so-called Kumano University, an annual three-day gathering in Shingū originally founded in 1990 by Nakagami as a local cultural event. This gathering attracted many young readers, journalists, artists, scholars, and writers, including Mobu Norio (b. 1970) and Enjō Tō (b. 1972), Akutagawa

---

9. Hasumi, Watanabe, Asada, and Karatani 1994, 18.
10. NKZ 2:242.

Prize winners in 2004 and 2011, respectively. While noting the importance of this "Nakagami boom"[11] in drawing attention to the writer's work, Livia Monnet criticizes the discourse of male scholars who promoted the boom as the masculinist canonization of Nakagami's literature. While I support Monnet's position and later discuss the details of her argument, I also wish to acknowledge that the activities of these *zenshū* editors contributed enormously to the confirmation of Nakagami's position in the genealogy of modern Japanese literature. By 1999, however, Nakagami's complete works had been published, and Karatani observed that as chief editor of the collection, his "mission was complete."[12] Once the complete works appeared, Karatani and his coeditors became less involved in Kumano University and the Nakagami boom gradually came to an end.

Since the early 2010s, Nakagami's narratives have received renewed attention through the publication of revised anthologies, e-books, and through a number of stage and film adaptations. The most significant difference between the previous Nakagami boom and today's trend is the shift in attention from the male characters, who were the focus of much previous commentary, to the women who feature in these narratives. The novel *Nichirin no tsubasa* (*Wings of the sun*, 1984), which features seven aged Burakumin women and their wanderings around Japan after dismantlement of their *hisabetsu buraku* homeland, was adapted as a stage performance by contemporary visual artist Yanagi Miwa (b. 1967). *Keibetsu* (*Scorn*, 1992), which depicts the experiences of a woman stripper, and *Sen'nen no yuraku* (*A thousand years of pleasure*, 1982), which features the aged Burakumin woman Oryū no oba (Aunt Ryū) and her inner voice narrating the tragedy of her marginalized community, were made into films in 2011 and 2012, respectively.[13] Nakagami's depiction of

---

11. Monnet 1996a, 15.

12. Karatani 2000, 7.

13. See *Keibetsu* 2011 and *Sen'nen no yuraku* 2012.

Oryū no oba as the *kataribe* (storyteller) of her *hisabetsu buraku* has been extensively discussed by literary commentators and scholars. In 2015, a box of audiotapes on which Nakagami recorded interviews with elderly Burakumin women who lived in Kasuga was discovered by his daughter, Nakagami Nori (b. 1971), who is also a writer. Based on these tapes, Japan's public broadcaster, NHK, produced a documentary film, televised in 2016, titled *Roji no koe chichi no koe: Nakagami Kenji o sagashite* (*Voice from the roji, voice of my father: In search of Nakagami Kenji*). As profiled in the title of Eve Zimmerman's insightful study of Nakagami's work, *Out of the Alleyway*, the term *roji*, often translated as "alley," is the expression Nakagami used to refer to his *hisabetsu buraku* homeland.

In a panel discussion at the 2017 Cultural Typhoon international cultural studies conference, held at Waseda University in Tokyo, these tapes were the subject of a presentation by one of the directors of the NHK documentary, Okada Tōru. Okada explained that intonation and dialect, in addition to reluctance and reticence on the part of the speakers, made the recordings of the women's voices rather unclear. He nonetheless noted that as he listened to these aged women's recollections of their poverty; ill health; harsh working conditions as *jokō* (factory women), *jochū* (maids), or *jorō* (prostitutes); being sold by their parent(s) to a brothel; and their general impression of life as Burakumin women, he was struck by how their stories resonated with the lives of the women depicted in Nakagami's novels.[14] These women's stories were about those things that "people do not openly talk about, the things that they refuse to talk about to outsiders," to borrow an expression from Nakagami's travel journal, *Kishū: Ki no kuni ne no kuni monogatari* (*Kishū: A tale of the country of trees, the country of roots*, 1978, hereafter *Kishū*).[15]

Okada further acknowledged that involvement in the documentary was probably very difficult for some participants, given that the

---

14. Okada 2017.
15. *Kishū* appears in NKZ 14:481.

film circulated information about both the people and the area in which they reside in a Burakumin context.[16] As further discussed below, many people remain silent about their Burakumin identity to avoid discrimination. Okada felt that the cooperation of the people of Kasuga and their willingness to be interviewed during the production process was a function of their great respect for Nakagami.[17] For them, Nakagami was the sole writer who had excavated the hidden voices of their mothers and sisters and unflinchingly inscribed them into his narratives. This ability to represent the voices of silenced people is the subject of this book.

Aim of This Book

How does a writer represent the voice of the voiceless? This is the primary question in my reading of the literature of Nakagami Kenji. My project explores his representation of the voices of voiceless (*mukoku*) people who are socially oppressed by mainstream hegemonic structures in Japan. Although Nakagami achieved prominence as a writer of Burakumin narratives, his representations of the marginalized include ethnic minorities, people with disabilities, illiterate people, the poverty-stricken, the aged, and sex workers. Notwithstanding his privileged position as a writer, Nakagami was conscious that the silenced voice he sought to "hear" and "represent" had been pushed beyond the margins and prevented by oppressive social structures from ever being heard. This contradiction, which I refer to as the paradox of representing the silenced voice, is the theme of the book. To understand this paradox, I draw on the work of the Indian American scholar Gayatri Chakravorty Spivak (b. 1942), who has theorized the "(im)possibility" of representing the voice of "subalterns," people who are oppressed at multiple levels by ideologies such as imperialism, patriarchy, and heteronormativity.

---

16. Okada 2017.
17. Okada 2017.

Arguing that the Burakumin, especially women, and other oppressed people depicted in Nakagami's narratives are Japan's "subaltern," I analyze Nakagami's writing through the framework of Spivak's theory. In the discourse used by Spivak, these subaltern people are often "foreclosed," a word used to indicate the silencing of those without power. While there is a large body of Japanese-language Nakagami scholarship and a growing body in English, there is no other study that reads this writer through Spivak's groundbreaking ideas. It is important here to emphasize that this is not an attempt to situate my project in the field of postcolonial studies. Rather, I appropriate aspects of that theoretical paradigm to inform my reading of Nakagami's work.

In her work, Spivak seeks to reveal and transcend the complicity of the West (or the North, to borrow from Italian theorist Antonio Gramsci [1891–1937]) in the suppression of the marginalized in the non-West (Gramsci's South). I argue that Nakagami similarly seeks to interrogate the relationship between mainstream hegemonic structures and the marginalized in Japan. In other words, his narratives have a strong geopolitical perspective in that they reveal the "otherness" of his homeland, Kumano, which the writer identifies as Japan's marginalized "South." As will be discussed in greater detail, Nakagami's geopolitical perspective is a key theme of the book.

I am particularly interested in drawing on Spivak's work, supplemented where appropriate by the ideas of feminist and queer studies theorists such as Judith Butler (b. 1956) and Eve Kosofsky Sedgwick (1950–2009), to profile Nakagami's depiction of marginalized Burakumin women. I wish to help Nakagami's readers hear these women's voices which, with the notable exception of the elderly Oryū no oba, have been largely overlooked in existing scholarship. While Nakagami's male characters have received ongoing attention, little interest has been shown in the women these men sexually violate. Prior to considering these women, I revisit the voices of key male characters to better understand their role in suppressing the stories of the women. By reviewing the conflicts between masculine pairs such as father/son, half-brother/half-brother,

and male friend/male friend, I will note how masculinist homosocial practices rationalize the male conflicts depicted and render
meaningless the voices of the women nearby. To explore the writer's
depiction of the male voice, I read a selection of Nakagami's early
autobiographical works, such as a 1968 essay about his half-brother
and the short story "Rakudo" ("Paradise," 1976). I revisit his best-
known work, the Akiyuki trilogy, consisting of "Misaki" ("The
Cape," 1976), *Kareki nada* (*The sea of withered trees*, 1977), and *Chi no
hate shijō no toki* (*The end of the earth, supreme time*, 1983).

The second half of the book focuses directly on Burakumin
women's voices. Chapters 4 and 5 introduce key women from the
Akiyuki trilogy, who are almost entirely absent as subjects with
agency from existing Nakagami scholarship. While some scholarship does discuss Satoko, the prostitute who unknowingly commits incest with her half-brother, Akiyuki, this is generally merely
in terms of her being a prop or a foil for Akiyuki himself. While I
make reference to Oryū no oba from *Sen'nen no yuraku*, perhaps the
most celebrated woman from Nakagami's texts, I do so mainly to
compare her shamanlike narrative powers with the absence of
these powers in two older women from the Akiyuki trilogy. These
women are Yuki, a former prostitute, and Moyo, a traumatized
mute. I profile these women whose subalternity stems not only
from their Burakumin status but also from the fact that as uneducated and sexually stigmatized subjects, their voices are silenced
and foreclosed. Importantly, this act of silencing is committed by
the hegemonic mainstream from outside *and* within their marginalized community.

My close reading of Nakagami's representation of the voice of
women such as Satoko, the incestuous sister; Yuki, the former prostitute; and Moyo, the woman who cannot speak, is this book's key
contribution to existing Nakagami scholarship. The polarized critiques of Nakagami's works as either complicit in or challenging the
masculinist activities that result from patriarchal systems and phallocentric ideologies essentially regard his narratives as a representation of the male voice. This approach runs the risk of considering

his women characters simply as objects to mirror the activities of the men. This, I would argue, can be the case even with commentary on Oryū no oba, the most widely discussed woman character from the Nakagami corpus. Although there is a sizable body of scholarship around Oryū no oba, it generally focuses on her role as the "data-bank"[18] of the community, rather than probing the subjectivity of the character. Spivak's work on the "sexed subaltern subject," which is further explained in chapter 1, has been instrumental in permitting me to "hear" the voices of these women whose significance can easily be elided by the power of the males in Nakagami's texts.

The analysis that follows includes interpretation of a number of key texts from the Nakagami corpus not yet discussed in English-language scholarship. These include the fictional work "Rakudo," read by those who have compiled biographies of Nakagami (such as Takazawa Shūji and Takayama Fumihiko) as an autobiographical story depicting events based on the author's private life. As far as I am aware, however, no scholar inside or outside Japan has conducted a close reading of this work, even though consideration of "Rakudo" is arguably essential for a full understanding of Nakagami's literary project. I have also tried to profile Nakagami's own voice, as heard in public lectures and conversations with other writers. In this way, I hope to broaden the pool of English-language material available for consideration by scholars interested in this writer's work.

Given that my primary aims are to give voice to previously silenced women characters and provide new interpretations of the women's voices depicted in well-discussed works such as the Akiyuki trilogy and *Sen'nen no yuraku*, I am unable to refer in any detail to Nakagami's very important mid- and late 1980s works, such as *Nichirin no tsubasa*, *Kiseki* (*The miracle*, 1989), *Sanka* (*Paean*, 1990), and *Izoku* (*A different clan*, unfinished). Neither do I refer to writings related to Nakagami's overseas experiences or his "subcultural" writ-

---

18. Asada 1996, 29.

ing, such as manga plots. These works are insightfully analyzed in detail by key Nakagami scholars such as Hasumi Shigehiko, Karatani Kōjin, Yomota Inuhiko, Takazawa Shūji, Watanabe Naomi, Tomotsune Tsutomu, Kurata Yōko, and Asano Urara in Japan and Nina Cornyetz, Anne McKnight, and Anne Helene Thelle in English-language scholarship.[19] I refer readers to these scholars' work and to my own essay on *Keibetsu*, Nakagami's final complete novel.[20]

Nakagami and the Burakumin Context

Although Nakagami is known as a Burakumin writer, and much of his writing is indeed set in a Burakumin context, not all of his material provides representations of Burakumin life. His work further depicts the diversity of backgrounds among Buraku people, including those who, like the writer himself, received financial and economic benefits from the democratic systems introduced at the time. Given this Burakumin emphasis, I briefly introduce key historical and sociopolitical aspects of that experience before embarking on my analysis of the writer's works.

Many scholars have noted the Burakumin are a social group that, unlike other minority groups such as Ainu, Okinawan people, or resident Koreans, are ethnically indistinguishable from the mainstream majority in Japan.[21] The precise definition of the term *burakumin*, however, remains "contentious."[22] This is because the word —which only came into circulation in the 1950s before appearing regularly in press reports by the 1970s—arose from a set of prejudi-

---

19. See Hasumi 1994, Karatani 2006, Yomota 1996, Takazawa 1998 and 2002, Watanabe 1994 and 1999, Tomotsune 2003 and 2010, Kurata 2010, Asano 2014, Cornyetz 1999, McKnight 2011, and Thelle 2010.

20. Ishikawa 2012.

21. For example, see Price 1972, Zimmerman 1999b and 2007, Sugimoto 2014, and Bondy 2015.

22. Sugimoto 2014, 204.

cial beliefs relating to the persons so defined. These beliefs were associated first with the claim that those concerned lived in "particular, geographically confined communities" called *buraku*, or *hisabetsu buraku*.[23] Second, it was said that Burakumin were decedents of the so-called outcaste group of the Tokugawa feudal system, the members of which lived in segregated communities, where some residents engaged in work such as butchery and leather work. The third belief was that Buraku people continued to work in industries carried over from those feudal occupations, which were sometimes collectively referred to as *buraku sangyō* (Buraku industries). These assumptions can be divided into three elements: residence, genealogy, and occupation.[24] This "trinity" of preconceived understandings regarding Buraku people were largely accepted as reality by wider society until the early 1970s. Such notions lost credibility because of the dramatic changes that occurred in Burakumin communities following the *Kōdo keizai seichō* (rapid economic growth) that occurred in Japan between the mid-1950s and early 1970s.[25] These changes were accelerated by the Special Measures Law for Assimilation Projects (1969–1979) that was introduced during the economic growth period and extended until 2002 as the Special Measures Law for District Renewal. The policies associated with these laws were designed to improve the physical environment of *hisabetsu buraku*, increase social welfare and public health support, and initiate educational programs.[26] According to Noguchi Michihiko, any "obvious characteristics" of Buraku people that may have once operated have been lost through complicating factors, such as an increasing number of people settling in and moving out of precincts designated as Buraku communities, marriage between Burakumin and non-Burakumin, and the decreasing number of people with a

---

23. Sugimoto 2014, 207, and Saitō 2017, 1.

24. Saitō 2017, 1–2. For further details, see Inoue 1969.

25. This book follows the official definition of the era of rapid economic growth, which is from 1955, when the economic boom known as *Jinmu keiki* commenced, until the 1973 oil crisis. See Tsuchida 2005, 118.

26. Saitō 2017, 1–2. For further details, see Noguchi 2000.

Buraku background who engage in the *buraku sangyō*.[27] These observations provide insights into the complicated social factors Nakagami was forced to navigate in terms of his personal circumstances and the broader literary context in which he worked.

According to Buraku kaihō jinken kenkyūsho (Buraku Liberation and Human Rights Research Institute), there are an estimated 6,000 Burakumin communities throughout Japan with a population calculated roughly at 3 million.[28] The exact size of this population is difficult to confirm. This is because people identify as Burakumin at their own discretion, and there are many who seek to avoid discrimination by intentionally abandoning Burakumin identity and relocating to a non-Burakumin community.[29] In other words, while many actively participate in antidiscrimination campaigns organized by groups such as Buraku kaihō dōmei (Buraku Liberation League, BLL) or Zenkoku chiiki jinken undō sōrengō (National Confederation of Human-Rights Movement in the Community, Jinkenren for short),[30] others try to conceal their Burakumin back-

---

27. For further details, see Noguchi 2000.

28. *Buraku mondai, jinken jiten* 2001, 736.

29. While the Assimilation Projects were intended to improve the standard of living of residents, many rejected the government designation of their communities as *dōwa chiku* (assimilation areas), that is, *hisabetsu buraku* registered by administrative agencies as areas toward which municipal assimilation policies applied. See *Buraku mondai jiten* 2000, 316. According to the last official survey conducted in 1993 by the Ministry of Internal Affairs and Communications, the number of *dōwa chiku* was 4,442, with a total population of 2,158,789. See *Buraku mondai, jinken jiten* 2001, 736. There are at least 1,000 areas for which the status remains the subject of dispute between the government and community groups. See Sugimoto 2014, 204.

30. The Jinkenren refuses to use the term *burakumin* in its title because this group claims that "Buraku discrimination no longer exists." The Jinkenren and the Japanese Communist Party (JCP) members regard the completion of the Assimilation Projects in areas registered by municipalities as *dōwa chiku* as a sign that these precincts, and therefore Buraku discrimination, have been eliminated. The Jinkenren and the JCP strongly criticize the 2016 enactment of the Law on the Promotion of the Elimination of Buraku Discrimination (Buraku sabetsu no kaishō no suishin ni kansuru hō) as perpetuating Buraku

ground. The actions of the latter are sometimes seen in terms of the saying "neta ko o okosu na" ("don't wake the sleeping baby"), an aphorism that expresses some cynicism toward those who hope to avoid difficulty by remaining silent about their identity as Burakumin.[31]

While several decades of national policy, such as the Special Measures Laws referred to above, saw some improvements in income levels and educational achievements, averages continued to lag behind those of non-Burakumin,[32] and the gap between Buraku people and non-Burakumin remained conspicuous even after the measures came to an end in 2002.[33] Furthermore, the reduction in government funding in recent years has led to a decline particularly in community-based activities, including the after-school *kodomo kai* (children's club), such as the one Nakagami attended as a child,[34] which were intended to supplement regular schooling. Also withdrawn were funds for organizing meetings at which Burakumin children and young people could discuss Burakumin issues and human rights.[35] Notwithstanding several decades of government policy and advocacy campaigns, some mainstream Japanese con-

---

discrimination and division between Buraku and non-Buraku communities. See "Buraku sabetsu eikyūka hō ga seiritsu," *Shinbun Akahata*, December 10, 2016, and "Jinken to buraku (dōwa) mondai seminā," *Chiiki to jinken*, February 15, 2017, 1–4.

31. Uchida 2014, 239–41.

32. During the period of Nakagami's writing, for example, the percentage of Burakumin receiving "livelihood security support," dropped from 76 percent in 1975 to 52 percent in 1993, but this remained almost twice as high as non-Burakumin. For further details, see Tipton 2008, 211, Sōmuchō 1995, 4, and Neary 2009, 79.

33. Uchida Ryūshi's 2009–2010 survey of 851 young Buraku people (age between 15 and 39) indicated that 19.6 percent did not complete a high school education. Given that the national average is 7.5 percent, levels of Burakumin educational achievement were low compared with the national average. See Uchida 2011b, 73–74.

34. Nakagami and Karatani 1997, 328.

35. Uchida 2009, 12–59; 2011a, 12–59; 2011c, 12–47.

tinue to avoid contact with Buraku people. In the 1970s numerous different lists were published denoting names and locations of Burakumin communities, indicating the entrenched nature of discrimination against Burakumin and the desire on the part of some mainstream Japanese to avoid contact with them. These lists were secretly edited and sold by private detective agencies to more than 220 Japanese firms and an indefinite number of individuals throughout Japan.[36] One of the lists, which was titled *Dōwa chiku chimei sōkan (A comprehensive list of assimilation areas)*,[37] contained the following preface: "For personnel managers working on employment issues, and families worried by problems to do with the marriage of their children, these [Buraku issues] are quite burdensome. Hoping that we can help to solve these problems, we have decided to go against public opinion at this time and create this book."[38] Understandably, the Osaka branch of the BLL vociferously protested against the editors, sellers, and buyers of these lists. Nevertheless, in 1985, *mimoto chōsa* (private investigation into one's background) was still being undertaken based on these lists. As a result, the Osaka prefectural government introduced An Ordinance to Regulate Personal Background Investigations Conducive to Buraku Discrimination. In 2011, following the 2007 exposure of the habitual investigation by land developers to identify *hisabetsu buraku* precincts, the ordinance powers were expanded to include regulation of discriminatory investigations of land in addition to the activities of private investigators.[39]

Clearly, discriminatory practices against Burakumin have continued into the twenty-first century; one such example is the "Serial discriminatory postcards incident" (Renzoku tairyō sabetsu hagaki jiken). From May 2003 to October 2004, over four hundred postcards and letters containing threatening and discriminatory lan-

---

36. Tomonaga 2005, 4–5.

37. *Buraku mondai jiten* 2000, 417.

38. Quoted in Tomonaga 2005, 4.

39. "Tochi sabetsu chōsa o kisei" *Kaihō shinbun*, November 7, 2011.

guage were sent anonymously to many people of Burakumin descent. Zainichi Koreans and Hansen's disease sufferers also received these letters. The culprit was an unemployed thirty-four-year-old man who was eventually sentenced to two years in prison. In court he testified that although he thought of himself as being superior to those to whom he sent postcards, he himself remained unemployed. The implication was that the "less qualified" Burakumin had taken away his job. Explaining that he had read a best-selling book series titled *Dōwa riken no shinsō* (*The truth about Buraku privileges*, five volumes published between 2002 and 2005), which accuses the Burakumin of having received unfair social concessions and being closely related to the organized crime group known as yakuza, he said he decided to harass Buraku people to relieve his social frustrations.[40] This incident demonstrates that Burakumin can easily become targets for the frustration of non-Buraku people experiencing financial or other social difficulties.

It should be noted that the 2016 Law on the Promotion of the Elimination of Buraku Discrimination was enacted to address new types of discrimination, including internet-based attempts to identify and disclose the location of Burakumin communities. One such attempt was made by a group called Tottori-Loop, which, since 2005 operates a website disclosing information on *hisabetsu buraku*. They assembled the information through interpreting various printed publications, including assimilation education textbooks, newspaper and journal articles, scholarly works, survey reports, administrative documents, and data collected from visiting *dōwa chiku*. The group also manages the publishing company Jigensha, which publishes lists of *hisabetsu buraku* and books on issues relating to minorities such as Burakumin, Zainichi Korean, Ainu, and Okinawan people. The website and publications include personal information about Buraku activists and often severely criticizes activists, the government, the BLL, and other human rights organizations as promotors of "*dōwa* privilege." Tottori-Loop has been the plaintiff

---

40. For further details, see Uramoto 2011.

in a number of court cases in which they demanded the release of information by selected municipalities relating to *hisabetsu buraku*. The group has also been defendants in cases mainly brought by the BLL and some municipalities.[41] Although diminishing in terms of employment problems, discrimination remains an issue in terms of social practices, such as marriage between Burakumin and non-Burakumin.[42]

Buraku people have been discriminated against since the beginning of the modern era because they are associated in the public imagination with the "outcaste" groups of premodern Japan. Prior to the modern era, outcaste people were pejoratively referred to as *eta* (great filth) or *hinin* (nonhuman) and were forced to stay in segregated rural hamlets. Residents of these hamlets often engaged in occupations such as animal slaughtering, crafting leather, weaving straw, and making footwear.[43] The term *eta* derived from the fact that these occupations have some association with the "defiling" elements of death or soil.[44] Ian Neary argues that discrimination against leather workers, which he notes occurs around the world, is "in some ways quite understandable" because the "putrid smell" of the raw leather makes it appear to be "dirty work." Many leather workers become "literally marked" for life with the dyes used for processing. In Japan, discrimination of this nature against Buraku people also derived from a perception of *kegare*, the "spiritual pollution" believed to stem from that community's association with dead

---

41. See Osaki 2016 and Akuzawa 2016.

42. To understand the issue of marriage between a Burakumin and non-Burakumin couple in Japanese society today, I refer to three publications: Kurihara Miwako's 2008 autobiographical novel, *Tarō ga koi o suru koro made ni wa* (*By the time Tarō falls in the first love*), Uchida Ryūshi's 2014 book, *Buraku mondai to mukiau wakamono tachi* (*Young people who face Buraku issues*), and Saitō Naoko's 2017 book, *Kekkon sabetsu no shakaigaku* (*Sociology on marriage discrimination*).

43. See "Eta" in *Buraku mondai jiten* 2000, 26, and Tsujimoto M. 1999, 65–69.

44. See *Daijisen*, 291 and 2244. Also see Yokochi Samuel 2008, 181, and Price 1972, 6–30.

animals.[45] This spiritual pollution was traditionally given as the reason for the segregation of Burakumin from mainstream society.[46]

Although Neary explains that both Shinto and Buddhist traditions to some extent have "prejudices associated with the actual and spiritual defilement,"[47] the term *kegare* is important particularly as a concept in Shinto, Japan's indigenous religion. Referencing *Engishiki* (*Procedures of the Engi era*, 927), a fifty-volume corpus of regulations for ancient Japanese government administration and ceremonies, Tsujimoto Masanori explains that typical causes of *kegare* are contact with any form of death—human or animal—childbirth, disease, and menstruation. The *hinin* often engaged, for example, in disposal of animal carcasses and the burial of unidentified corpses.[48] Subsidiary causes can include contact with soil or dirt.[49] In *Kegare to ōharae* (*Impurity and purification*, 2009), Yamamoto Kōji extends this belief by arguing that the essence of *kegare* includes taboo violations, such as treason and subversion of the social order. According to Yamamoto, *kegare* can have an adverse impact on the person directly affected and the community to which they belong.[50] Yamamoto explains that *kegare* is a social concept that was established as an attempt to evade phenomena that disturb the social order and therefore evoke instability and abhorrence.[51] Accordingly, traveling entertainers, prostitutes, and those who begged for a living were regarded as "impure." The itinerant lifestyle of such people, derogatorily referred to as *kawara mono* (riverside wanderers), was consid-

---

45. Neary 2010, 7.

46. McCormack 2002, 87.

47. Neary 2010, 7.

48. Amos 2011, 42. According to Amos, in the Edo era, outcaste groups were also acknowledged as official punitive arms, such as guard and executioner, by the shogunate. Their special duties, which were bestowed by the authority, accentuated their idiosyncrasy and marginality in local communities.

49. Tsujimoto M. 1999, 36.

50. Yamamoto 2009, 15–73.

51. Yamamoto 2009, 82.

ered morally reprehensible.[52] Criminals and rebellious tenant farmers were also degraded as *hinin* and segregated from society.[53]

Yotsu (four), which implies death and association with animals, is a pejorative term used in reference to Buraku people. In the travel journal *Kishū*, Nakagami discusses the meaning of "four":

> It is said that "four" is pejorative. The most important reason that the number "four" is regarded as pejorative is because it has been a derogatory name for Burakumin. ... Since, "four" implies "four-legged beast" and "death," it is abhorrent. This is certainly the case. For people who live within the conventions of civilized society, the bestial nature of man—the might of living things and the power of death—are abhorrently fearful. However, people cannot exist without the might of living beings and cannot ignore the power of death. "Four" induces awe.[54]

Because the Chinese reading for "four" (*shi*, 四) is a homophone for "death" (*shi*, 死), "four" is often considered in Japan to be ritually ominous.[55] Since ancient times, death as *kegare* has traditionally been held in both awe and abhorrence. Discrimination against the Burakumin stems from that awe and abhorrence toward *kegare*, a sense that is still deeply rooted in the psyches of people today.[56] *Buraku*

---

52. Takeuchi and Takayanagi 1994, 226. *Izu no odoriko* (*The Izu Dancer*, 1926) by the winner of 1968 Novel Prize in Literature, Kawabata Yasunari (1899–1972) is a good source for understanding the social status of traveling entertainers in the Taisho era.

53. Hatanaka 2004, 69–71.

54. NKZ 14:672.

55. Also see Margherita Long's discussion on "death" and "four" in the Japanese context. See Long 2006, 2.

56. The internationally acclaimed film *Okuribito* (2008, *Departures*, 2008, dir. Takita Yōjirō), for example, features a male protagonist whose wife and close friends are disgusted when they discover that he has become a mortician. The film's narrative demonstrates how the sense of *kegare* is still deeply rooted in the psyche of many people, both non-Burakumin and Burakumin, in contemporary Japan.

mondai jiten (*Concise encyclopedia of Buraku issues*, 2000) defines *kegare* as a "false consciousness," which, through a long history of control, has been politically and religiously entrenched and spread by the hegemonic mainstream as "ideology." Regarding the concept of *kegare* as a cause of the discriminatory culture of Japan,[57] the BLL regards its liberation campaign to be a form of denunciation (*kyūdan*) that will enlighten people and thus enable them to see through and work to eliminate entrenched social ideologies of this nature.[58]

The historical nature of discrimination against Burakumin is evident in the words of the *Suiheisha sengen* (*Declaration of the Levellers' Society*, 1922), one of the first documents to demand human rights and self-determination for Burakumin. Given the significance of this statement, I quote it in full here:

> *Tokushu* Burakumin [Residents of special hamlets] throughout the country: Unite!
>
> Long-suffering brothers! Over the past half century, the movements on our behalf by so many people and in such varied ways have yielded no appreciable results. This failure is the punishment we have incurred for permitting ourselves as well as others to debase our own human dignity. Previous movements, though seemingly motivated by compassion, actually corrupted many of our brothers. Thus, it is imperative that we now organize a new collective movement to emancipate ourselves by promoting respect for human dignity.
>
> Brothers! Our ancestors pursued and practiced freedom and equality. They were the victims of base, contemptible class policies and they were the manly martyrs of industry. As a reward for skinning animals, they were stripped of their own living flesh; in return for tearing out the hearts of animals, their own warm human hearts were ripped apart. They were even spat upon with ridicule. Yet, all through these cursed nightmares, their human pride ran deep in their blood. Now, the time has come when we

---

57. See "Kegare" in *Buraku mondai jiten* 2000, 112.
58. See "Kyūdan" in *Buraku mondai jiten* 2000, 86.

human beings, pulsing with this blood, are soon to regain our divine dignity.

The time has come for the victims to throw off their stigma. The time has come for the blessing of the martyr's crown of thorns.

The time has come when we can be proud of being *Eta*.

We must never again shame our ancestors and profane humanity through servile words and cowardly deeds. We, who know just how cold human society can be, who know what it is to be pitied, do fervently seek and adore the warmth and light of human life from deep within our hearts.

Thus is the *Suiheisha* born.

Let there be warmth in human society, let there be light in all human beings.[59]

Through legislative initiatives in the early years of the Meiji era (1868–1912), including the 1871 Emancipation Edict (*kaihō rei*) and the 1872 abolishment of the feudal class system,[60] the *eta* and *hinin* became *heimin* (commoners). This gradually became *shinheimin* (new commoners),[61] a categorization that immediately marked the person

---

59. This is cited from Buraku Liberation League Tokyo, "Suiheisha sengen eibun," see http://blltokyo.net/siryou/kiso/suiheisya_sengen3.html (accessed March 19, 2019).

60. Although upper-class samurai became part of the new aristocracy (*shizoku*) through the abolishment of the feudal class system, the majority of the samurai joined peasants, artisans, and merchants as commoners (*heimin*). For further details, see Tipton 2008, 44, and Kadooka 2016, 14–15. The abolishment of the Tokugawa hereditary social hierarchy was also intended to end special feudal rights so that a new system of land ownership and tax could be established. For further details, see Kurokawa 1999, 24–25.

61. Kurokawa 2016, 10–11. It is difficult to calculate an exact population of *shinheimin* at that time. According to a 1935 survey by the Chuō yūwa jigyō kyōkai (Central Integration Project Council), there were 5,361 Burakumin districts, the population was 99,968, and the ratio was 1.44 percent to the total population. Western Japan has more Burakumin districts and bigger communities than eastern Japan, where communities were often small and scattered across the area. For further detail see Kurokawa 2011, 12.

involved as a former *hinin*. As Burakumin writer Kadooka Nobuhiko notes, the *Suiheisha* declaration is accordingly a critique not merely of the *yūwa* (integration) policies of successive government administrations in modern Japan but also of those Burakumin who, by willingly accepting and often profiting from the *kaizen* (remedial) project promoted by wealthy power-brokers in their community, debased the human dignity of Burakumin.[62] By asserting the association of Buraku people with specialized occupations—such as slaughtering animals, the very occupations that drew allegations of *kegare*, rather than complying with the official government line of "liberty" and "equality"—the declaration worked to affirm Burakumin otherness and give a call to action for self-liberation.

According to Karatani, the emergence of the nation-state saw discrimination play a key role in the process of establishing a Japanese national "identity." Because this process was maintained (or reinforced) by excluding those who deviated from the mainstream, it resulted in the exclusion of the *shinheimin*.[63] Kurokawa Midori explains that through the dramatic social change brought by Meiji government policies, which included the introduction of a new educational system (*gakusei*), conscription, and land tax reform, many ordinary people experienced financial difficulties. In seeking a scapegoat for their misfortunes, they directed their anger and frustration at the *shinheimin*. As a result, former *eta* and *hinin* became the target of brutal discriminatory practices, including murder, torture, bodily harm, arson, and destruction of property.[64] These were re-

---

62. Kadooka 2016, 29.

63. Karatani also noted that this exclusion operated with respect to other groups, such as Ainu. See Karatani's comment in his round-table discussion, Asada, Karatani, Okuizumi, and Watanabe 2000, 256–57. In this context, the term *shinheimin* soon took on the same derogatory implication as the earlier terms, *eta* and *hinin*. Through some trial and error, the word *burakumin* eventually came into general use in Japan in the late 1950s and was adopted for common use by the media and academic circles in the 1970s. For further detail, see Teraki 1998.

64. See Kurokawa 2011, 34, and Uesugi 2010, 58–63.

ferred to collectively as "riots against the Emancipation" (*kaihō rei hantai ikki*), or "riots against the new policies" (*shinsei hantai ikki*).[65] Kurokawa notes that there were at least twenty-four cases of these forms of aggression recorded across western Japan. In *Sen'nen no yuraku*, Nakagami depicts fictional episodes of violence against Burakumin communities arising from the Emancipation Edict as recalled by the aged woman Oryū no oba.[66] These will be further discussed in chapter 5.

Even after the Emancipation Edict and campaigns that followed by prewar Burakumin activists, discrimination and poverty continued to prevent many Burakumin children from attending school.[67] According to Nakagami, the idea of compulsory education only became a reality for Burakumin communities after World War II.[68] Thus, while his older half-brothers and half-sisters were denied such an opportunity, Nakagami—born in 1946—received the benefits of literacy from the new education system that accompanied postwar democracy. In a 1991 discussion with Karatani, Nakagami describes himself as a *bungaku shōnen* (boy who loved reading), even though there were no books in his home. To compensate for this, Nakagami borrowed material from his classmates, school libraries, and the book collection of the after-school children's club, *kodomo kai*.[69] It is thus easy to understand why he refers to himself as "the first child born from the encounter of Burakumin and letters."[70]

---

65. Kurokawa 2011, 34.

66. *Sen'nen no yuraku*, in NKZ 5:103–4.

67. NKZ 15:306. Also see Kurokawa 2011, 63.

68. NKZ 15:306. Also see Takazawa 1998, 6–7.

69. Nakagami and Karatani 1997, 328.

70. NKZ 15:306. This statement in his essay titled "Ki no mama no kora" ("Children in the natural state") was published in *Kaihō kyōiku* (*Liberation education*), a magazine published by a Buraku liberation organization called Zenkoku kaihō kyōiku kenkyū kai (All Japan Research Society for Liberation and Education). This essay was published in 1982, the year he published *Sen'nen no yuraku*, and the work gained a reputation.

Following the 1977 publication of *Kareki nada*,[71] the sequel to the Akutagawa Prize–winning "Misaki," Nakagami was hailed as "the standard-bearer" of younger writers born in the postwar era.[72] This was also the year he set out on a pilgrimage through the Kishū region to collect material for the essays that became the travel journal *Kishū*. In the half decade or so that followed, the writer produced in quick succession a series of fictional and nonfictional works related to the Kishū region. These included, in order of publication, the collection of short stories titled *Mizu no onna* (*A woman of water*, 1979), the novel *Hōsenka* (*Touch-me-not*, 1980), the essay collection "Monogatari no keifu" ("Genealogy of narratives," 1979–1985), the short story collection *Sen'nen no yuraku* (1982), and the novels *Kii monogatari* (*A tale of Kii*, 1977–1984) and *Chi no hate shijō no toki* (1983). Unlike works such as "Rakudo," "Misaki," and *Kareki nada*, which appeared prior to widespread knowledge of Nakagami's Burakumin background and the writer's "voluntary" declaration of himself as being from a *hisabetsu buraku*, the works listed above were written following this information becoming public.

It is difficult to pinpoint precisely when Nakagami revealed his Burakumin background. Suga Hidemi asserts that this aspect of his identity was unknown at the time of the *Kishū* serialization.[73] Margherita Long, on the other hand, argues that since "the Kii Peninsula is known for its outcast communities," and since Nakagami was "famous as an autobiographical Kii writer," his Burakumin background must have been an "open secret" among *Kishū* readers.[74] In her reference to Long, Cornyetz adds that this was particu-

---

71. *Kareki nada* also won the 1977 Mainichi shuppan bunka shō (Mainichi Publication Culture Prize) and the 1978 Geijutsu senshō shinjin shō (The New Face Award of the Ministry of Education), but Nakagami was not satisfied with these prizes. *Kareki nada* was the first of six nominations for the Tanizaki Jun'ichirō Award, but he never achieved his apparent desire to win this prize. See Takayama 2007, 375.

72. Suga 2000, 663.

73. Suga 1999, 161–63.

74. Long 2006, 6 and 30.

larly the case for "readers in Kansai, or the Southern parts of Japan's main island," who were more likely to understand the outcaste context, than "those in Kantō, or the Northern half, where there had been historically far fewer outcaste hamlets."[75] Because both views are ultimately based on speculation, it is difficult to judge which is more accurate. Buraku studies scholar Noguchi Michihiko cites a passage from *Kishū* that reads: "[between my Burakumin interviewer and myself] there is a silent understanding of the fact of being the discriminated against" in support of his argument that Nakagami did, in fact, reveal his Burakumin identity in that narrative.[76] Although there are undoubtedly certain readers who, like Noguchi, detect a declaration of Burakumin identity in Nakagami's words, I argue that the passage is too nuanced to be definitive.

In my view, any ambiguity around Nakagami's Burakumin background was clarified by 1978 when the writer formed the Buraku seinen bunka kai (Buraku youth cultural group) in Shingū and organized a series of twelve monthly lectures titled "Hirakareta yutaka na bungaku" ("All-inclusive flourishing literature"). Each lecture featured a well-known intellectual from Tokyo, including poet and philosopher Yoshimoto Takaaki (1924–2013), politician and novelist Ishihara Shintarō (b. 1932), and novelist and Buddhist nun Setouchi Jakuchō (b. 1922). The cultural group's activities were, however, severely criticized by the Shingū BLL as "merely related to literature which has nothing to do with liberation."[77] Nakagami and other cultural group members came into direct conflict with the Shingū BLL over issues of employment and housing for Kasuga people. As a result, the cultural group members eventually withdrew from the Shingū BLL to establish the Kasuga BLL.[78] During that time, Nakagami worked tirelessly as an ideological leader of the cultural group and a representative of the Kasuga BLL. After eight

---

75. Cornyetz 2010, 127.

76. Noguchi 2001, 86. For the original text, see NKZ 14:668.

77. NKZ 15:259.

78. Moriyasu 2003, 8–9.

sessions, the lecture series was canceled, mainly because of differences of opinion in the Kasuga BLL about strategies to counteract discrimination against Kasuga people.[79] In a statement published in the *Mainichi shinbun*, Nakagami reflected that although the lectures were "fruitful for him as a writer," the conflict in which he was embroiled left him with a sense of "defeat."[80]

Also provocative to scholars seeking to clarify Nakagami's Buraku identity was the 1977 round-table conversation published in *Asahi journal* with established novelists Noma Hiroshi (1915–1991) and Yasuoka Shōtarō (1920–2013). During this discussion, titled "Shimin ni hisomu sabetsu shinri" ("The discriminatory psychology hidden in the psyche of the Japanese people"), Nakagami concealed his Burakumin origins and invented a character, "a writer whom I know." The statement below features two voices: the first is Nakagami's own voice using the first-person pronoun *boku* (I), and the second is that of "a writer whom I know," expressed in third person.

> In my case, whenever I witness discrimination, somehow, I cannot help going to extremes. ... A writer whom I know says that for now he is still sane because he's writing novels, but if he entered politics, honestly, his only recourse would be to toss a bomb. ...
>
> Thinking about discrimination, a bomb is the only answer. While I realize that for me, politics means literary politics, I'm not yet sure what I'm trying to blow up, I seem to just be making my way in the dark on some mission of self-destruction.
>
> In other words, I'm in despair. For me, there is no solution whatsoever to discrimination.[81]

This powerful passage provides important insights into the price Nakagami paid to address matters of discrimination and give a

---

79. Moriyasu 2003, 8–9.

80. NKZ 15:259–60.

81. Nakagami, Noma, and Yasuoka 1999, 58–59.

voice to those who experienced discrimination. To restate this in
more literary terms, the challenge facing the writer was to create
narratives that would eliminate discrimination while simultaneously
being plunged into despair at being forced to work within the narrative structures of Japanese literature, "structures" that were themselves "discriminatory."[82] This is one of the most important perspectives of Nakagami's writing. As influential literary critic and
Nakagami specialist Hasumi Shigehiko pointed out, Nakagami was
a writer of epoch-making works that illustrated the discriminatory
operation of contemporary narrative structure.[83] (I investigate this
point in greater detail in chapter 3.) Former Suiheisha Museum di-
rector Moriyasu Toshiji pointed out that for Nakagami "the issue of
hisabetsu buraku" was "largely a problem of culture [rather than a
sociopolitical issue],"[84] and thus his ideas were "undoubtedly irrec-
oncilable with [the view of] the BLL."[85] For the BLL, political action is an absolute necessity in the fight against the discrimination
directed toward Buraku people and the compromised living environment they experience as a result.[86]

Nakagami's sense of being defeated by discrimination is evident
in the anecdotes he relates about the experiences of the "writer
whom I know" during the Noma and Yasuoka round-table discussion. Although this Burakumin "writer" explained his background
to his wife prior to their marriage, he feels unable to read BLL magazines in front of her when in Tokyo. He always reads this material

---

82. Nakagami, Noma, and Yasuoka 1999, 55.

83. Hasumi 1984, 292–93.

84. Nakagami and Karatani 1997, 330.

85. Moriyasu 2003, 8. In his interview with activist poet Tanigawa Gan
(1923–1995), Nakagami gave the label "Lenin" to former BLL leader Matsumoto Jiichirō (1887–1966), reflecting Nakagami's view of Matsumoto's dictato-
rial leadership of the organization. Nakagami explains that he never simply
agrees with the BLL because he is a person related to BLL members and a descendant of the former *hinin* who, according to Tanigawa, often antagonize each
other. See Nakagami and Tanigawa 1995, 51–53.

86. Moriyasu 2003, 8.

when returning to his hometown. Given that this "writer whom I know" made no attempt to conceal his circumstances from his wife, we can assume that at one level he wished honestly to share his background information with others. Nakagami continues: "But, he says, he cannot help but feel that [the Burakumin context] is taboo. 'I don't want to look at it,' that's how he feels. So, in that sense, he half *passed* as being in the mainstream. Yet, while there are things he doesn't want to look at, there is also a part of him that feels a longing [*ito'oshii*] [to identify as Burakumin]."[87] Through this account, Nakagami is able to provide insights into the sensibility of a man who "feels his Burakumin context as a taboo" while desperately "longing" to identify himself as a member of the community. As Tsujimoto Yūichi points out, *ito'oshii* (or *itoshii*) is a recurring word in Nakagami's texts that expresses the feelings of Burakumin protagonists in narratives such as "Misaki" and *Kareki nada*.[88] By drawing on this particular term during the round-table, Nakagami conceivably tried to express an important theme of his narratives to Noma and Yasuoka. While those writers had also created narratives of the Burakumin, neither expressed "despair" at their literature in terms of its complicity with discrimination. Given that, in the *Suiheisha sengen* and BLL discourse, feeling "his Burakumin context as a taboo" is prohibited to a self-affirmative Burakumin, who is required to be "proud of being *Eta*," and thus Nakagami could not have voiced his inner thoughts without the invented "writer whom I know."

According to Takazawa, Nakagami invented this fictitious writer on Noma's advice. As a senior writer of the Japanese literary community (*bundan*) and member of the Central Committee of the BLL, Noma judged that it would have been "unwise" for Nakagami to declare his Burakumin identity during the round-table.[89] In a

---

87. Nakagami, Noma, and Yasuoka 1999, 59–60.

88. Tsujimoto Y. 1999, 188. Watanabe Naomi (1996) also focuses on Nakagami's use of the term *itoshii*.

89. Takazawa 1998, 93.

1991 discussion with Karatani, Nakagami explained the context from his perspective:

> [At the 1977 round-table], I did speak about [his *buraku* identity] directly, but I asked that they "please edit it out." "Please write it as someone else's story." It's not a big deal that I come from a *hisabetsu buraku* background. This is unimpeachably true, but I told them to explain it in terms of the things that I had heard happened to someone else. So it's not really true; it was my own story. When that conversation happened, in one sense I was aware that it had finally started. By which I mean—that if you look at the bottom of my literature, or the thorough way I see things, *hisabetsu buraku* issues absolutely come through.[90]

Citing this passage, Anne McKnight emphasizes the fact that Nakagami's Burakumin background and experience were revealed but simultaneously concealed. Borrowing Jacques Derrida's phrase "under erasure," McKnight points out that Nakagami's statement demonstrates his Burakumin identity is an identity that is effaced while remaining legible.[91] I borrow the term "effaced legibility"[92] from McKnight to refer to the means by which Nakagami cancels the signified aspect of his identity while making the sign visible to voice his perspective of discrimination or, more precisely, his "despair" at whether discrimination can ever be eliminated.

As a result of this potentially ongoing despair and the effacement of the Buraku aspect of his identity, Nakagami could not avoid plunging into a "Kafkaesque" (to use his word) state of mind. Empathizing with Nakagami's crisis, Karatani responded to this comment by his friend and fellow writer as follows:

---

90. The passage was translated by Anne McKnight (2011, 72–73). For the original, see Nakagami and Karatani 1997, 331.

91. McKnight 2011, 73.

92. McKnight 2011, 73.

I see. Although you refer to Kafka, Kafka never saw his Jewish identity as the basis [of his literature.] Everyone, however, knows that he is Jewish. Your case is different. If you declare [your Burakumin identity], it will become your "basis." Even if you don't, it will become your "basis" in another way. This is a double bind. …

So, here, an important point to consider is that [in their writing of the Burakumin] it was the Buraku issue that Yasuoka and Noma approached first of all—I have no desire to criticize them, but it's a huge trap. … I think it is very damaging for a writer to create narratives from a single basis.[93]

As Karatani went on to point out, because Nakagami did not commit himself as a writer who participated in the Burakumin liberation movement, he "eventually became opposed to the BLL."[94] However, Nakagami made a new form of Burakumin declaration by voluntarily "becoming a Burakumin,"[95] which, in Karatani's words, involved "declaring a basis in order to efface it."[96] In response to this comment, Nakagami explained that he always invalidated the basis from which he worked and "exposed my grazed self" to ensure that his writing was "entirely new and ceaselessly present." For him, "Anything can be a drama,"[97] and his narratives are indeed full of drama. In other words, his writing is arresting, highly emotional, and *itoshii*, longing for a firm basis. Nakagami's view of "becoming a Burakumin" is discussed in greater detail along with selected narratives in later chapters.

Nakagami's birth place, Kasuga, was one of the *hisabetsu buraku* areas designated for "improvement" in terms of the 1969–1979 Assimilation Projects. The Kasuga reform project, which aimed to de-

---

93. Nakagami and Karatani 1997, 332–33.
94. Nakagami and Karatani 1997, 333.
95. Nakagami and Yasuoka 1980, 365.
96. Nakagami and Karatani 1997, 333.
97. Nakagami and Karatani 1997, 333–34.

velop Shingū's Burakumin areas, began in 1977.[98] This was part of modernization and urbanization policies implemented throughout peripheral areas of Japan at that time. In the past, Kasuga was divided from the other areas of Shingū by a hill known as Garyūzan. By 1981, this hill and the old buildings of the Kasuga Buraku that lay behind the hill had been bulldozed and effectively obliterated. In their place, the government authorized the building of a small apartment complex and a main street.[99] Ostensibly, the Assimilation Projects were enacted to efface the difference between Burakumin and non-Burakumin. Nakagami, however, noticed the negative reaction of the broader mainstream society to the reforms.

> I have heard the word "reverse discrimination": if there really is such a word it should be used to denote the demolition of *hisabetsu buraku* by the wave of urbanization and modernization. Old buildings were demolished and new buildings constructed. Roads were nicely bituminized. Although these improvements were done basically through demands to urbanize and modernize, people say "why does this occur only in *hisabetsu buraku*?" "Reverse discrimination" is a deceitful expression made by those who claim that only Buraku people have access to these improvements, which in fact work to tyrannize the *hisabetsu buraku* and the people discriminated against.[100]

The phrase "reverse discrimination" is a reminder of how modern policies intended to address the unequal position of Burakumin in Japanese society merely created new narratives of marginalization. As Nakagami observed, the Assimilation Projects could never benefit Buraku people in terms of eliminating discrimination. Rather, the effacement of difference merely fostered a new form of discrimination against Burakumin otherness.

Nakagami also became aware that the reform of the *hisabetsu bu-*

---

98. Takazawa 2002, 326.
99. Takazawa 1998, 257.
100. NKZ 14:678.

raku marked oppression against Burakumin residents in terms of land ownership.

> If there really is a Buraku issue, I think it is land ownership. Whether legal or illegal, people built their homes on land on which they settled in close quarters with each other. As they became older, the authorities demolished those houses and built new structures. ... Although it is obvious that the *hisabetsu buraku* ... is being caught up in urbanization of the area, Buraku inhabitants feel anxious about their land ownership. Whose is the land on which they have lived for many generations? Or what will become of their leaseholds? That is to say, I believe that land ownership is the most significant aspect of the Buraku issue and that on the Kii Peninsula, the nation of darkness where there is not much flat land [suitable for building accommodation], this hardcore Buraku issue is especially problematic.[101]

Most of the land that encompassed the Kasuga precinct and the Garyūzan hill was registered as belonging to Tamaki Sameru (1885–1961), a non-Burakumin former chairman of Shingū City Council, and three other local non-Burakumin figures.[102] In his autobiographical story "Karasu" ("Crows," 1982), Nakagami gives an account of stories from local Burakumin who were not aware that by stamping their seal on blank paper when they borrowed money from "a certain Tamaki," they were being cheated out of their land.[103] "Karasu" also narrates how Tamaki cheated an aged Burakumin woman, Ochie no oba, out of her land and how her house was demolished without any consultation with her about the leasehold.[104] Although detailed research into the history and transi-

---

101. NKZ 14:675.

102. Takazawa 1998, 153, and NKZ 6:435. Tamaki Sameru was a nephew of a local doctor, Ōishi Seinosuke (1867–1911), who was falsely regarded as one of the traitors in the 1910–1911 High Treason incident.

103. NKZ 6:435.

104. NKZ 6:435.

tion of the *dōwa* district in Shingū by Wakamatsu Tsukasa and
Mizuuchi Toshio was unable to confirm the authenticity of these
particular stories,[105] we can nonetheless assume that practices of
this nature did occur to some extent. Given the BLL definition of
Buraku issues (*buraku mondai*) as social issues related to the humiliation of Burakumin and violation of their rights,[106] such complicity
between the landowner and the authorities is a concrete example, as
Nakagami claims, of *buraku mondai*. Important here is the fact that
without Nakagami's narrative of Ochie no oba, the experience of
this aged woman would be totally invisible. Through his writing she
is seen as a party discriminated against by the hegemonic mainstream. She is voiceless and foreclosed. This is in stark contrast to
the manner in which those subject to, for example, discrimination
in marriage and employment had their problems taken up and publicly declared *buraku mondai* in denouncement campaigns conducted
by the BLL. This focus on the invisibility and voicelessness of an
aged Burakumin woman is just one example of Nakagami's representation of the foreclosed voice of the marginalized.

The obliteration of the landscape of the *hisabetsu buraku* homeland, which Nakagami saw as a "tyrannical"[107] exercise of power
against the Buraku community through the capitalist (urbanizing
and modernizing) erasure of social difference and otherness, is one
of the most important motives for his production of Burakumin
narratives. As apparent in his collection of autobiographical-style
writings (including "Karasu"), and the fictional series titled *Kumano
shū* (*A collection of Kumano stories*, 1984), Nakagami perceived complicity in the dismantlement process between the landowner, the city of
Shingū, and groups of Burakumin traders, all of whom were involved in erasing *hisabetsu buraku* in the area for their own economic
benefit. In *Kumano shū*, the author further revealed that his family,

105. Wakamatsu and Mizuuchi 2001, 80.

106. See "Buraku mondai" in *Buraku mondai jiten* (2000, 423–24) for the
definition of the term.

107. NKZ 14:678.

which operated a small construction company, made huge profits by dismantling the Kasuga landscape and displacing people who had made their homes there for generations.[108] In this regard, the efface-ment of his birth precinct was for Nakagami a form of Burakumin community self-implosion that revealed the structural nature of the cyclic repetition of discrimination inside and outside of community.

The third and last volume of the Akiyuki trilogy, *Chi no hate shijō no toki*, narrates the final days of the Burakumin homeland and community during its dismantlement by the city of Shingū, groups of Burakumin traders, and a landowner named Sakura, whom Nakagami fictionally depicts as a retired Shingū man who remains politically influential behind the scenes. My interpretation of this work focuses on Nakagami's literary representation of the Kasuga community—the so-called *roji* (alley)—as a particular Burakumin community located on the Kii Peninsula, a geopolitically and his-torically marginalized area of Japan. Nakagami's understanding of the area as "the nation of darkness" alerts readers to the fact the *roji* is a narrative site that is the home of oppressed people. In other words, this place is metaphorically located within the wider hege-monic myth of mainstream abhorrence toward and exclusion of dif-ference. This work was, I argue, a literary response to the personal crisis Nakagami experienced at the erasure of the landscape of Ka-suga and his family's involvement in this process. As he writes in *Kumano shū*, this lost homeland had once been "an endless book,"[109] that is, the inexhaustible source of his narrative.

It is productive to approach Nakagami as a writer who interro-gates the social structures resulting in discrimination against those marginalized people, especially Burakumin, oppressed by the hege-monic mainstream community. As suggested, however, it is impor-tant to be aware that this marginalization can occur both within

---

108. For further detail see "Karasu" in *Kumano shū*, in NKZ 5:425–38. *Ku-mano shū* includes six fictional works and eight essays serialized in the magazine *Gunzō* between 1980 and 1982.

109. NKZ 5:228.

and without the *hisabetsu buraku*. As McKnight points out, the Sayama incident, which involved claims of false accusations against a Burakumin man and was considered one of the most controversial postwar cases of discrimination against Burakumin, particularly marked a turning point[110] in Nakagami's development as a writer and in the cultivation of his understanding of the term *discrimination*.

In 1963, in the city of Sayama, Saitama prefecture, twenty-four-year-old Ishikawa Kazuo (b. 1939), a member of the Sayama Burakumin community, was arrested on charges of rape, robbery, and murder of a local high school girl. Following a conviction that relied heavily on his own confession, Ishikawa was sentenced to life imprisonment. He insisted, however, that he had made a false confession after being isolated and threatened by police. In 1977, the Supreme Court turned down Ishikawa's appeal without hearing the case.[111] Ishikawa served thirty-two years in prison while maintaining his innocence. Since being released on parole in 1994, with his wife and other supporters, Ishikawa has continued to seek a retrial to have the conviction overturned.[112] The following is Nakagami's comment on the incident in the 1977 round-table conversation with Noma and Yasuoka. "The reality of the rape and murder of the girl … in Sayama demonstrated the terror felt by the settled [non-Burakumin] residents of the area at the thought that their [community] myth about [the sanctity of] sex had been violated and I would say that's why these people were convinced that [a Burakumin per-

---

110. McKnight 2011, 72.

111. The Sayama incident also demonstrates the destructive tensions that exist to some extent between the BLL and the JCP. Proclaiming themselves the main supporters of the accused, in a statement that confirmed the deep political divisions that separated the BLL and the JCP, the BLL was highly critical of Ishikawa's lawyer, who was a JCP supporter (Tainaka 1977, 2–3). These two groups have been longtime rivals since disagreement arose in the 1960s over policies related to the Special Measures for Assimilation Projects (Tipton 2008, 186).

112. For further detail about the Sayama incident, see *Sayama* 2013.

son] must have been the criminal."[113] This passage demonstrates Nakagami's view of the structure of discrimination. For him, the conviction of a young Burakumin man in the Sayama incident resulted from the "frame-up"[114] that was a consequence of the panic that gripped non-Burakumin residents who were terrified by the vicious crime that took place in and violently disturbed the peace of their small community. The uncanny circumstances of the murder invoked the non-Buraku people's latent abhorrence of the unconventionality of the Burakumin residents and the otherness that arose from their being *kegare*, spiritually polluted. As a result, non-Buraku people could instantly believe, without concrete evidence, that a young Burakumin man must be the offender.

In his later essays, Nakagami sees discrimination as a "narrative" established through particular elements, such as "sex, violence, and religion."[115] Religion includes formal religious practices and the widely held informal beliefs or myths that have currency in certain communities. For Nakagami, the Sayama incident was a typical case that demonstrated discrimination as narrative while profiling the three elements of sex, violence, and religion. Rather than drawing attention to discriminatory practices that might be labeled "Buraku issues," Nakagami draws on this triad as illustrative of the way hegemonic ideologies construct discrimination against marginalized people. Accordingly, the textual analysis chapters that follow will give close attention to the frequent depiction of sex, violence, and religion in Nakagami's narratives of the lives of people who are socially oppressed.

Although much of his writing draws on his own experiences and the experience of those in his community, Nakagami interestingly did not use the term *burakumin* in his fictional narratives. Burakumin critic Hirano Hidehisa notes in his 1982 essay that there

---

113. Nakagami, Noma, and Yasuoka 1999, 17.
114. Nakagami, Noma, and Yasuoka 1999, 17.
115. NKZ 15:167.

were readers who were therefore unaware that Akiyuki's birthplace Kasuga—the *roji*—was a *hisabetsu buraku*.[116] In the late 1980s, I was one of those readers who did not realize the Burakumin context of the writer and his narratives. One of the first stories I read was "Misaki." At that time I lacked the comprehension and knowledge to detect the Burakumin context, and my response was related to the fact that there was no direct reference to Burakumin or *hisabetsu buraku* in the narrative or the writer's notes. The fact that the protagonist is never represented as a victim of non-Burakumin discriminatory practices or as a person distressed by his Burakumin identity contributed to my inability to interpret the "meaning" behind Nakagami's text.

Nakagami's unique approach to the production of narratives with a Burakumin context becomes obvious when his work is compared with that of other novelists who produce what might be referred to as Burakumin literature. Perhaps the most well-known Burakumin character in modern Japanese literature is Segawa Ushimatsu, the protagonist of *Hakai* (*The Broken Commandment*, 1906) by Shimazaki Tōson (1872–1943). Aware that he is oppressed by *buraku sabetsu* (discrimination against Burakumin), Ushimatsu seeks to involve himself in the nascent Buraku liberation movement. This is also the case with the young male protagonists from renowned long works such as *Seinen no wa* (*A circle of youth*, 1947–1971) by Noma Hiroshi and *Hashi no nai kawa* (*The River with No Bridge*, unfinished work intermittently written between 1958 and 1992) by Sumii Sue (1902–1997). Noma's non-Burakumin municipal officer protagonist and Sumii's young Burakumin hero have a strong sense of justice and voluntarily commit to becoming involved as organizers in the Buraku liberation movement.[117] Because the principal aim of Noma and Sumii was to address discrimination against Burakumin in modern Japanese society, these authors depicted young men who were resentful of mainstream discriminatory practices against Bu-

---

116. Hirano 1982, 285.
117. See Noma 1971 and Sumii 1993.

rakumin and sought to became enthusiastic liberation movement activists. Motifs of this kind do not appear in Nakagami's fictional narratives, and the writer's most famous creation, Akiyuki, never aspires to engage in political activism as a means of "liberating" himself or his community.

In *Kareki nada*, Akiyuki is aware of a number of discriminatory practices against *roji* people, including himself. Although Akiyuki and his lover, Noriko, the daughter of a wealthy Shingū timber merchant, discuss the possibility of marriage, Noriko's father is opposed to such a union.

> [Noriko tells Akiyuki that] her father said that "He [Akiyuki] comes from the area where we used to have our other house, doesn't he?" "What do you mean, 'other house'?" Noriko had asked. Her father explained that this was a house built for family members who suffered from incurable consumption and who would eventually die. It was built to avoid any inconvenience for other members of the family who could then concentrate on their work even after the patient died. Confining the ill to such a house where they could be cared for by a resident nurse and a doctor who visited regularly was much better for the sake of patients as well as a family's reputation than having the patient in hospital.

"You rich people live a different life, don't you?" Akiyuki teased Noriko.[118] As Noguchi explains, the father's story demonstrates the marginality of the *roji*, Akiyuki's birthplace, as a place stigmatized by the mainstream society to which Noriko's family belongs. Her father's opposition to a legal union between the couple also implies that the discriminatory attitude toward marriage between a Burakumin and non-Burakumin operated in some contexts even in the mid-1980s. Akiyuki, however, does not really show resentment at being discriminated against.[119] Noguchi argues that Nakagami's de-

---

118. NKZ 3:303.
119. Noguchi 2001, 78–79.

piction of Akiyuki's "indifference"[120] toward *buraku sabetsu* marks the author's desire to write to express the oppressed voice of his "alter ego."[121] Akiyuki is the illegitimate son who is obsessed with hatred toward his biological father as the source of the fragmentation of his *roji* family. Furthermore, by depicting a young hero who is disinterested in *buraku mondai*, Nakagami tries to avoid having his narrative read as a literary denunciation of the social and political injustice experienced by Burakumin or as literary support of the Buraku liberation movement.

Akiyuki's indifference to Buraku issues is a feature he shares with many other of Nakagami's *roji* characters. For example, Akiyuki's mother, Fusa, the heroine of *Hōsenka*, is also depicted as unaware of *Buraku sabetsu*. As Hirano notes, single mother Fusa has no time to think about the social injustices practiced against her *roji* community because she is desperately fighting on behalf of her five children to survive each day.[122] I also argue that as an illiterate woman, she has no access to the discourse of Buraku liberation and its male-initiated theorization and activism. Hirano considers Nakagami's depiction of Fusa to be a precise representation of the uneducated and poverty-stricken people who made their homes in the *hisabetsu buraku*.[123]

In support of this view, Hirano cites a passage from a prison notebook of the Sayama incident convicted man, Ishikawa Kazuo, who referred to the poverty he experienced as a child. Ishikawa writes: "It was only after I lodged an appeal to a higher court and began researching for that appeal that I finally understood the fact that I had been discriminated against because I had lived in 'Maeppara' of 'the 4th district of Sugawara' and that this was 'Buraku discrimination.'"[124] While Ishikawa had initially been aware that poverty had made him the subject of discrimination, he was unable

---

120. Noguchi 2001, 79.

121. Kobayashi 2009, 110–12, and Tansman 1998, 257.

122. Hirano 1982, 284.

123. Hirano 1982, 282–90.

124. Cited in Hirano 1982, 287. For the original text, see Ishikawa 1977, 275.

to see this as *buraku sabetsu*, "discrimination against Burakumin." Like Fusa, Ishikawa received limited schooling. This illiteracy prevented him from recognizing that his village, Maeppara (literally meaning "front field") was a *hisabetsu buraku*. For Ishikawa, Maeppara was no more than his hometown, where his poverty-stricken family and neighbors lived in the same "field," helping and arguing with each other.[125] This closely parallels the situation Nakagami depicts in his representation of the *roji*, the slumlike homeland of marginalized people. Like Ishikawa, it is only after Akiyuki has been imprisoned that he realizes the *roji* is a place of historical and political discrimination. Unlike the first two narratives of the Akiyuki trilogy, *Chi no hate shijō no toki* unambiguously depicts Akiyuki and the *roji* as located in a Burakumin context through, for example, the use of derogatory labels such as *eta* and *yotsu* in reference to the people who reside there.

Existing Critique

An extensive corpus of Nakagami scholarship exists in both Japanese and English. In the Japanese-language field, there are essay collections by Buraku studies scholars, such as Noguchi, Hirano, and Moriyasu, and commentaries by self-identified Burakumin writers, such as Hijikata Tetsu (1927–2005) and Uehara Yoshihiro (b. 1973).[126] While these discuss Nakagami's works as a Burakumin writer's representation of Buraku people and the *hisabetsu buraku*, more important in terms of this discussion is the approach of Japanese literature commentators, such as Etō Jun (1932–1999), Hasumi, and Karatani, who interpret Nakagami's literature as the culmination of the development of the Japanese "novel" (*shōsetsu*).

Etō reads Nakagami's material as being in the tradition of the masterpieces of the literary naturalist movement that depicted the

---

125. Ishikawa 1997, 263–89.
126. See Hijikata 1992a, 1992b, and Uehara 2017, 8–17.

lived experience—"real life"—of the Japanese people.[127] Hasumi regards Nakagami's narratives as a unique *shōsetsu* form that critically reveals the "law" controlling the narrative depicted in the text.[128] I discuss this position in detail in chapter 3. Two of the best-known commentaries on Nakagami's work are *Sakaguchi Ango to Nakagami Kenji* (*Sakaguchi Ango and Nakagami Kenji*, 1996) by Karatani and *Kishu to tensei: Nakagami Kenji* (*Nobility and reincarnation: Nakagami Kenji*, 1996) by Yomota. Karatani's essay collection approaches Nakagami's writing from a deconstructionist position influenced by Paul de Man (1919–1983). Yomota's *Kishu to tensei* examines Nakagami's narratives by articulating the intertextuality with Asian and Western narratives that is a feature of Nakagami's narratives. *Hyōden: Nakagami Kenji* (*Critical biography of Nakagami Kenji*, 1998), by Takazawa Shūji, is the most detailed biography of Nakagami. Hasumi, Karatani, Yomota, and Takazawa regard Nakagami's work as a challenge to the hegemony of the conventional system of narrative (*monogatari*). Taking a historical perspective toward Japanese literary studies, Watanabe Naomi's *Nihon kindai bungaku to "sabetsu"* (*Modern Japanese literature and "discrimination,"* 1994) and *Fukei bungaku ron josetsu* (*Introduction to a theory of lèse-majesté literature*, 2006) reads Nakagami's material by tracing the genealogy of Japanese narratives representing the Burakumin. In doing so, Watanabe asserts a view of Nakagami's writing as a critique of modern Japanese literature and the manner in which representation in that mode continuously entrenches discrimination against Buraku people. The approach of these scholars often draws on poststructuralism to critique the hegemonic patterns, rules, and ideologies that control language and representation in texts.

In 1986, accompanied by Karatani and Asada, Nakagami traveled to France at the invitation of the symposium Japon des Avantgardes. He engaged in dialogue with eminent poststructuralist the-

---

127. Etō 1996, 144.
128. Hasumi 1984, 305.

orist Jacques Derrida (1930–2004).[129] After this event, many of Nakagami's major works were translated into French with the support of French publisher Fayard, which also published French translations of the work of Colombian writer Gabriel García Márquez (1927–2014). Fayard was active in the campaign that resulted in García Márquez being awarded the 1982 Nobel Prize in Literature. According to Karatani, Fayard's support was based on the publisher's belief that, more than any other writer, Nakagami had the potential to be the next García Márquez.[130]

There are only two major publications of Nakagami's writing translated into English: *The Cape and Other Stories from the Japanese Ghetto* (translated by Eve Zimmerman) and *Snakelust* (translated by Andrew Rankin), which are both short story collections. There are also English translations of two other short stories. They are "Fushi" (1977; translated as "The Immortal" by Mark Harbison), published in *The Showa Anthology: Modern Japanese Short Stories* (1985), and "Hanzō no tori" (1980; translated in 1982 as "Hanzo's Bird" by Ian Hideo Levy) published in booklet form. In-depth English language scholarship into the writer's narrative began only after his death in 1992. Scholars such as Mark Morris, Mats Karlsson, and Anne McKnight have explored the relationship between Nakagami's texts and the literature of William Faulkner (1897–1962). As was the case with García Márquez, it was Faulkner's work that inspired Nakagami to revive the oral histories of the peripheral "South" of his community as a means of contesting the official histories of the elite. A comparative study of Nakagami and Faulkner (and/or García Márquez) is an approach frequently seen in Japanese and English scholarship. Morris's 1996 article titled "Gossip and History; Nakagami, Faulkner, García Márquez" and McKnight's 1999 article "Crypticism, or Nakagami Kenji's Transplanted Faulkner: Plants, Saga and Sabetsu" explore the influence of Faulkner's litera-

---

129. Nakagami and Derrida 1996, 10.
130. Karatani 2012b, 4.

ture on Nakagami in terms of writing narratives of oppressed peoples who reside in a society's peripheral South. Karlsson's book, *The Kumano Saga of Nakagami Kenji* (2001), focuses on the Akiyuki trilogy to provide a comparative study of Nakagami and Faulkner and to use narratology theory to investigate the writer's narrative style.

A significant body of Nakagami scholarship addresses the representations of violence toward women that often feature in the writer's narratives. As Karlsson notes, "probably more so than in Japan," Nakagami's disturbing depictions of this nature are "the single most contentious feature" for feminist and other academics in the West.[131] This is not to say that Nakagami's work is dismissed out of hand by those scholars who question these representations. Like a number of critics inside and outside Japan, Livia Monnet, for example, reads Nakagami's writing as demonstrating a strong degree of misogyny and phallocentrism. She nonetheless concedes that these works effectively reveal the violent nature of the social structures that create masculinist perspectives. Monnet's strongest critique is reserved for key Japanese male scholars, such as Karatani and Asada, whose efforts were largely responsible for canonizing Nakagami,[132] and whom she regards as justifying the writer's depiction of a "heroic-macho-violates-woman-as-nature" discourse.[133] The masculinist textual politics of prominent Japanese male critics is repeatedly criticized by scholars such as Nina Cornyetz and Eve Zimmerman. I consider their concerns in greater detail below.

In her book, titled *Dangerous Women, Deadly Words: Phallic Fantasy and Modernity in Three Japanese Writers* (1999), Cornyetz adopts a psychoanalytic reading of the work of three Japanese writers: Izumi Kyōka (1873–1939), Enchi Fumiko (1905–1986), and Nakagami. She includes chapters on Nakagami's poems, short stories, and the Akiyuki trilogy. In her 2007 work, *Out of the Alleyway: Nakagami Kenji and the Poetics of Outcaste Fiction*, Zimmerman uses a biographical ap-

---

131. Karlsson 2014, 11.
132. See Monnet 1996a, 1996b.
133. Monnet 1996b, 234.

proach to interpret the Kumano narratives as a product of the writer's life experience. McKnight's 2011 book, titled *Nakagami, Japan: Buraku and the Writing of Ethnicity*, on the other hand, includes Nakagami's 1960s writing, the late 1980s texts on Korea, and subcultural works produced in collaboration with manga artists. McKnight examines these works from the perspective of Nakagami as a writer of "high literature" who "writes the ethnicity" of the Burakumin. I refer in greater detail to the discussions of these three scholars in my analysis of Nakagami's Kumano narratives.

On a number of occasions, Nakagami explained that the aim of his writing was to reveal the "archetype of narrative"—he uses the word *monogatari*—and destroy the "laws and codes" of Japanese literary language and convention that justify discrimination against difference. For Nakagami, this amounted ultimately to an attempt to "make new literature."[134] Not all scholars agree that he was successful in this endeavor. In *Negotiating Identity: Nakagami Kenji's Kiseki and the Power of the Tale* (2010), which focuses on Nakagami's later narrative *Kiseki*, Anne Helene Thelle criticizes Nakagami as a writer who "remains trapped in the language and conventions of Japanese literature."[135]

Buraku studies scholars and Burakumin writers often criticize Nakagami's narrative as "insufficient"[136] in terms of narrating an accurate history of Buraku reality or the "complete liberation of the human."[137] This objective was proclaimed as the core of art for Burakumin by activist poet and the former chair of the Buraku Liberation Literary Prize Committee, Teramoto Satoru (1913–1966). Edward Fowler also criticizes the Burakumin identity of Nakagami's characters as "almost inconsequential" in his "mythologized" narrative settings. Fowler argues that Nakagami's narrative lacks a "visceral sense of marginality [or] characters who wrestle head-on

---

134. See NKZ 15:140–56, and Nakagami 1999a, 224–39.

135. Thelle 2010, 217.

136. Noguchi 2001, 91. Also see Kurokawa 2016, 189 and 242, and Hijikata 1992a.

137. Teramoto 1992, 94–106.

with their Burakumin-hood," qualities that he argued were apparent in novels by Hijikata Tetsu.[138] Scholars such as McKnight, Tomotsune, and Asano, however, have reevaluated the significance of Nakagami's narratives, essays, and commentary—especially those that clearly demonstrate the Burakumin context—as discourses in the trajectory of the Buraku protest and liberation movement.[139] In doing so, these scholars try to articulate the possibility of Nakagami's work being interpreted as effective activism in the literary, historical, social, and political framework of Buraku discourse, or, to borrow McKnight's term, as "Buraku rhetorical activism."[140]

Many of the scholars I have referred to here, regardless of whether they are Burakumin, non-Burakumin, Japanese or non-Japanese, commonly assert that Nakagami's works demonstrate the distinction between "difference" (*sai*) and "discrimination" (*sabetsu*). This distinction was not something Japanese novelists were particularly aware of prior to Nakagami's emergence. Scholars such as Karatani, Watanabe, and Takazawa, moreover, see Nakagami's motive for becoming a writer of narratives of the socially marginalized as wanting to assert the difference between the identities of these groups and the mainstream. This is in contrast to any motive to provide a literary representation of the "liberation" of Buraku people from discrimination, something that Nakagami "despaired" would ever be realized. In Karatani's sense—which is based on neo-Freudian psychoanalysis and poststructuralist theory—identity is not the goal but the starting point of any process of self-consciousness.[141] Given this view, I regard Nakagami's representation of identity in his narratives and his self as unstably multiple and even self-contradictory.

It is apparent from the foregoing that Nakagami's literature provokes ongoing discussions that demonstrate the Derridean critique

---

138. Fowler 2000, 34.

139. See McKnight 2011, Tomotsune 2003 and 2010, and Asano 2014.

140. McKnight 2011, 6.

141. For example, see Karatani's discourse in Nakagami and Karatani 1997.

of the "original" text. According to Derrida, since the origin is only a "trace,"[142] the authority of any text is provisional.[143] To Derrida, linguistic meaning is an unstable phenomenon: at all times, and in all places, *différance* (difference and deferral) applies.[144] The ambivalent status of Nakagami's narrative confirms the fact that *différance* always intrudes into literary representation, thus preventing completeness of meaning.[145]

Structure Overview

My study does not situate Nakagami literature in the frame of Buraku discourse, nor does it seek to place the writer in some trajectory of Japanese literature. Rather, I approach his works as pragmatic texts that demonstrate the interdisciplinary theory of the literary representation of oppressed peoples, generally Burakumin, whose voices are silenced and foreclosed by the hegemonic mainstream from outside and within their marginalized communities. These voiceless people are those who, because of multiple reasons such as being poor, illiterate, immigrant, orphaned, or aged, have no access to education. They were not able to access modern ideologies of Buraku activist discourse, such as equality, liberation, declaration of Buraku identity, or denunciation of discrimination against Burakumin. In Nakagami's narratives, these people are often women. As already noted, my close reading of the writer's representation of the voices of these Burakumin women is this book's key contribution to existing Nakagami scholarship.

The book consists of six substantive chapters. While providing some discussion of Nakagami's work, chapter 1 mainly sets forth a framework for considering the writer's narratives. Chapters 2–6

---

142. Derrida 1976, 61.

143. Spivak 1976, 19.

144. See Derrida 1982, 3–27, and Sim 2002, 5–6.

145. Derrida 1976, 101–8.

provide close readings of selected texts. The underlying objective is to discuss Nakagami's representation of the voice/s of subject/s oppressed by hegemonic norms or ideologies.

Chapter 1 sets out to clarify the theme of the book, which is the paradox of representing the silenced subaltern voice. I have noted that the principal theoretical element of my discussion is Spivak's argument around the (im)possibility of the subaltern speaking. Having said that, I want to state clearly that I am not a postcolonial scholar, and I do not intend to give a postcolonial reading of Nakagami's work. Rather, I am appropriating what I regard as a highly relevant aspect of Spivak's scholarship that, I argue, creates possibilities for a new reading of Nakagami. There may be some postcolonial scholars who regard my analysis as inadequate in terms of the principles of that field of study. This is to misunderstand my use of Spivak's ideas. Although my book does not seek to situate Nakagami's material in a postcolonial literary context, I do argue that applying aspects of Spivak's scholarship to Nakagami's texts provides new insights into this Japanese writer's narratives.

An important element of Nakagami's work is his attempt to represent as much as possible the voices of those to whom he himself referred as the *mukoku* (the silenced)—those people who have no voice in society. I am particularly interested in applying Spivak's perspective, developed through her readings of Karl Marx (1818–1883) and Antonio Gramsci, of representing the sexed subaltern voice from the South to Nakagami's ideas of those who are silenced or without a voice. The main Spivak texts I reference are her short 1988 essay, "Can the Subaltern Speak?"[146] and her 1996 essay collection titled *A Critique of Postcolonial Reason: Toward a History of the Vanishing Present.* Spivak is known for her extremely complex language.

---

146. "Can the Subaltern Speak?" was first published in the journal *Wedge* in 1985, as "Can the Subaltern Speak?: Speculations on Widow Sacrifice"; reprinted in 1988 as "Can the Subaltern Speak?" in Cary Nelson and Larry Grossberg's edited collection, *Marxism and the Interpretation of Culture;* and revised by Spivak as part of her "History" chapter in *A Critique of Postcolonial Reason: Toward a History of the Vanishing Present,* published in 1999.

As evident from Terry Eagleton's harsh critique of the "obscurantism" of *A Critique of Postcolonial Reason,* her style of composition can discourage not only nonspecialist readers but also academic readers, including Eagleton, who largely agree with Spivak's position.[147] In drawing on Spivak's work to inform my theoretical approach, I openly admit the difficulty of interpreting and decoding her writing, which, constructed as it is from an abundant knowledge of and deep insight into a wide range of theoretical fields, endlessly poses new puzzles. I would like to stress my impression of Spivak's writing as (to borrow from Stephen Morton's lucid explanation) her challenge against "the common-sense assumption that clear, transparent language is the best way to represent the oppressed."[148] In other words, by refusing to adhere to the systematic conventions of Western critical thought, her sometimes opaque writing acts as a critique of the power structures entrenched by "rational" language. Like that of Spivak, Nakagami's writing was often the subject of criticism, in his case by Japanese literary specialists who claimed that his language did not follow conventional grammar or idiomatic expression.[149]

In her essays, Spivak attempts to articulate the voices of silenced subalterns, voices that cannot be heard through representations based on hegemonic Western theories or on models of political resistance and social reform. For Spivak, this is because Western intellectuals cannot help but rely heavily on Kantian/Hegelian/Marxist perspectives of subjectivity and class consciousness in their mode of representation (writing). As a result, they often ignore geopolitical determinations in their construction of "the history of Europe as Subject" and their narratives of the dominant North.[150] These intellectuals thereby suppress non-Europe and the non-West, thereby closing out the history of the subordinate South. The geopolitical

---

147. Eagleton 1999, 3–6.
148. Morton 2003, 5.
149. Maruya 1989, 388–90.
150. Spivak 1988a, 271.

context is a critical element of Nakagami's narratives,[151] which often depict the otherness of Kishū Kumano, a site viewed by the writer as Japan's marginalized South that exists in the shadow of the mainstream Japanese North.

Before arguing Spivak's view, I present background information about Kishū Kumano by referring to Nakagami's essays, interviews, and travel journals. I examine Spivak's critique of ideology, hegemony, the subaltern, and her discussion on the role of the intellectual, which references Gramsci and noted Palestinian American commentator Edward W. Said (1935–2003). Based on Gramsci's and Spivak's ideas of the "intellectual," I investigate Nakagami's ambivalence about his role as a member of the silenced Burakumin community who is nevertheless privileged as a "person who has (written) language."[152] The challenges inherent in the act of representation will be investigated by reading Marx's interpretation of this issue, in addition to the ideas of more contemporary theorists such as Spivak and Karatani. I close the chapter with an analysis of an example of Nakagami's representation of the voices of *mukoku* Kumano Burakumin from the 1978 travel journal *Kishū*.

Chapter 2 focuses on Nakagami's early writings and a short novel titled "Rakudo" (1976). A number of prominent themes feature in his late 1960s writing. These include criticism of Japanese New Left writers, recollections of his "uneducated" half-brother's violence and suicide, and reflections on then nineteen-year-old Nagayama Norio (1949–1997), who shot and killed four people in 1968. First, through an analysis of nonfiction material produced by Nakagami from 1965 to 1969, I profile two elements that were frequently represented in literary production and discussed in academic writing during this period: the masses (*taishū*) and loss (*sōshitsu*). Nakagami felt sympathy for those involved with the fiasco of the New Left and initially affiliated with that group. He soon

---

151. See Nakagami's comment in a 1985 discussion with Murakami Haruki. Nakagami and Murakami 1985, 22–23.

152. NKZ 14:613.

became aware, however, that the sense of loss in his inner landscape and that experienced and represented in literary terms by student movement activists who identified themselves as representatives of the voiceless masses had very different foundations. Nakagami's early writings have already been discussed by many key scholars of his work. I supplement these with a detailed discussion on the intertextual relationship between Nakagami's late 1960s texts and the contemporaneous perspective of two Japanese critics: Yoshimoto Takaaki, regarded as one of postwar Japan's most important social commentators, and Akiyama Shun (1930–2013), whose 1967 essay examines the inner landscape (*naibu*) of transgressive youth. By referencing these scholars' texts, I articulate Nakagami's motives for writing—giving representation to—hidden voices that express a sense of loss.

The last half of chapter 2 focuses on Nakagami's short story "Rakudo," modeled to some extent on the writer's experiences and family background. Through reading this "autobiographical" yet fictional *shōsetsu*, I demonstrate how Nakagami represents the voices of a violent young husband and the silence of his battered wife, which contrasts strongly with the spoken voice of the former, in the context of the Japanese family in the modern "my home era." This discussion draws on Spivak's theories and the gender critique given by Mizuta Noriko (b. 1937) of the "discourse of man" depicted in modern Japanese literature.

Chapter 3 gives a close rereading of Nakagami's most well-known work, the Akiyuki trilogy: "Misaki," *Kareki nada*, and *Chi no hate shijō no toki*. This chapter particularly focuses on Nakagami's depiction of the voice of a transgressive man who is oppressed by the fragmentation of the relationship between him and his family and also his subaltern (Burakumin) community during the dismantlement of the Kumano Burakumin homeland. I give particular attention to how Nakagami's theory of *monogatari* operates to depict the voice of the Kasuga Burakumin. Of particular importance is the third novel in the trilogy, *Chi no hate shijō no toki*. Unlike *Kishū*, "Rakudo," "Misaki," or *Kareki nada*, each of which appeared prior to the writer's announcement of his Burakumin community links, *Chi no hate shijō no toki* was written following Nakagami assuming responsibility, as the only recognized Burakumin novelist of the time, to depict the Burakumin voice. As noted, in this novel the *roji* is unambiguously represented as associated with the outcaste context in a manner not articulated in previous works. The dismantlement of the outcaste community in the name of national urban planning and capitalist progress in *Chi no hate shijō no toki* is investigated by referring to the theory of community argued by Zygmunt Bauman (1925–2017). Thus, although this chapter provides an overview of "Misaki," and *Kareki nada*, the focus of the textual analysis is on how Nakagami, a writer who consciously chose to "become a Burakumin,"[153] represents the Burakumin voice in *Chi no hate shijō no toki*.

I also discuss the Akiyuki trilogy as an example of Nakagami's unique writing practice that derived from overlaying the modern Japanese Western-influenced naturalist literature mode with the more traditional Japanese narrative (*monogatari*) mode. In doing so, I examine Hasumi's interpretation of *Kareki nada* as a narrative that reveals the code of *monogatari*. In discussing this narrative of the son's patricidal challenge, I focus on the breaking of family taboos by the male protagonist, Akiyuki, including incest with his half-sister and the murder of his half-brother. Akiyuki's transgressive acts are interpreted as implying the cyclic repetition of a family tragedy.

Chapter 4 investigates the voice of the sister, Satoko, who has an incestuous relationship with Akiyuki. There is considerable discussion in both Japanese and English scholarship of Akiyuki's breaking the incest taboo with his half-sister as a substitute for patricide. Although a number of these commentaries reference Satoko, little attention has been given to her vulnerability or her response to the incest. My discussion profiles Satoko's subjectivity by considering her as a sister whose sexuality is exploited as a strategic weapon in

---

153. Nakagami and Yasuoka 1980, 365.

Akiyuki's bitter conflict with his father. This conflict, I argue, is the son's attempt to bond with the father. Drawing on Sedgwick's study of male "homosociality," I discuss Satoko's subalternity as an object of dispute in her father and half-brother's homosocial bond. I consider Satoko as, to borrow Spivak's phrase, "the sexed subaltern subject" who has "no space" to speak in modern patriarchal society.[154]

A key element of chapter 4 is the analysis of Nakagami's interpretation and, in turn, my reinterpretation of "Kyōdai shinjū" ("A brother-sister double suicide"), a folk song featured in the Akiyuki trilogy that implies the playing out of a mythic family tragedy in Kasuga. This ballad, which is drawn from the rich oral history of the Kasuga *Buraku*, narrates the incestuous love between a young woman and the brother who loves her. Drawing on the representation of "sister" (*imo*) in the work of Yanagita Kunio (1875–1962), the father of folklorist studies in modern Japan, and on the ideas of prominent feminist theorist Judith Butler, I analyze the sister in the "Kyōdai shinjū" ballad as an archetype of all "sisters" who are required to suppress their desire and sometimes sacrifice their lives in the name of the patriarchal state.

Chapter 5 discusses Nakagami's representation of old women or *oba* from Kumano. To articulate the significance of the *oba* in Nakagami's narratives, I first investigate Nakagami's reading of the work of well-known woman author Enchi Fumiko (1905–1986) to provide insights into his view of the tradition of the "old woman" (*omina/ōna*) as a storyteller of *monogatari*, narrative.[155] Based on this discussion, I examine Nakagami's depiction in *Sen'nen no yuraku* (1982) of the aged *roji* woman, Oryū no oba, as a Burakumin *omina*. Drawing on Spivak's theories discussed in chapter 1, I further discuss how Nakagami presents Oryū no oba's silenced voice.

Oryū no oba has a special status that derives from her role as *omina* who passes down *monogatari* to the younger generation in the community. In contrast, I consider Yuki and Moyo, two aged out-

154. Spivak 1999, 307.
155. NKZ 15:242.

caste women who feature in the Akiyuki trilogy, as *oba* who can never assume the voice of community storyteller. While Yuki is an aged eldest sister who once worked as a prostitute to support a fatherless Burakumin family, Moyo is a single aged woman who became mute when she was young after being raped by outcaste men. This final chapter investigates how Nakagami depicts the (im)possibility of these sexed women's voices speaking to or being heard by the community while also demonstrating how the writer presents an alternative representation of their voiceless voices.

CHAPTER 1

The Paradox of Representation

Geopolitical Perspective of Kishū Kumano

Gayatri Chakravorty Spivak is one of a number of women postcolonial theorists whose work has been instrumental in profiling gender matters regarding those on the margins of society. Most notably, Spivak has been at the forefront of the push to give a voice to the silenced and the dispossessed. This chapter conducts a detailed discussion of the applicability of Spivak's critique of representing the voice of the silenced subject to Nakagami's perspective of *mukoku*, the silenced or those without a voice. Focusing on the geopolitical perspective of Nakagami's writing, which is an important element in the work of scholars such as Spivak and postcolonial scholar Edward Said, I argue that Nakagami, like Spivak and Said, attempted to represent the silenced voice of Japanese society's "Other."

Knowledge of Kishū Kumano[1] is essential to an interpretation of Nakagami's narratives because an understanding of the relevance of this location is critical to interpreting the oppressed status of the

---

1. The expression *Kishū Kumano* refers to the Kumano region of the Kii Peninsula. This region is often simply referred to as Kumano. Unless specifically wishing to invoke some use of the term *Kishū* by Nakagami, I generally refer to this area as Kumano.

53

writer's characters. Nakagami's narratives depict the otherness of Kishū Kumano, long regarded as *komoriku*, a hidden country, on the periphery of Japan. In his 1978 travel journal *Kishū: Ki no kuni ne no kuni monogatari* (*Kishū: A tale of the country of trees, the country of roots*, hereafter *Kishū*), Nakagami portrays this region as "the nation of darkness" where the "losers" have settled.[2] The term *losers* implies those who incurred social stigma (*kegare* in Yamamoto's sense) through defeat or social marginalization, including ancient exiled nobles, rebellious farmers, and modern anarchists and socialists.[3] The expression "nation of darkness" suggests that Nakagami's view of Kishū Kumano as a historical site geographically situated as the inverse of the ancient capital Kyoto where the emperor, the symbol of *hare* (purity or glory), once lived.[4] In other words, this nation of darkness is juxtaposed against the center of Japan, the political entity that operated under the brilliant auspices of the sun goddess. Traditionally renowned as a spiritual spot for healing abhorrent diseases like leprosy, Kumano was also known since ancient times as a place for salvation. Pilgrims, regardless of rank, sex, or place of residence, came to pay homage at the three shrines of Shingū, Hongū, and Nachi, collectively known as Kumano Sanzan. It was thus depicted paradoxically in folklore and myth as a sacred yet ominous realm of death and a place of revival that was inhabited by the marginalized and ostracized.[5] As a realm of death, it was *kegare* (polluted).

I have noted Yamamoto's view of *kegare* as including social dissent. In modern Kishū Kumano, this social dissent was most evident in the so-called High Treason incident (Taigyaku jiken, 1910–1911). This was an alleged 1910 socialist-anarchist plot to assassinate Emperor Meiji, and it led to the mass arrest of leftists and the execution of twelve accused, including prominent anarchist Kōtoku

---

2. NKZ 14:676.

3. NKZ 14:676 and Yamamoto 2009, 15–73.

4. NKZ 15:63.

5. Nakagami and Tomioka 1996, 233–34. Also see Karlsson 2001, 2–4, and Cornyetz 1999, 170–71.

Shūsui (1871–1911), in 1911. Since the postwar era, the incident has largely been regarded as a fabrication by the state. It also resulted in the conviction of six defendants from Shingū, the so-called Shingū Group, and the execution in January 1911, of two of them. This included local doctor and sometime physician to Kōtoku, Ōishi Seinosuke (1867–1911), regarded by authorities as the Shingū Group leader.[6] The Taigyaku jiken made a strong impression on Nakagami and is a theme that repeatedly erupts in his fictional narratives. In the 1977 essay titled "Watashi no naka no Nihonjin: Ōishi Seinosuke" ("A Japanese man on my Mind: Ōishi Seinosuke"), Nakagami discusses the incident and the brutality of the sentences visited on Ōishi and the other Shingū convicted. This short work confirms the author's view of Kishū Kumano as a place that was historically "consigned to the cold" by the political center.[7] The extract from this essay given below begins with reference to the *Kojiki* (*A Record of Ancient Matters*), the text compiled in 712 to justify the imperial authority of the time.[8] The Tōsei, or defeat of the area by the mythical Emperor Jinmu, mentioned in the opening line was invoked repeatedly by Nakagami as a metonym for the subjugation of the local area by the center.

> Kumano was the place to which the Emperor Jinmu came for the Tōsei [conquest of the East] and where, according to the *Kojiki*, "a large bear [could be seen] faintly moving around; then it disappeared. Then Kamu-yamato-iware-biko-no-mikoto [the Emperor Jinmu] suddenly felt faint; his troops also felt faint and lay down."[9]
> Kishū Kumano is always in darkness. Although situated close to the culture of the Kinki area, it is under the shadow of the Ya-

---

6. For further details about the Shingū Group and Ōishi Seinosuke, see Hartley 2013.

7. NKZ 14:367.

8. The narrative of Jinmu Tōsei is also written in *Nihon shoki* (*The Chronicle of Japan*, 720). In this book, however, I focus on the *Kojiki* narrative, which Nakagami cited in his essay "Watashi no naka no Nihonjin: Ōishi Seinosuke."

9. Descriptions in brackets are my annotations in this citation. I cited Philippi's translation of the *Kojiki*, with some modifications. See *Kojiki*, 167.

mato Court. Throughout the Edo era, into the last days of the
Tokugawa shogunate, and even after the Meiji Restoration, the
Kishū clan could not find their way into the halls of power. It
might sound dramatic, but Kumano has always been consigned to
the cold despite being featured in Japanese history since the time
of ancient myth.[10]

Donald L. Philippi, the English translator of the *Kojiki*, notes that
the reference to a "large bear" (*kuma*) signifies the unruly Kumano
mountain deities, who initially transformed themselves into the
form of a bear that cast a spell over Emperor Jinmu and his men.
Jinmu was revived by a magical sword, whereupon the Kumano
deities were "magically quelled."[11] In the *Kojiki*, the derogatory attitude of the center toward the people of Kumano is evident by the
fact that the latter are depicted as "men with tails." Philippi cites
commentary suggesting that early Japanese believed that indigenous people who lived in the mountains, given their "primitive"
stage of cultural development, were animal-like and were therefore
referred to as having tails.[12]

Noting that the Kii Peninsula, on which Kumano is located, is
"a peninsula of darkness," Nakagami goes on to observe that it was
"no mystery"[13] that Kishū Kumano was the home of various groups
that had rebelled against authority. He gives details of the derogatory assumptions made by those conquering the people who fled to
and were exiled or executed in Kumano. This included those defeated in the Saika ikki (Saika riots, 1577–1585), an uprising in Saika

---

10. NKZ 14:367.

11. This part is written in *Kojiki* as follows: "At the very time that he [Jinmu]
received that sword, all of the unruly deities in the KUMANO [*sic*] mountains
were of themselves cut down." Philippi notes in an annotation that "the magic
power of the heavenly sword was in itself sufficient to vanquish immediately all
the unruly deities." See *Kojiki*, 167.

12. See Philippi's commentary in *Kojiki*, 170.

13. NKZ 14:367.

against Oda Nobunaga (1534–1582), a brutal warlord who initiated political unification in early modern Japan. The leader of this uprising was the son of the lord of Saika Castle, Suzuki Magoichi (circa sixteenth century; birth and death dates uncertain), whose followers, armed with guns, were one of the most highly skilled and technologically advanced military units of the time.[14] Ryūzō, the father of the eponymous protagonist of the Akiyuki trilogy, is depicted through intertextuality with the legend of Magoichi to emphasize his resentment toward authority. Further discussion of the use of this legend is found in chapter 3.

Nakagami regards the matters referred to above—the Taigyaku jiken, the Jinmu Tōsei, and the Saika ikki—as representative of the culture of political defeat that has marked the people of Kishū Kumano since ancient times.[15] He notes that in the modern era, too, an event such as the High Treason incident was "inevitable" because Kishū Kumano people had an innate tendency to rebel against authority.[16] The history of Kumano given here confirms the status of the area as *komoriku*, hidden country.

Nakagami's representation of Kishū Kumano as a "nation of darkness" resonates with the etymology of the term *Kumano*, meaning both "field of bears" (熊野) and "the edge of a field" (隈野). In a 1985 interview with Jacques Derrida, Nakagami explained the paradox of the Kumano toponym:

> Kumano is a strange place. Kumano means the edge of the field.
> ... To sum up, the edge is a place in which there is no land, or the
> margin of something. ... We can probably define Kumano as a
> place which exists nowhere, or as a place which exists even though
> it is invisible. So, as a land, Kumano is a place of paradox; it is a
> sort of paradoxical land. That is to say, ... Kumano is a place in
> which inside and outside stick together, a place that is at once in-

---

14. *Daijisen*, 1033, and Teraki 1991, 66–67.
15. NKZ 14:367.
16. NKZ 14:367.

side and outside. It is a place that eternally circulates, and since there are no breaks or divisions, it is a place that exists as a borderless zone.[17]

In response, Derrida suggests that Nakagami's perspective when writing of Kumano is "not an ideological, philosophical or political justification of literature from the periphery," but a critique of the concept of peripherality.[18] Peripherality, as Derrida defines that concept in this interview, is something that presumes the binary structure of center/periphery. For the French thinker, the practice of "deconstruction," while acknowledging the necessity of periphery, at the same time seeks to critique the hierarchical nature of binary structures. Informed by this perspective, Derrida views Nakagami as a writer who, although on the edge of periphery, nonetheless rejects peripherality as an ideology and tries to "shake" the binary opposites that have already been "invalidated" from inside and outside.[19] A critique of binary opposites is acknowledged as one of the most important aspects in the work of Derrida and also of Spivak, who translated Derrida's *De la Grammatologie* (1967, translated as *Of Grammatology* in 1976). It is also, as I further argue, a crucial element of Nakagami's writing.

Nakagami's unique interpretation of periphery is demonstrated in his construction of Kumano as "Japan's South." This view was influenced by William Faulkner's ideas regarding the "curse" of the American South. According to Faulkner, this curse is "slavery, which is an intolerable condition—no man shall be enslaved—and the South has got to work that curse out."[20] As Nakagami noted in his 1985 lecture titled "Faulkner, hanmo suru minami" ("Faulkner, the luxuriant South"), Faulkner's literature largely enabled him to conceptualize and write about Kumano as a geopolitically margin-

---

17. Nakagami and Derrida 1996, 13.

18. Nakagami and Derrida 1996, 18–19.

19. Nakagami and Derrida 1996, 18–19.

20. Faulkner 2003, 287.

alized South.[21] My interest in this book is in Nakagami's literary representation of the silenced people in the Japanese version of the "cursed" Southern community. In the main textual analysis section of the book, I examine Nakagami's narratives as (borrowing Faulkner's words) an attempt to "work out" the "intolerable condition" or "the curse" visited on the marginalized people of Kumano, the Japanese South. Although there is no slavery in Kumano, the area was "cursed" by social conditions that dehumanized *hisabetsu buraku* residents in a manner that might be seen as similar to slavery in some aspects.

Ideology, Hegemony, and the Subaltern

No discussion of geopolitics can proceed without reference to the work of Antonio Gramsci. Theorists like Spivak and Said developed their postcolonial perspective of the world by drawing on elements of Gramsci's work, including the Italian theorist's notion of "hegemony," his history of the "subaltern" class, and his trenchant critique of "the role of intellectuals." As Kang Okcho notes, these key aspects emerged through Gramsci's attempt to understand how his homeland, Sardinia, had been stigmatized in Italy as the "backward"[22] South.[23]

Gramsci is remembered as a founding member and leader of the Communist Party of Italy. Imprisoned between 1926 and 1937, he died one month after his release at the age of forty-six. Gramsci's radical involvement in communism was grounded in his questioning of why the Italian South was considered backward in relation to the more affluent North. His 1926 unfinished essay, "Some Aspects of the Southern Question," demonstrates his geopolitical observations of southern Italy. He argues:

---

21. NKZ 15:542–43.
22. Gramsci 2000, 173.
23. Kang 1999, 129.

It is well known what kind of ideology has been disseminated in myriad ways among the masses in the North by the propagandists of the bourgeoisie: the South is the ball and chain which prevents the social development of Italy from progressing more rapidly; the Southerners are biologically inferior beings, semi-barbarians or total barbarians, by natural destiny; if the South is backward, the fault does not lie with the capitalist system or with any other historical cause, but with Nature, which has made the Southerners lazy, incapable, criminal and barbaric. ... The Socialist Party was to a great extent the vehicle for this bourgeois ideology within the Northern proletariat. The Socialist Party gave its blessing to all the "Southernist" literature of the clique of writers who made up the so-called positivist school.[24]

Expressions such as "lazy, incapable, criminal and barbaric," which were directed toward the Italian South, were reiterated through "a variety of forms such as articles, tales, short stories, novels, impressions and memoirs" produced by intellectuals and scientifically authorized as the "nature" of people from the South. Moreover, "southernist" literature was claimed by mainstream northern members of the Socialist Party to be "the science of the proletariat." Gramsci criticized this socialist penchant for "science" as bourgeois propaganda that fostered oppression against the "wretched and exploited" southerners.[25] The essay also demonstrates how Gramsci considers ideology and its power over society. In *The German Ideology* (1845–1846), Karl Marx and Friedrich Engels (1820–1895) note with respect to ideology that "the ideas of the ruling class are in every epoch the ruling ideas. ... The class which has the means of material production at its disposal, has control at the same time over the means of mental production."[26] As implied by the foregoing quote, which demonstrates the writer's animosity toward other Italian socialists, "the ruling idea" of the dominant group concerns not

---

24. Gramsci 2000, 173–74.
25. Gramsci 2000, 174.
26. Marx and Engels 1970, 64.

only the hierarchical pair of ruling class/proletariat but also other alternative pecking orders complicated and intertwined with various binary concepts such as center/periphery, northern socialists/southern socialists, literate/illiterate, and culture/nature. These processes operate within and outside a class position or class consciousness. The dominant group imposes its view as a common-sense ideology through a distorted construction and representation of artificially created social binary opposites in a manner that greatly advantages their position of power. This, in effect, was Gramsci's theory of hegemony.

In *The Prison Notebooks* (1929–1935), Gramsci conceptualizes hegemony as the power of ideology that serves to justify the interests of dominant groups. The term *hegemony* initially referred to the dominance of one state within a confederation. It is now generally understood through Gramsci's argument to mean domination achieved through a combination of "force" and "consent."[27] Drawing on Gramsci, Dominic Strinati defines the process of hegemony as follows: "Dominant groups in society, including fundamentally but not exclusively the ruling class, maintain their dominance by securing the 'spontaneous consent' of subordinate groups, including the working class, through the negotiated construction of a political and ideological consensus which incorporates both dominant and dominated groups."[28] In the exercise of hegemony, the ideology of the dominant group receives commonsense "spontaneous consent" from other groups in a way that justifies the dominance of the ruling elite. Like Gramsci's "southerners," any group that voluntarily or involuntarily deviates from the ideology is marginalized. From this perspective, Japan's Buraku people can be seen as the people of the metaphoric South. In the case of Kumano Burakumin, the metaphor is literal.

Subaltern, meaning "of inferior rank,"[29] is a term that originally

---

27. Loomba 1998, 30, and Ashcroft, Griffiths, and Tiffin 2007, 106–8.
28. Strinati 1995, 165.
29. Ashcroft, Griffiths, and Tiffin 2007, 198.

appears in Gramsci's work in reference to the socially oppressed. Subaltern groups are subject to the social hegemony of the dominant classes. With this in mind, Gramsci sets out to formulate the methodological criteria by which it might be possible to recover the "necessarily fragmented and episodic" history of the subaltern classes so that the voices of this group might be heard.[30] This process, however, is not without difficulty.

> There undoubtedly does exist a tendency to ... unification in the historical activity of these groups, but this tendency is continually interrupted by the activity of the ruling groups. ... Subaltern groups are always subject to the activity of ruling groups, even when they rebel and rise up. ... Every trace of independent initiative on the part of subaltern groups should therefore be of incalculable value for the integral historian.[31]

I argue that Gramsci's focus on subaltern history has a parallel in Nakagami's focus on Burakumin oral folklore. For Nakagami, Burakumin folklore has "incalculable value" because it expresses the "trace," identified by Gramsci, containing the hidden voice of those who, like Italian southerners and Japanese Burakumin, have been marginalized by "the activity of the ruling groups." I have noted how Nakagami considers the geopolitical subalternity of Kishū Kumano to result from the putative "backwardness" of this southern region in relation to the hegemonic center of Japan. Given their common positions, Gramsci's notes on the nature of subaltern history evoke Nakagami's view of Burakumin history as oral folklore. In a later chapter, the intertextual presence of Burakumin folklore in Nakagami's narratives will be discussed from the Gramscian geopolitical perspective with reference the "Kyōdai shinjū" ("A brother-sister double suicide") ballad that appears in *Kareki nada*.

Since the late 1970s, Gramsci's texts have been interpreted in a deconstructionist way by a number of scholars, including Spivak,

---

30. Gramsci 1971, 54.
31. Gramsci 1971, 55.

Said, and the members of Ranajit Guha's Subaltern Studies group. Said uses Gramsci's concept of hegemony—a form of power relation that, while it suppresses, dominates others by consent[32]—to explain certain forms of cultural power in civil society, including the workings of Orientalism. Guha applies the term *subaltern* "as a name for the general attribute of subordination in South Asian society, whether ... this is expressed in terms of class, caste, age, gender and office [*sic*] or in any other way."[33] Said evaluated the work of Subaltern Studies group scholars as an analogue of attempts "to articulate the hidden or oppressed accounts of numerous groups—women, minorities, disadvantaged or dispossessed groups, refugees, exiles, etc."[34] Drawing on the views of Guha and Said, we can identify members of *hisabetsu buraku* communities also as subalterns on the margin of society because of issues such as class, gender, location, sexual orientation, ethnicity, or religion. For Buraku people, subalternity is most often related to their location within a *hisabetsu buraku* precinct.

While I concur with the views of Said and Guha regarding the subaltern as a general concept to indicate the socially marginalized, I wish particularly to draw on and emphasize Spivak's view that the "true" subalterns are people "whose identity is its difference."[35] Spivak further explains the term *subaltern* as "the description of everything that doesn't fall under strict class analysis."[36] In this context, the subaltern becomes an idea that can be appropriated for various kinds of people or groups that are socially marginalized and silenced—*mukoku*, to borrow Nakagami's term—because of their "difference." This is the case even if some in the group have access to wealth. It is important to note that this difference not only exists between groups, it can also operate within groups or within what appears to be an homogeneous community. Drawing on Ania

32. Said 1988, vii.
33. Guha 1982, vii.
34. Said 1988, vi.
35. Spivak 1999, 272.
36. Spivak 1990, 141.

Loomba's discussion of Spivak's proposition "Can the subaltern speak?," I argue that the dominant and the subjugated are positioned concurrently within several different discourses of power and resistance. The relationship between them is ceaselessly "intersected" and "spliced" by various forms of power relations.[37] Nakagami's Kumano narratives depict the most oppressed Burakumin who are the targets of discrimination from the hegemonic mainstream because this operates both outside and within the *hisabetsu buraku*.

The issue of the intellectual, the learned person whose task is often to support the consolidation of hegemonic structures, has considerable importance in Gramsci's work. Nakagami saw himself as a "person who has a (written) language" and can therefore represent the voice of the silenced.[38] He was nonetheless very aware that the written word paradoxically has the power to silence the voice of oppressed people who, because of subaltern markers such as gender, age, or illiteracy, can never assume the role of political or cultural representative for their communities. Nakagami's view of the contradiction inherent in his being a representative (intellectual with a voice) of the voiceless Burakumin community resonates with the views of scholars who use a deconstructive approach to interpret Gramsci's ideas on "the role of intellectuals."[39] Since Gramsci's writings can be "fragmentary" and "unsystematic,"[40] in the discussion that follows I draw on Said's interpretation of the Italian thinker's ideas on "the role of the intellectual" (presented in Said's 1993 lecture collection, *Representations of the Intellectual*).

According to Said, Gramsci argues that there are two types of intellectual: traditional and organic. Traditional intellectuals are

---

37. Loomba 1998, 231–45.

38. NKZ 14:613.

39. Noting that "all men are intellectuals but not all men have in society the function of intellectuals," Gramsci argues that while both "the specialist" or "layman in the sense of 'profane, non-specialist'" have an intellect and use it, they are not all intellectuals by social function. See Gramsci 2000, 303.

40. Mouffe 1979, 170.

specialists such as "teachers, priests, and administrators, who continue to do the same thing from generation to generation."[41] Gramsci criticizes the sense of privilege held by traditional intellectuals and their identification of themselves as "autonomous and independent of the dominant social group."[42] This sense of entitlement results in these intellectuals abrogating any responsibility to change the social and political system from which they benefit. On the contrary, their ideology essentially functions to justify and consolidate the hegemony of the ruling group. Organic intellectuals are people such as "the industrial technician, the specialist in political economy, the organizers of a new culture, of a new legal system, etc."[43] While Gramsci sees these people as directly connected to "classes and enterprises that used intellectuals to organize interests, gain more power, [and] get more control," he also regards them as actively advocating to "change minds and expand markets." In other words, unlike traditional intellectuals who "seem more or less to remain in place, doing the same kind of work year in year out," organic intellectuals are "always on the move, on the make."[44] Because of this incessant movement, which he regards as suggesting a willingness to embrace social and political change, Gramsci pins his hope on these organic intellectuals to create a counterhegemony for the subaltern group. To borrow Spivak's words with reference to Gramsci, the intellectual's role is to advocate for the "subaltern's cultural and political movement into the hegemony."[45] For Spivak,

---

41. Said 1996, 4.

42. Gramsci 1971, 7–8.

43. Gramsci 1971, 5.

44. Said 1996, 4. To cite Gramsci's explanation: "It can be observed that the 'organic' intellectuals which every new class creates alongside itself and elaborates in the course of its development, are for the most part 'specialisations' of partial aspects of the primitive activity of the new social type which the new class has brought into prominence." Said insists, "There has been no major revolution in modern history without intellectuals; conversely there has been no major counter revolutionary movement without intellectuals."

45. Spivak 1999, 269.

the desire of the responsible intellectual must be to realize a social structure in which subalterns do not remain subalterns but can embark on a track to become effective members of the citizenry.[46] As noted already, the geopolitical perspective is a starting point when considering the representation of the subaltern. I briefly discuss that perspective in relation to Spivak, noting how this also relates to Nakagami.

Spivak and Nakagami: Writers of Hybridity

Gayatri Chakravorty Spivak was born in 1942 as the daughter of a Brahmin family in Calcutta.[47] A permanent resident alien of the United States and nonresident Indian with citizenship, Spivak sees herself as a "bilingual person" who has "two faces."[48] In a 1993 interview with Alfred Arteaga, Spivak discusses her desire to involve herself in the cultural activities of West Bengal by positioning herself "as a person with two fields of activity, always being a critical voice so that one doesn't get subsumed into the other."[49] This position is also evident in her ideas on the role of the translator. As a translator of Bengali writer Mahasweta Devi (1926–2016), for example, Spivak considers translation a project that must paradoxically consider both the necessity and the impossibility of representation. As a reader of original texts, she claims that a translator "must have the most intimate knowledge of the rules of representation and permissible narratives which make up the substance of a culture, and must also become responsible and accountable to the writing/translating presupposed original [sic]."[50] This claim can be explained as the voice of a hybrid who assumes an "irreducible cultural translation" in their identity to be *both* the colonial subject and

---

46. Spivak, Takemura, and Ōhashi 2008, 129.
47. Spivak and Arteaga 1996, 16.
48. Spivak and Arteaga 1996, 18.
49. Spivak and Arteaga 1996, 18.
50. Spivak 2000, 1.

the Eurocentric economic (and intellectual, in Spivak's case) migrant.[51] This position demonstrates Spivak's hybridity as both a privileged writer and as the West's other.[52]

As the translator of Derrida's *Of Grammatology*, Spivak engages with, while ultimately challenging, the influential French intellectual activity of the late 1960s that encompasses theories related to such groundbreaking notions as deconstruction, second-wave feminism, and poststructuralism. The "philosophy of 1968" presented in Luc Ferry and Alain Renaut's 1985 essay, *Le Pensée 68* (translated as *French Philosophy of the Sixties: An Essay on Antihumanism*), includes commentary on Foucault's *The Order of Things* (1966), Deleuze's *Difference and Repetition* (1968), and Derrida's *Writing and Difference* (1967).[53] Acknowledged as an influential founding text of postcolonial studies, Spivak's 1988 essay "Can the Subaltern Speak?" can be seen as a critique that deeply engages with the philosophy of 1968. Spivak's essay, for example, provides a critical reading of a dialogue between Michel Foucault (1926–1984) and Gilles Deleuze (1925–1995) on the topic of the intellectual representation of "society's Other."[54] In the 1996 essay collection *A Critique of Postcolonial Reason: Toward a History of the Vanishing Present*, Spivak revisits the issue of representation. (I examine her criticism of Foucault and Deleuze's perspective of representation in a later section of this chapter.)

Spivak's identification of herself as "a critical voice" can inform our understanding of Nakagami's identification of himself as a "person who has language" to represent the silenced voice. It is clear that these writers' social backgrounds differ markedly. While Nakagami was a member of Japan's marginalized Burakumin community, Spivak was born into a family of Brahmins, the highest caste in India. Rather than focusing on the class difference, I em-

---

51. Spivak and Milevska 2006, 72.

52. Hybridity is one of the most important aspects of Spivak's "reason"—that is, her motive—for seeking to contribute to the creation of new transcultural forms within the contact zone produced by colonization.

53. See Ferry and Renaut 1990.

54. Spivak 1988a, 271.

phasize their common status as privileged individuals who migrated from a peripheral homeland (colonial India for Spivak and the Ka-suga *hisabetsu buraku* for Nakagami) to the hegemonic center (the United States for Spivak and Tokyo mainstream Japanese society for Nakagami).[55] In doing so, I profile Nakagami's position as a hybrid writer "with two fields of activity," whose "critical voice" is situated between mainstream written language and the spoken language of his outcaste community with its large number of prewar-born people without education. In his interview with Jacques Derrida, Naka-gami explains that the aim of his narratives is to "recover the *katari mono bungei* (the oral tradition)" of people belonging to the lower strata of Japanese society. Nakagami also explains that his intertex-tual appropriation of the oral folklore of the illiterate community of his origins is his own "strategy" to "give [literary] representation" to political and cultural issues about Japan's outcastes.[56]

In spite of Nakagami's stated aim, his writing demonstrates the impossibility of the "successful" written representation, according to literary convention, of the spoken language of his peripheral homeland. This can be seen from the dismissive position some-times taken toward Nakagami by members of the mainstream cul-tural community, a position that is apparent in comments by Maruya Saiichi (1925–2012) regarding Nakagami's *Kiseki* (*The miracle*, 1989), which was nominated for the 1989 Tanizaki Jun'ichirō Literary Award. Maruya, like his fellow judges, Yoshiyuki Jun'nosuke (1924–1994) and Ōe Kenzaburō, was a graduate of the University of Tokyo—Japan's most prestigious academy—and a major literary figure of the time.[57] Maruya criticized *Kiseki* as "lacking polish" (*chōtaku o kaku*), claiming that the text did not follow conventional

---

55. Spivak 2000, 1.

56. This is a category that Nakagami argued included the emperor in addi-tion to the Burakumin, the group commonly understood to be referred to as outcaste. See Nakagami and Derrida 1996, 29.

57. Nakagami was nominated for the Tanizaki Jun'ichirō Literary Award six times. He was unsuccessful each time.

Japanese grammar or idiomatic expression.[58] Nakagami responded to this criticism in a lecture delivered while he was in attendance at the 1990 Frankfurt Book Fair in Germany:

> Those comments by other [Japanese writers] on the clumsiness of my written Japanese are, to me, nothing other than a clear statement which demonstrates that there is still an unassailable distance between *Japan* and *myself.* ... These writers criticise Japanese as written by me, a person who left the illiterate world to enter the world of letters, that is to say, the world of the formal Japanese language.
>
> Such comments vividly remind me of the time I first learnt Japanese characters. They make me recall the anxiety that I felt at that time. So, too, do they summon up the inexpressible anger and the strange sense of isolation that I once experienced. ...
>
> Therefore, I can do nothing but ask: how do *Japan* and *I* connect with each other? Do we overlap or disconnect? Is what I write even *Japan*? Am I a *Japanese*? These are my questions.[59]

Through his mastery of letters, Nakagami regarded himself as isolated from the "illiterate world," in other words, from the Burakumin community. Even so, he also regarded himself as isolated through his nonmastery, in terms of the demands made by Maruya, of the "world of the formal Japanese language," and mainstream Japanese society. Like Spivak, who positions herself "as a person with two fields of activity, always being a critical voice so that one doesn't get subsumed into the other,"[60] Nakagami seeks to speak with a "critical voice" to question his paradoxical social position, a position he sees as neither central nor peripheral.

The questions that Nakagami asks about his identity recall the deconstructionist problematization of identity in oppositional terms.

---

58. Maruya 1989, 388–90.
59. Nakagami 1999a, 345; emphasis in original.
60. Spivak and Arteaga 1996, 18.

An understanding of the social operation of binary opposites is a key aspect in the work of Derrida and Spivak. Each discusses how presence or identity is established only by an absence. We can apply this to Nakagami's situation by noting that the Burakumin are the "Burakumin" only because they are *not* the non-Burakumin. Discrimination against the weaker pair of a binary, such as the periphery or impurity, inevitably occurs in the establishment of social identification. The "weaker" of the pair is excluded from the mainstream of a community, which demands a consistent and exclusionary identification with the power components of the group. To challenge the hierarchy involved in binary oppositions, Nakagami voluntarily retains a sense of hybridity and paradox within himself to write narratives that represent the spoken word. In the discussion that follows, Nakagami's literary representation of oral folklore, such as "Kyōdai shinjū," is interpreted as a product of the writer's radical reflection on binaries such as central/peripheral and literate/illiterate.

The Theory of Representation

Any intellectual who tries to articulate the hidden—or subjugated—voice of subaltern groups or undertake the task of disclosing the consciousness of the socially marginalized must understand the significance of the process of "representation." In "Can the Subaltern Speak?" and its sequel work, *A Critique of Postcolonial Reason*, Spivak reads Marx's view of representation as given in *The Eighteenth Brumaire of Louis Bonaparte* (1852) to highlight the necessity and impossibility of representation. *The Eighteenth Brumaire* examines the 1851 coup d'état instigated by Charles-Louis Napoléon Bonaparte (1808–1873) and the consequent despotism of his rule (1852–1870).

In his classic analysis of the French democratic parliamentary system of the time in *The Eighteenth Brumaire*, Marx explains that the relationship between a "democratic representative" and the "represented" is that of "the political and literary representatives" and "the petty bourgeoisie." He asserts that even though both belong to the bourgeoisie, given the former's education and elite position, political and literary representatives are "as far apart as heaven and earth" from the people they represent.[61] Thus, a representative system inevitably includes a hierarchy between the hegemonic representative—who controls the system—and the represented. In *Rekishi to hanpuku* (*History and Repetition*, 2004), Karatani reads this passage, noting that Marx emphasizes the severance of political parties and their discourse from the lived experiences (and suffering) of the members of an actual class.[62] Karatani explains that in the representative system, the discourse of representatives (political parties) can never be considered equivalent to the interest of "actual [small-holding peasant/worker] classes." This is because the discourses—including the rationale for decisions made and actions taken—are completely "arbitrary" and "independent" from the consciousness of this actual class. Citing Kenneth Burke's view, Karatani concludes that actual classes are "class unconscious" and are only made conscious of their position as a (small-holding peasant/worker) class when they are able to see through (and understand the deceit of) the discourse of the hegemonic representative.[63]

According to Karatani, Marx's objective in *The Eighteenth Brumaire* is to reveal the "mystery"[64] or riddle (*nazo*)[65] that made an emperor of Louis Napoléon Bonaparte. Karatani argues that Marx rejects attributing Louis Napoléon's assumption of power to his ideas, strategies, or character. Instead, continues Karatani, Marx's text asserts that only through mechanisms such as political representation or cultural representation—representations that are "arbitrary" and "independent" from class—is power exercised. Moving beyond the bourgeoisie to develop this paradox, moreover, Marx

---

61. Marx 1963, 50–51.
62. Karatani 2012a, 8.
63. Karatani 2012a, 8–10. In this discussion, Karatani refers to Kenneth Burke's 1966 book *Language as Symbolic Action: Essays on Life, Literature, and Method*.
64. Karatani 2012a, 10.
65. Karatani 2004, 14.

discusses the small-holding peasant as the lowest strata of the hier-archy of the democratic parliamentary system. He argues that this group of people form a class, "in so far as millions of families live under economic conditions of existence that separate their mode of life, their interests, and their culture from those of the other classes, and put them in hostile opposition to the latter."[66] He asserts that given that "there is merely a local interconnection among these small-holding peasants," the group simultaneously and contradicto-rily does not constitute a class. Since the "identity of their interests begets no community, no national bond," and there is "no political organization among them," they cannot be said to have a class con-sciousness.[67] Marx goes on to point out:

> They are consequently incapable of enforcing their class interest in their own name, whether through a parliament or through a convention. They cannot represent themselves [*sich vertreten*], they must be represented [*vertreten werden*]. Their representative must at the same time appear as their master, as an authority over them as an unlimited governmental power that protects them against the other classes and sends them rain and sunshine from above. The political influence of the small-holding peasants, therefore, finds its final expression in the executive power subordinating society to itself.[68]

In this passage, small-holding peasants are discussed as silenced people who are only capable of forming a class—we might say of articulating a position or, in Spivakian terms, expressing their voice—when they are represented by a "representative" from their own group. However, they reject this in favor of a "representative" from the elite class. Karatani sums up Marx's view of small-holding peasants as a class with neither its own representatives nor a dis-course—voice—that would either represent or protect its own class

66. Marx 1963, 124.
67. Marx 1963, 124.
68. Marx 1963, 124.

interests. The group must therefore be represented by someone else. The most puzzling element of the "mystery" that Karatani regards as the core of Marx's discussion is the fact that rather than seeking a representative from their own group, small-holding peasants consciously cast their ballots for Louis Napoléon as their "emperor." If they had chosen someone from their own group, this representative would have been able to take these "voiceless" people into the political arena and thereby give them a political voice.[69]

Said and Spivak both discuss Marx's passage referring to the small-holding peasant. In *Orientalism* (1978), Said cites Marx's ironic assertion, "Sie können sich nicht vertreten, sie müssen vertreten werden" (They cannot represent themselves, they must be represented), when critiquing "the Orientalist, poet or scholar, who, believing that the Orient cannot do this for itself, diligently represents this space to 'render its mysteries plain for and to the West.'" According to Said, this Orientalist "representation" is always justified by the cliché that "if the Orient could represent itself, it would; since it cannot, the representation does the job, for the West, and *faute de mieux*, for the poor Orient." Said's commentary emphasizes the need for such representations to be understood "*as representations*," not as "natural" depictions of the Orient.[70] This argument refers to the West's Orientalist practices rather than the subalternity of the Orient. We can apply Said's ideas to writers—or, to borrow Nakagami's words, people who "have language"—whose representations confirm the hegemonic power of elites in their literary production and thus act to silence subaltern people or even create new subaltern groups.

In *A Critique of Postcolonial Reason*, Spivak reads this passage as Marx's ironic view of how Louis Napoléon fraudulently represented the small-holding peasants while simultaneously suppressing this group as "revolutionary" subjects opposed to bourgeois interests. Perceptively noting that there are two senses of representation—

---

69. Karatani 2012a, 15–16.
70. Said 1995, 20–21.

"representation as 'speaking for' as in politics," and "representation as 're-presentation' as in art or philosophy"—Spivak points out that Marx's German text clearly demonstrates the difference between these two senses of representation. In the passage cited above that refers to the small-holding peasants, Marx uses *vertreten* to mean "represent" in the sense of speaking for as in politics, rather than *darstellen* ("re-present" as in art or philosophy). Nevertheless, in this passage, Marx tries to articulate small-holding peasants as social "subjects" whose consciousness is suppressed by the parliamentary representative and dislocated from and incoherent for those, such as writers and artists, who represent these peasants in cultural production. Furthermore, the representation of the small-holding peasants undertaken by elite writers and artists is completely dislocated from the lived experiences of this group. In her textual analysis of Marx's discussion of the small-holding peasant, Spivak argues that in addition to exposing the fraudulent nature of elite parliamentary representation, Marxist scholars have a responsibility to expose the fraudulent nature of elitist cultural representation, including literature.[71]

While she respects the position of Marx, Spivak criticizes other elites, including Foucault and Deleuze, for what she regards as their carelessness in confusing the two senses of representation. In her critique, she cites several passages from the commentary given by Deleuze in "Intellectuals and Power: A Conversation between Michel Foucault and Gilles Deleuze" (1972). In this work, Deleuze declares, "There is no more representation; there's nothing but action"—particularly "action of theory and action of practice which relate to each other as relays and form networks."[72] Noting serious flaws in this argument, Spivak disputes these claims.

> Since theory is also only "action," the theoretician does not represent (speak for) the oppressed group. Indeed, the subject is not

---

71. Spivak 1999, 256–60.
72. Foucault and Deleuze 1977, 205–17.

seen as a representative consciousness (one re-presenting reality adequately). These two senses of representation—within state information and the law, on the one hand, and in subject-predication, on the other—are related but irreducibly discontinuous. To cover over the discontinuity with an analogy that is presented as a prop reflects again a paradoxical subject-privileging. *Because* "the person who speaks and acts ... is always a multiplicity," no "theorizing intellectual ... [or] party or ... union" can represent "those who act and struggle."[73] Are those who act and *struggle* mute, as opposed to those who act and *speak*? These immense problems are buried in the differences between the "same" words: consciousness and conscience (both *conscience* in French), representation and re-presentation.[74]

As Marx argues in *The Eighteenth Brumaire*, the elite representative (both parliamentary and cultural) deprives the social subject of "representative consciousness (one re-presenting reality adequately)." In Spivak's interpretation of the Foucault–Deleuze conversation, the men simply believe that (as a result of their own "insightful" theories and actions) the oppressed can be heard and will have influence in the wider society.[75] Although she does not accuse the French thinkers of deliberate oppression, she does argue that they efface the subaltern voice. Most important, in their representations of the subaltern, Deleuze and Foucault "systematically ... ignore the question of ideology and their own implication in intellectual and economic history."[76] Spivak writes, quite damningly in fact, that what many leftist intellectuals display is often nothing more than a list of "politically uncanny subalterns" they have known. She goes on to accuse these intellectuals of self-constructing as "transpar-

---

73. These words in quotes are cited by Spivak from Foucault and Deleuze 1977, 206.

74. Spivak 1999, 256–57, emphasis in original by Spivak from Foucault and Deleuze 1977, 206.

75. Spivak 1999, 257.

76. Spivak 1999, 249.

ent." In other words, Spivak accuses those concerned of making themselves invisible in the process of the oppressive representation of subaltern groups. In this way, they abrogate responsibility toward those groups.[77]

To Spivak, the projects undertaken by scholars like Foucault or Deleuze are merely reports on the "nonrepresented subject," which, in spite of the claims made by the authors, provide nothing more than a superficial analysis (which, Spivak contends, is not actually an analysis) of the operation of "the power and desire of the [hegemonic] Subject." Their work provides no opportunity for the oppressed to speak. Citing Said, Spivak criticizes Foucault's view of power for obliterating "the rôle of class, the rôle of economics, the rôle of insurgency and rebellion." She rejects the Foucault–Deleuze conversation for the inability of either to see that difference existed between terms such as "representation" and "power." She argues that Deleuze and Foucault belong to "the exploiters" side of the international division of labor. No matter how sincerely they might try to critique the constitution of the global hegemony of Europe and the West, they are irretrievably caught within the process of the production of the Other in which Europe and the West engage. Spivak appropriates Foucault's phrase "epistemic violence" to refer to the interest of the intellectual whose secret power and desire persistently constitute "the Other as the Self's shadow."[78] The Foucault–Deleuze conversation is a good example of how, even in conversations between those Gramsci would surely have regarded as potential organic intellectuals, the hegemonic discourse of the intellectual entrenches the oppression of the subaltern.

Spivak asks whether "the intellectual" or even the "indigenous" representative—whom she refers to as the "native informant"—can "represent" the subaltern voice.[79] In her terminology, the native informant is a member of the subaltern group who is co-opted

---

77. Spivak 1999, 257.
78. Spivak 1999, 265–66.
79. Spivak 1999, 283.

by the dominant group. Seen as a "blank" on whom dominants can impress their ideas, the native informant is thus "generative of a text of cultural identity that only the West or Western-model discipline could inscribe."[80] As apparent from her title, *A Critique of Postcolonial Reason*, Spivak warns that the discourse of postcolonial/colonial studies can possibly become an "alibi" that serves "the production of current neo-colonial knowledge." This alibi emerges when a native informant from "the South," that is, the subaltern space, expresses their silenced voice for the interest of "the North," that is, hegemonic mainstream. In doing so, they become the "self-marginalizing" or "self-consolidating" postcolonial subject. This transformation removes the possibility of legitimate "native" information—information related to actual lived experience—being delivered by the informant.[81] Since the discourse of such a postcolonial subject inevitably assists the domination of the South by the North, their discourse must also support the North's penchant for the "binarism" which, with the hierarchies of meaning inherent in pairs such as center/periphery, culture/nature, and male/female, works to institutionalize discrimination.[82] Such binarism continually creates new forms of oppression for the marginalized. This mechanism is what I call "the paradox of representing the silenced voice."

Although she suggests that the "true" subaltern group is "gender-unspecified," Spivak nonetheless observes that her analysis often reveals "the poorest woman of the South" as the most deprivileged subaltern.[83] She calls these women whose voices are erased by the multiple working of ideologies such as imperialism, patriarchy, and heteronormativity the "foreclosed native informant."[84] There is an important distinction between foreclosed native informants whose voices are never heard and self-consolidating native

---

80. Spivak 1999, 6.

81. Spivak 1999, 1–6.

82. Ashcroft, Griffiths, and Tiffin 2007, 18–21.

83. Spivak 1999, 6.

84. Spivak 1999, 6.

informants whose voices are co-opted by the hegemony. Whereas the latter entrench the position of power elites, the former struggle to have their voices heard at all. This will become evident in the discussion in chapter 5 that draws on Spivak's ideas to present the aged Burakumin woman in Nakagami's narratives as the "most" oppressed woman of Kumano, that is, of the Japanese South.

As was the case with Europeans who sought to represent the East, and French theorists who failed to understand their complicity in the production of the Other, the gulf between subalterns and the intellectuals—including educated indigenous subjects (native informants) such as Guha—who try to "represent" the voice of subalterns is, to borrow Marx's terminology, as great as the gulf between "heaven and earth." These "elite" intellectuals are therefore inevitably positioned as outsiders by the perceived "nonelite" members of subaltern society. Spivak foregrounds the imbalance between the elite and the nonelite within subaltern society.[85] The ever self-consolidating native informant who represents their silenced voice for the interest of hegemonic mainstream society is inevitably paradoxical. This is because if a subaltern were able to "represent" their own voice then, by definition, that person would cease to be a subaltern who cannot be heard by others. This, I argue, is the dilemma in which Nakagami found himself.

In the face of the epistemic violence that must inevitably be committed by the intellectual in the process of representation, Spivak poses the question: "can the subaltern speak?"[86] She further inquires, "How can we touch the consciousness of the people, even as we investigate their politics?,"[87] and "What might the elite do to watch out for the continuing construction of the subaltern?"[88] She notes that matters relating to "the subaltern woman" seem to be the most challenging aspect of these questions.

---

85. Spivak 1999, 271–308.
86. Spivak 1999, 269.
87. Spivak 1999, 272–73.
88. Spivak 1999, 281

In so fraught a field, it is not easy to ask the question of the consciousness of the subaltern woman; it is thus all the more necessary to remind pragmatic radicals that such a question is not an
idealist red herring. Though all feminist or antisexist projects cannot be reduced to this one, to ignore it is an unacknowledged
political gesture that has a long history and collaborates with a
masculine radicalism that renders the place of the investigator
transparent. In seeking to learn to speak to (rather than listen to
or speak for) the historically muted subject of the subaltern
woman, the postcolonial intellectual *systematically* "unlearns" female privilege [that is of the woman scholar]. This systematic unlearning involves learning to critique postcolonial discourse with
the best tools it can provide and not simply substituting the lost
figure of the colonized.[89]

Donna Landry and Gerald Maclean, editors of *The Spivak Reader*
(1996), explain that coming to terms with the "loss" or disadvantage
associated with the "systematic unlearning" of privilege is one of
"the most powerful tasks" Spivak sets for her readers.[90] Noting that
there is no "contemporary metropolitan investigator" who is not
influenced by "the masculine-imperialist ideological formation,"[91]
Spivak acknowledges that she herself is a privileged intellectual. For
her, the "unlearning project" must start from the articulation of the
scholar-subject's attachment to hegemonic formations—"by *measur-
ing* silences, if necessary—into the object of investigation."[92] When
we try to find how to "speak to (rather than listen to or speak for),"
we realize that our privilege has become an obstacle, that is, a "loss"
or disadvantage in terms of the activity in which we are engaged.
According to Spivak, unlearning our knowledge permits us to con-
front and invalidate masculine-imperialist discourses that lead to
oppression. Thus, in her words, intellectuals must "critique post-

---

89. Spivak 1988a, 295.
90. Landry and Maclean 1996, 4.
91. Spivak 1999, 283.
92. Spivak 1999, 284.

colonial discourse with the best tools it can provide" so that we can
eventually "touch the consciousness of the people" without involving a "continuing construction of the subaltern."[93] In his writing,
Nakagami adopts a number of strategies—which are not always
successful—to depict the defiance of women against masculinist
practice. These attempts closely parallel Spivak's call for a need to
critique postcolonial discourse "with the best tools it [i.e., postcolonial discourse] can provide."

In her analysis of the socially silenced woman, Spivak profiles
the dead Indian women subjected to sati, the Hindu practice of a
widowed woman's self-immolation on her husband's funeral pyre.
These women's voices were effaced by the mixed workings of imperialist and domestic patriarchies, both of which were complicit in
the oppression of women in colonial India. The Hindu practice of
sati (literally, good wife) was banned by the British Raj in 1829
within its territories in India. This abolition was historically regarded by the West as a "case of white men" gallantly "saving brown
women from brown men."[94] In opposition to this interpretation,
modern Indian nativists such as Pandurang Vaman Kane (1880–
1972) praised the sati ritual as symbolic of the "ideals of womanly
conduct" and evidence of "the cool and unfaltering courage of Indian women."[95] As Spivak notes, by insisting that "the women actually wanted to die,"[96] these "benevolent and enlightened"[97] male
nativists claimed to give the burned widows a voice and thereby
transform them into subjects—rather than objects—of the sati
practice. Spivak goes on to point out that this merely made the
women scapegoats in male justifications of patriarchy and nationalism. Such justifications are logically of the same category as the ra-
tionalization of colonialism by "white" men who saw their rule over
India as their burden to establish a "good society" in an otherwise

93. Spivak 1999, 281.
94. Spivak 1999, 287.
95. Spivak 1999, 294.
96. Spivak 1999, 287.
97. Spivak 1999, 294.

"uncivilized" part of the world. Spivak critiques nativist thought as nothing but a parody of the "nostalgia for lost origin."[98] In other words, she points out that nativist discourse is merely the essentialist assumption that native cultures remain unchanged in spite of the violent impact of colonial rule. The erroneous assumption of the native culture and its representatives is that it is able to recover itself at any time to its former or precolonial state. Spivak argues, however, that for the practice of sati, this is obviously not the case. In the nineteenth century, this custom presented a new dilemma for Indian women. If these women chose to become a sati they consented to a domestic patriarchal norm. If they did not, they were regarded as traitorous followers of imperialism.

In the nineteenth century, Indian women were subjected to this dilemma regardless of class. In Spivak's analysis of the muted woman, she references the Rani (Indian queen, the wife of a Raja) of Sirmur as the embodiment of this dilemma in that she was removed from her "no doubt patriarchal and dissolute" husband and managed by "a young white man."[99] Thus, rather than becoming a sati in the conventional sense, she was taken against her will to become the sati of "the commercial/territorial interests of the East India Company," which the young white man represented.[100] Whether a nineteenth-century Indian woman should become a sati or nonsati became *the* issue around which colonizers and nativists vied in defending the legitimacy of their respective ideologies. Because neither had any interest in the voice of the real-life Indian woman, both denied her the right to assert herself as a subject. In this context, "there [was] no space from which the sexed subaltern subject [could] speak."[101]

In contrast to the examples of sati and the Rani, Spivak sees the suicide of a young unmarried woman activist as a subaltern inter-

---

98. Spivak 1999, 287-88.
99. Spivak 1999, 233–34.
100. Spivak 1999, 277.
101. Spivak 1999, 307.

vention into—or a "rewriting" of—the social text of sati-suicide. In 1926, during the struggle for Indian independence, activist Bhubaneswari Bhaduri (birth uncertain, although Spivak speculates she was only sixteen or seventeen at the time of her death), hanged herself while menstruating. Based on a letter Bhubaneswari wrote to her sister, Spivak explains that the girl committed suicide because she was frustrated by her inability to commit to terrorist activity. Concerned that her family might think the cause of her death was an "illicit pregnancy," she waited for her menstrual cycle to begin before taking her own life. Because Bhubaneswari's family saw her simply as a sati-to-be, they never understood the reasons for her activism or her suicide. The "physiological inscription" to which she was subjected demonstrates that the motive for suicide by an Indian woman of the time could only ever be rationalized within a framework of the "legitimate passion by a single male." Through interviews with the girl's family, Spivak realized that Bhubaneswari's voice could never be heard in the imperial and patriarchal context because both her family and the colonizers regarded her suicide as a complete "puzzle," an "absurdity," and "a case of delirium."[102]

Spivak concedes that given their privileged status, neither the noble Rani of Sirmur nor Bhubaneswari, a metropolitan middle-class girl, were "true" subalterns. What Spivak emphasizes here by offering the narratives of these women, however, is the impossibility of the voice of the gendered subject effectively speaking or being heard. In the colonial text, the Rani only appeared as an object to be controlled by either colonizers or nativists. Although Bhubaneswari tried to "speech" her self-conscious responsibility for her death by making her own body an "instrument,"[103] ultimately (and tragically) the legitimacy of her "speech act"[104] was refused by her family and

---

102. Spivak 1999, 307.

103. Spivak 1999, 273.

104. Spivak 1999, 273. I see Spivak's use of the term "speech act" as similar to the use by John Langshaw Austin in *How to Do Things with Words* (1962). Austin discusses the term as a performative utterance issued to intend significance as a socially valid verbal action. See Austin 1962, 45–52. Based on this concept, Spi-

wider society.[105] Spivak explains, "once a woman performs an act of resistance without infrastructure that would make us recognize resistance, her resistance is in vain."[106] This is the case regardless of a woman's class or status. It is also the case for men of low social status. Spivak referred to this excluded political and social position, which denies a subject access to civil society, as "subalternity."[107] Her view provides a key perspective to my analysis of Nakagami's depiction of marginalized characters, particularly his Burakumin women. These women include Satoko, a prostitute who unknowingly commits incest with her half-brother, and Yuki, who was sold to a brothel as a fifteen-year-old to support her fatherless family. Like Bhubaneswari, these women are constructed, to use Spivak's words, as puzzles, absurdities, and cases of delirium. Their attempts to express their voices to resist their hegemonic center were inevitably "in vain." As we will see in later chapters, these women had no access to any infrastructure that might have permitted recognition of their resistance.

In the conclusion of "Can the Subaltern Speak?," Spivak noted that because the subaltern cannot speak, it is the duty of intellectuals to re-present them. While this presents the intellectual with a challenging contradiction, Spivak argues that she (the intellectual) "must not disown" this "circumscribed" task "with a flourish."[108] In

---

vak sees Bhubaneswari's suicide as a statement of her subjectivity expressed by using her own body.

105. In addition to being refused at the time of her death, Bhubaneswari's voice continues to be refused today. This is apparent in the narrative of the activist's family given by Spivak in *A Critique of Postcolonial Reason*. She notes how Bhubaneswari's great-grandniece brought "jubilation" to the whole family when she was promoted to an executive position in a US-based transnational corporation. While Bhubaneswari fought as an activist for national liberation, her great-grandniece works as a representative of globalization that is legitimated and manipulated by the new empire. As Spivak remarks, this is also an example of the "historical silencing of the subaltern." See Spivak 1999, 311.

106. Spivak and Milevska 2006, 60.

107. Spivak and Milevska 2006, 72.

108. Spivak 1988a, 308.

A Critique of Postcolonial Reason, Spivak admits that her earlier conclusion that the subaltern cannot speak was an "inadvisable remark."[109] Drawing on Abena Busia's "positive" comment that, after all, Spivak is "able to read Bhubaneswari's case, and therefore she (Bhubaneswari) *has* spoken in some way,"[110] Spivak apparently acknowledges that, although difficult, it is possible for a subaltern to have their voice heard to some extent. In interrogating notions of representation, we have already seen Spivak's critique of the geopolitical determination of the West, including her critique of the role of the intellectual. In addition, we noted how it is essential for the intellectual to "unlearn" privilege to "hear" the subaltern voice. By actively committing to these principles, it is possible to support the "subaltern's cultural and political movement into the hegemony," which Spivak sees as the most important role of the (postcolonial) intellectual. One of the underlying assumptions of this book is that although situated in a very different context, Nakagami had the same approach as Spivak to the representation of the silenced voice in Japan. Accordingly, the discussion that follows returns repeatedly to Spivak's ideas in mapping the contours of Nakagami's work.

Representation of the Foreclosed Burakumin Voice

Before discussing the paradox of representation and Spivak's related question "Can the subaltern speak?" in relation to Nakagami's work, it is necessary to revisit—following Spivak's injunction—the geopolitical parameters of the Kumano writer's textual production. Almost all of Nakagami's writing is set in or references the geographical site of Kishū Kumano (as discussed in a previous section of this chapter). The travel journal *Kishū* is a particularly good example of Nakagami's use of the geopolitical that also provides ex-

---

109. Spivak 1999, 308.
110. Busia 1989, 102–3. Cited in Spivak 1999, 309.

cellent insight into Nakagami's consciousness of the fraught process of representing the silenced voice.

From March to December 1977, to serialize a travel journal in the magazine *Asahi journal*, Nakagami undertook an intermittent nine-month journey through the Kii Peninsula. During this time, he visited over twenty *hisabetsu buraku* communities. While traveling, he encountered, observed, and recorded various forms of discrimination against Buraku people. His purpose in undertaking this journey was to know "what people do not openly talk about, the things that they refuse to talk about to outsiders."[111] *Kishū* demonstrates Nakagami's attempt to discover the significance of the silences that were evident in interviews with Burakumin and non-Buraku people during his journeys. Nakagami was struck by the complex nature of the discriminatory practices he encountered on his travels. Noting that "the word 'discrimination' is too simple," he concluded that: "'Discrimination' needs to be classified in terms of the spectra of those discriminating and those being discriminated against."[112]

In one section of *Kishū*, Nakagami gives an account of a meeting convened by local people in Koza, a small town at the southern tip of the Kii Peninsula. These people had previously requested a correction to material that Nakagami had published about discrimination against Burakumin fishermen from the Nishimukai precinct in Koza town. Nakagami had written that Nishimukai Burakumin fishermen, newcomers to the profession, were discriminated against by traditional Koza fishermen opposed to the entry of new players to the local industry. The meeting attendees objected to this claim. The group had also complained about Nakagami's description of the town as "gloomy," a word that was seen as antagonistic to the Koza town administration's efforts to promote the area and downplay Burakumin issues.[113]

---

111. NKZ 14:481.
112. NKZ 14:598.
113. NKZ 14:613.

To be honest, … I expected to be severely denounced by the people from the *hisabetsu buraku*. This is because I have language. No
matter the circumstances, those who have written language are
obliged to be "criticized" by those with no written language. For
now, I will refer to those with no written language as voiceless
people. I had [previously] seen my role as taking the language of
the voiceless and releasing this back to them in order to give it
shine and energy. However, there were no voiceless people at the
meeting that was held in the community center at Nishimukai,
Koza. Those who attended the meeting to request a correction of
the "facts" that I had written were probably there to represent the
voiceless people. I was left with an impression of their politeness
toward me as a writer of language. I cannot help thinking why.[114]

In this statement, Nakagami demonstrates the multiple layers of
hierarchy that operate even within a seemingly homogeneous group
in terms of the relationship between the representatives and the
represented. We see Nakagami, the writer or intellectual in the
Gramscian sense who has "written language," the local native informant Burakumin representatives at the meeting, and the local
voiceless—in his word, *mukoku*—Buraku people who did not attend.

Influenced by 1968 New Left student activism in Japan, the
young Nakagami was an enthusiastic reader of Marx.[115] His writing
about the meeting with the people of Nishimukai demonstrates his
uncertainty about his position in his community, an uncertainty
that I argue was influenced by Marx's interrogation of the relationship between the represented and those who represent them. During
the meeting, Nakagami realized that, since the local representatives
have come to speak, they are not actually completely voiceless (*mukoku*) people. Therefore, it is impossible for him to hear the "real"

---

114. NKZ 14:613–14.
115. Nakagami included the Marx and Engels work *The German Ideology* in
his 1984 book list, "Monogatari/han-monogatari o meguru 150 satsu" ("150
books about narrative/anti-narrative"). See Nakagami 1998, 249.

voice of the voiceless. This is primarily the point Spivak makes in her essay on the subaltern voice. Like the Indian sati, who is unable to voice her position through multiple layers of oppression of patriarchal colonialism and nativist nationalism, the voiceless Buraku people experience a state of absence as subjects before intellectuals. We should recall here Busia's note that Spivak recovering Bhubaneswari's voice, which demonstrates some possibilities for the silenced voice to be heard. I will discuss Nakagami's writing of the voice of a fisherman's wife in Nishimukai who privately speaks to the writer.

Not only does subalternity operate on the grounds of structures such as class, race, and gender, there is also, as confirmed in much of Nakagami's work, a hierarchy in modes of "representation" that gives greater value to written over spoken language. Since Nakagami's generation had received the education denied to Burakumin in the past, he had access to the written word. He discusses how the local (uneducated) representatives who attended the meeting in Koza saw the power of the writer's words over their spoken language. Often denied formal education, the subaltern is also denied access to the more powerful mode of written representation. As a writer Nakagami held a "privilege" in Spivak's sense, and thus he lost the power to hear the voice of the "voiceless." (This is in spite of the fact that he originally had the background of a historically silenced Burakumin.) As previously noted, this paradox is suggested in Loomba's observation that the dominant and the oppressed are positioned simultaneously within several different discourses of power and resistance. The trinity—Nakagami, the indigenous representatives, and the voiceless people—contains not only a three-step hierarchy but also various intersected, less visible relationships that create fluid states of both power and resistance.

After the formal meeting with the Burakumin representatives, Nakagami met informally with a local Burakumin couple. Emerging from behind her fisherman husband's back, the wife broke a taboo and engaged in a "confidential" talk with Nakagami. She explained that although newcomer Nishimukai Burakumin fishermen

were superficially able to use any port around Koza, there were unfair differences in charges for port use for the newcomers compared
with established Koza fishermen. Because the Nishimukai port
used by newcomers was, in the wife's words, "nominal," and without facilities, these Burakumin fishermen were in fact forced to use
other ports. Listening to her, Nakagami realized that "although
there is no fact of discrimination, there actually is structural discrimination."[116] He sees that this structural discrimination is evident in the administrative "inefficiency" of the Koza authorities
who, in a relatively small town, have formed two different coopera-
tives for established, mainstream fishermen and newcomer fishermen. I consider "structural discrimination" to be what Nakagami
aims to make public by representing the silenced voice. Here, this
silenced voice is that of the woman whose words are never "authorized" by either her husband—although he permitted his wife to
speak, when questioned by Nakagami the husband refused to confirm what she had said—or the other local men who attended the
meeting. The Burakumin woman who conversed confidentially
with Nakagami is the native who seeks to speak but whose voice is
never heard—except by the intellectual who assumes the responsibility of hearing and representing her voice. In Spivak's words, she
is a "foreclosed native informant."[117] I argue that Nakagami's writing demonstrates a commitment to the almost impossible task of
representing the voice of foreclosed subalterns such as this woman.

To Spivak, literary or cultural representation has the potential to
collapse the hegemony. Rather than through "the accessible abstract
in general—the matheme still contaminated by the human,"[118]
which Spivak understands to include systems of capital—it is
through the concrete literary mode that subaltern women such as
the Rani of Sirmur or Bhubaneswari (we might include the Nishimukai fisherman's wife) can "exceed" the hegemonic system. Drawing

---

116. NKZ 14:619.
117. Spivak 1999, 1–6.
118. Spivak 1999, 245.

on this view, I read Nakagami's writing as exceeding the mainstream normative Japanese system to reveal how "structural discrimination" against the marginalized is inherent in this system. My analysis of Nakagami's fiction will probe the writer's attempts to engage in a mode of representation that is not complicit in justifying the hegemony of division between the mainstream North and the subaltern South, nor with the forces that collude to maintain this division in Japan. Through this approach, I demonstrate how Nakagami refused to become a self-marginalizing or self-consolidating Burakumin informant.

CHAPTER 2

The Voice of
a Transgressive
Young Man

A Young Writer in Tokyo

Nakagami Kenji is a novelist particularly known for his depiction of the inner landscape of transgressive young men.[1] This propensity is evident even in early works, such as the writer's memoirs of the late 1960s New Left protests and poems that express his ambivalent feelings toward his family (especially his half-brother) and his Kishū Kumano homeland. This chapter presents examples of Nakagami's early writings in addition to the short novel "Rakudo" ("Paradise," 1976), as a means of providing insights into the young writer's literary development.

In 1965, the eighteen-year-old Nakagami left Kumano for Tokyo to take the entrance exam for the prestigious Waseda University. This was the year after the Tokyo Olympics, an event that saw Japan emerge from the humiliation of postwar defeat to project "an

---

1. These protagonists are variously characterized as paper boys, illegitimate sons, orphans, male prostitutes, criminals, or members of social minority groups such as Burakumin, Ainu, or Korean residents in Japan.

91

image of confidence as the newest member of the world's leading industrial nations."[2] By the late 1960s, Japan's role as special procurer for the US military during the Korean War and then Vietnam War had taken the country into an era of rapid economic growth (from approximately 1955 until 1973). In 1968, with its gross national product exceeding that of West Germany, Japan became the world's second most productive nation behind the United States. By the mid-1950s, however, the developing postwar economy led to "wide-spread consumerism" and "a cultural climate of personal self-interest and material wealth"[3] for many in Japan. With a 1956 Japanese economic white paper (*Keizai hakusho*) proclaiming "It is no longer the postwar era," Japan's social consciousness shifted from common memories of defeat in war to the possibility of new economic and social success. Yumiko Iida labels this the emergence of "mass (*taishū*) society."[4] Given the desire of the emerging consumer masses to be members of the bourgeoisie and construct a nuclear family, Hasumi Shigehiko refers to this period of individualism as the "my home era."[5] This phrase invokes the general desire to acquire significant material goods, such as a television and a car.

Following the high-speed economic growth enjoyed by Japan in the previous decade, there was an expansion of publicly funded Assimilation Projects, such as the urbanization of provincial areas, including Nakagami's hometown of Shingū and its surrounds. In this process Nakagami's stepfather became a successful builder who had the financial means to send his wife's son to an elite private university. Nakagami, however, never enrolled in university but remained in Tokyo as a *yobikō sei* (student of a school that prepares candidates for university entrance exams).[6] He soon stopped attending even

---

2. Iida 2002, 119.

3. Iida 2002, 95.

4. Iida 2002, 114.

5. Asada, Karatani, Hasumi, and Miura 2002, 171.

6. In a 1991 interview with Karatani, Nakagami mentioned that he never sat the entrance exam for any university. See Nakagami and Karatani 1997, 316.

those classes to spend most of his time listening to jazz, taking drugs, reading books, and writing poems.[7] In 1965 he became involved in writing for and editing (1967–1970) the coterie literary journal *Bungei shuto* (*Literary metropolis*). During this time, Nakagami served his apprenticeship as a writer. Tsushima Yūko (1947–2016) was a regular contributor to this journal, as was Kiwa Kyō (b. 1945), whom Nakagami married in 1970.[8]

In addition to engaging in literary activity, from November 1967 the twenty-two-year-old Nakagami began to participate in the violent New Left protests known in Japanese as *gebaruto* (from the German *gewalt*, employment of force). Increasingly frustrated by the endless war in Vietnam, the politics of the Japanese government concerning university administration, the pending 1970 renewal of the Treaty of Mutual Cooperation and Security between the United States and Japan, and the 1972 reversion of Okinawa, the student movement in the late 1960s became more radical and violent.[9] In the second half of the 1960s, overt social upheaval broke out following New Left anti–Vietnam War protests and university campus conflicts. Rather than focusing on the benefits of rapid growth, generated mainly by heavy and chemical industries and the con-

---

7. Information about Nakagami's life in Tokyo and his stepfather's benefit from the urbanization of Shingū is mainly based on Takazawa 1998 and 2002.

8. Karlsson 2001, 11.

9. In his 1968 autobiographical essay, "Kakuzai no sedai no fukō" ("The misfortune of the generation armed with wooden batons"), Nakagami wrote that he participated in the Haneda protest (1967) and later in the Ōji Field Hospital protest (1968–1969). See Nakagami 2012, 174. These protests were directed against Prime Minister Satō Eisaku (1903–1974) in defiance of his strong support for the US–Japan Security Treaty and tacit Japanese support for US military operations in Vietnam. These violent *gebaruto* protests led to the political radicalization of New Left youth and crisis events such as the United Red Army (1971–1972) hostage crisis in February 1972 at Asama Mountain Lodge and the Japanese Red Army (1971–2001) involvement in the May 1972 Lod Airport massacre. See Suga 2003, 109–16. Takazawa explains that Nakagami's involvement in the New Left *gebaruto* was restricted to the role of sympathizer rather than being a committed activist group member. See Takazawa 1998, 55.

struction boom, protesters questioned the "my home era" to focus on loss (*sōshitsu*). Along with material gains, economic growth resulted in various dystopic environmental outcomes, such as Mina-mata disease (caused by severe mercury poisoning), officially ac-knowledged in 1968 as the direct result of pollution.[10] Rapid economic growth also came at a high cost for workers in terms of problems such as stress from overwork and obsessive company loy-alty.[11] Drawing on Marxist theory, New Left members began to see the individual as alienated from both nature and community. While being one of the young violent students, Nakagami was ironically only able to live like a hippie, or to use the Japanese word, *fūten*, by taking advantage of the financial support of his successful step-father.[12]

Nakagami's 1968 short story, titled "Nihongo ni tsuite" ("On the Japanese language"), depicts a young *fūten* who is hired by a group of anti–Vietnam War activists to care for a deserting African American soldier for five days. This work was short-listed for the 1968 Gunzō shinjin bungaku shō (Gunzō Literary Award for New Writers) and was runner-up for the 1969 Sakka shō (a literary award organized by the coterie magazine *Sakka*, or *Writers*). In spite of being praised for its "freshness" of language,[13] "Nihongo ni tsuite" was also criticized as a work written by one of the many epigones of Ōe Kenzaburō. This was because the characters in the novella, in-cluding the young male protagonist and the African American sol-dier, are similar to those in Ōe's prize-winning short story "Shiiku" ("Prize Stock," 1957). Certainly, Nakagami had been subject to the influence of Ōe, the most radical writer in Japan at the time, whose ideas had strong appeal for 1960s literary youth. Yet as inferred in a

---

10. Suga 2003, 183.

11. For further details, see the NHK documentary film *Sengo 70 nen Nippon no shōzō: Purorōgu* (*Images of Japan 70 years after the war's end: Prologue*, 2015).

12. Takazawa 1998, 9–15.

13. Quoted in Takayama 2007, 139. This was an excerpt from a comment on "Nihongo ni tsuite" made in *Gunzō* (June 1968) by Noma Hiroshi, a member of the selection committee.

1979 conversation between Minakami Tsutomu (1919–2004) and Nakagami titled "Fūdo to shutsuji no uta" ("A Song of birthplace and climate"), the late 1960s was an experimental era when the young writer from Shingū struggled to overcome the influence of Ōe and establish his own literary identity.[14]

In 1958—a decade before the New Left *gebaruto* protest movement—Nakagami's eldest half-brother, Kinoshita Ikuhei, hanged himself at the age of twenty-four. Nakagami was twelve at the time and living with his mother who, leaving Ikuhei in Kasuga, had taken her younger son and daughters to make a new family with a man from a neighboring town.[15] In his 1982 autobiographical essay titled "Karasu" ("Crows"), Nakagami notes how in the few years before his death Ikuhei became an aggressive alcoholic who often made Nakagami and his mother the target of violent, drunken behavior.[16] His 1969 autobiographical essay titled "Hanzaisha sengen oyobi waga bokei ichizoku" ("Declaration of a transgressor and my matrilineal family"), explains that Nakagami's mother bore a total of six children to two different men, her first husband and later Nakagami's biological father. The mother then married a man with a son, and this man became Nakagami's stepfather.[17] Nakagami's biographer, Takazawa Shūji, argues that the writer's *jōkyō* (leaving for Tokyo) was an attempt to escape from his homeland with its complicated family background, including the pall created by his brother's death.[18] Yet while Nakagami may have escaped physically, his ambivalent longing for his half-brother intensified as he became aware of the significance of the absence of "writing" for his deceased sibling.

---

14. Nakagami and Minakami 1980, 174. Although Minakami does not specifically refer to Ōe, Takayama notes that Ōe is the writer implied in this conversation. See Takayama 2007, 140–41.

15. Nakagami's family background information is also based on Takazawa 1998 and 2002 and Zimmerman 2007.

16. NKZ 5:429.

17. NKZ 14:137–38.

18. See Takazawa 1998 and 2002.

Following his marriage in 1970, Nakagami cut his connection
with New Left activism and its hippie-like lifestyle. He also gave up
writing speculative avant-garde poetry. Instead, he worked hard at a
range of manual labor jobs to support his new family while enthusiastically writing a series of short stories (*tanpen shōsetsu*). These were
often narratives of transgressive acts by gloomy young men who
were represented as *yobikō sei* with a similar *jōkyō* experience as those
of the writer. "Haiiro no koka kōra" ("Greyish Coca-Cola," 1972)
and "Jūkyūsai no chizu" ("Map of a nineteen-year-old," 1973) are
typical examples of the writer's works at that time. Nakagami's short
story "Rakudo" (discussed in the last half of this chapter) is also
modeled to some extent on the writer's experiences and family
background.

As noted already, two strong threads run through Nakagami's
late 1960s self-writing. These are his sense of lament around the
ambivalent memory of his dead half-brother and criticism of elite
New Left activists who wrote about their sense of fiasco and loss
after the collapse of the 1960 protest against the ratification of
Anpo, the Treaty of Mutual Cooperation and Security between the
United States and Japan. In spite of strong popular opposition, the
renegotiated agreement was forced through the Diet by then Prime
Minister Kishi Nobusuke (1896–1987), leaving the New Left lead-
ers of the 1960s anti-Anpo protests feeling bereft and impotent.[19]
In spite of the violent nature of many protests of the time, Iida explains that New Left voices in the 1960s came to be increasingly
represented by "romantic," "mute," and aesthetically inclined expressions of political actions and ideas.[20] Nakagami criticized this
trend as "revolutionist sentimentalism."[21] While despising New
Left writers, Nakagami was nevertheless aware that unlike his illiterate half-siblings, he himself was one of the privileged youth who
committed themselves to literature and activism. In other words, he

---

19. Iida 2002, 115–16.
20. Iida 2002, 115.
21. NKZ 14:134.

saw himself as affiliated with the New Left while contradictorily holding that group in contempt.

In an essay written in 1968, Nakagami noted that Ikuhei's death provided one of the most important motivations for his becoming a writer. During the Anpo struggles, a girl student, Kanba Michiko (1937–1960), lost her life and became an icon of the movement. To Nakagami, Ikuhei's death had much greater social import than the death of what he regarded as a privileged girl. Ikuhei's death strongly affected Nakagami's sense of self.

> I keep writing although it's nothing about someone else but all about myself. Actually, the person who died in 1960 when, after the chaos of the Occupation era, Japan entered a time of imperialism was never Kanba Michiko, a University of Tokyo student, but my only uneducated Cain in the world—my own brother. What has happened in the ten years that have elapsed since then? It's for that reason that now I must take responsibility for everything that happened within my own self as a writer and also as an actual person.[22]

This juxtaposition and blurring of the "uneducated" Ikuhei with the prestigiously educated Kanba Michiko, who died two years after his brother, is one expression of Nakagami's view of the binary relationship between center and periphery, here expressed as literate and illiterate. Although Ikuhei's Burakumin background was not revealed in the essay—Nakagami had not made this aspect of his life public at the time—the binary relationship between non-Burakumin and Burakumin in terms of education was undoubtedly a key factor in the writer's mind. For this author, literacy was a critical aspect of the difference between himself and his brother, a difference that was literally one of life and death.

The vehemence of his critique of the "revolutionist sentimentalism" of the student movement is apparent in the passage below, in which Nakagami castigates a poet from the movement, Osada

---

22. NKZ 14:134.

Hiroshi (1939–2015). "Shut up, you unscathed bystander! The instant poet who describes himself as a fresh wanderer can never know the young man who died miserably by hanging himself, or know that among the bereaved who are brooding on that death, one suffers repeated bouts of insanity while another keeps scattering words like curses."[23] In 1965, the "instant poet," Osada, published a collection of verse titled *Warera shinsen na tabibito* (*We, the fresh wanderers*), dedicated as a "requiem" to the death of four young Anpo activists, including Kanba.[24] The monologue by the young man depicted in the title piece, "Warera shinsen na tabibito," tells of a former activist who overcomes the sense of defeat he felt after the Anpo struggle and moved on to share the future with his new wife. While the opening verse depicts the man's sense of remorse for "the dead" who lost their lives in "the spring time of our lives" (*seishun*),[25] the closing lines display his sense of hope at starting a family:

> Feeling fury toward poverty and misfortune
> Surrounded by the resounding echo of the flow of water through
>   the valley
> With sunlight playing like a spy through the trees
> We do nothing but remain standing without being forgiven
> . . .
> Love me
> My love
> As if holding time like a burning ball

---

23. NKZ 14:134.

24. These four Anpo activists are Kanba Michiko, Kishigami Daisaku (1939–1960, *tanka* poet and student of Kokugakuin University, committed suicide in 1960), Kayano Hiroshi (1935–1960, student of the University of Tokyo, died of an asthma attack), and Kusama Teruo (1935–1960, dramatist, died of overwork). In the subheading of his poem "Warera shinsen na tabibito," Osada refers to these four activists as "our fellows all with a letter K in their initials who died in 1960." See Osada 1965, 107–17. This subheading does not appear in the definitive edition of *Warera shinsen na tabibito*, published in 2012.

25. Osada 1965, 107.

My wife, I embrace you
Again and again I embrace you
…
The dead need neither wreath nor gravestone
For these dead met a perfect death
Give to us a child
Give us a child![26]

For Nakagami, Osada's poetry is a typical example of the deceit of the New Left *bungaku seinen* (young men who love literature) who identify *warera* (themselves) as "fresh," that is, as innocent, by exploiting the stories of others, here the dead activists. Osada's work can be read as a typical representation of what Iida refers to as the "romantic, collective and agonised" subject following the collapse of the Anpo movement.[27] This New Left sentimentalism can be also interpreted, in the words of Spivak, as "self-marginalizing" by the activists who, in spite of the fact that as elite writers they must always belong to the hegemonic center, construct themselves as helpless, wounded, Anpo conflict losers. They are, however, actually "self-consolidating"[28] and thereby bringing advantage to themselves by using the power of writing. As discussed in chapter 1, Spivak criticizes self-marginalizing subjects who ignore the fact that they have the power of representation and thereby conceal a desire to affiliate with the power structures of the hegemonic society.

Nakagami's biting critique of Osada's poem can be read as a criticism of both the exclusionary nature of the collective identification by New Left activists as "ourselves" and the lack of geopolitical perspective in their ideas. Although belonging to the same generation as the activists, neither Ikuhei, who committed suicide on March 3, 1958, nor his half-sister who suffered spasmodic bouts of insanity after Ikuhei's death, are ever implied in the *warera* as voiced

---

26. Osada 1965, 117.
27. Iida 2002, 126.
28. Spivak 1999, 6.

by the poet from the Tokyo center, Osada. Through his elite collective perspective, Osada mistakenly regards a "spirit that feels freshness after enduring chaos"[29] as the common sentiment of his generation in the mid-1960s.[30] Nakagami is deeply critical of the poet's ignorance of those such as his siblings who are "uneducated" youth on the periphery and have no written words to represent themselves and cannot be released from the mainstream discrimination directed against them. Furthermore, while the poet embraces his wife and longs for a child, Ikuhei died single and without children.

This idea of the new life for which the former activist, Osada, longed following the Anpo collapse closely parallels the notion of the everyday life of the Japanese masses (*taishū*) that emerged in the mid-1950s. The legitimacy of these masses was confirmed by spirited poet and radical theorist Yoshimoto Takaaki. Yoshimoto's antisectarian philosophy of independence, known as *jiritsu shisō*, had a strong influence on 1960s New Left students who were searching for strategies to help them operate collectively outside the authority structures. These structures ranged from the Japan Communist Party to university administrations. Nakagami was a keen reader of Yoshimoto's poems and essays, and it is reasonable to assume that he was influenced by that thinker's ideas.[31] Yoshimoto's "archetypical image of the masses" (*taishū no genzō*) can be seen in one of his early poems:

---

29. Osada 1965, 115.

30. The Anpo activism of 1960, however, declined rapidly after the passage of the treaty by default on June 19 and the consequent July 19 resignation of Prime Minister Kishi. As seen in a June 27 1960 article, published in the weekly magazine *Shūkan bunshū*, "Demo wa owatta, sā, shūshoku da" ("The demonstration is over, so now we need to look for a job"), the students returned to university to finish their degrees and find work. The employment rate of 1960 university graduates hit a postwar record of almost 100 percent. See Oguma 2005, 547.

31. For example, see Nakagami and Yoshimoto's 1983 conversation "Bungaku to genzai" ("Literature and the present") in Nakagami and Yoshimoto 2005, 48–81.

I respect the countless number of people who are born, marry, bear children, bring them up and grow old, your meager dinner on the table, your dismal religion, your life conflicts, your envy and so on. The humming of your innocent son …

On this evening, I wish you happiness …

And scholars, so-called artists and noisy verbose authorities, I wish that you would cease your contemptible talk, at least on this quiet evening.[32]

This verse, published in 1964, well demonstrates Yoshimoto's view. For him, the *taishū* are the people who feel no necessity to engage with or speak out about the current social and political situation. Partly because they understand that they have no power to influence current affairs, they feel there is nothing more important to them than their own everyday lives and futures. While the *taishū* are the people who can voluntarily choose to be political or nonpolitical, Nakagami's uneducated Burakumin family, without access to hegemonic political materials and practices, are unable to make that choice.

Yoshimoto conceptualized his theory of *taishū* by probing the war responsibility of the intellectual. During this process, he concluded that by the mid-1950s there was a severance between the generation that had been mobilized nationally for war and the generation that came of age after the war. Many writers and intellectuals from the older generation could no longer successfully express the common consciousness of society because their perspective was based on war experiences, which they felt were impossible to represent. Younger scholars, such as Yoshimoto and Etō Jun, on the other hand, commented on postwar society by critiquing these older intellectuals and valorizing contemporary writers. By the late 1950s, Yoshimoto had published a number of essays criticizing modernist intellectuals such as Maruyama Masao (1914–1996), prewar com-

---

32. Quoted in Okeya 1985, 76. For the whole poem, see Yoshimoto 1974, 15:74–81.

munist writers such as Kobayashi Takiji (1903–1933), and contemporary communists such as Miyamoto Kenji (1908–2007).[33] Because of their elitism or leftist fundamentalism, Yoshimoto saw these intellectuals as dismissive of and isolated from the "everyday life" of the average Japanese citizen. It was this average citizen from which he abstracted his famous *taishū no genzō* (archetypal image of the masses).[34] His criticism of academics and of leftist authorities, coupled with his theory of *taishū no genzō*, led to a significant paradigm shift in discourses related to the consciousness of the Japanese people. For Yoshimoto, the most important characteristic of the masses is their "independence" from intellectual enlightenment or intellectual organizations. This is the thinker's widely acknowledged concept of the "independence of the masses" *(taishū no jiritsu)*. With this premise, Yoshimoto insists that the real power of the masses is expressed through their own "contra-avant-garde communication."[35] By expressing their own voice (not the voice communicated on their behalf by intellectuals), they can try to be "independent" from the system. By the late 1960s, the popularity of this idea of the independence of the masses had made Yoshimoto a charismatic figure among New Left activists.[36] His theory of the deep structure of the Japanese masses was further developed in his 1968 essay *Kyōdō gensō ron (Common illusion)* which, in spite of its extremely complicated language, was enthusiastically adopted by activist students as a dominant element of their theoretical lexicon.[37]

Tanigawa Gan (1923–1995), an activist poet who was involved

---

33. Yoshimoto's criticism of modernist intellectuals and "anti-convert" communists, "Tenkō ron" ("Essay on conversion," 1958), *Gisei no shūen (The end of fiction,* 1960), and *Jiritsu no shisō teki kyoten (Theoretical base of independence,* 1966), were the most well-read essays among the Japanese New Left students in 1960s. These essays are included in Yoshimoto 1974, vol. 13.

34. Yoshimoto 1974, 13:349.

35. See Yoshimoto 1974, 13:87–101, and Kashima 2009, 49–50.

36. The notion of the "independence of the masses" is explained in Yoshimoto 1974, 13:87–101, and Kashima 2009, 49–50.

37. Oguma 2005, 649.

in anti-Anpo campaigns with Yoshimoto, nevertheless criticized the notion of *taishū no genzō* as merely an image of the "lower middle-class" of the old Tokyo downtown (*shitamachi*) where Yoshimoto was born. Tanigawa was also active in other campaigns, such as those involving atomic bomb victims, rural farmers, and Burakumin. For him, Yoshimoto was a thinker who, significantly in terms of the current discussion, was in the "unfortunate situation" of never having encountered "the Japanese *fukashoku senmin*" (literally "untouchables" a term sometimes also used for Buraku people).[38] Like Tanigawa, Nakagami saw Yoshimoto's view of the independence of the masses as restricted to the people of the "Edo *shitamachi*."[39] In a 1983 conversation titled "Bungaku to genzai" ("Literature and the present"), Nakagami told Yoshimoto:

> If you go to somewhere like Kishū even today, ... people will never open their hearts to you if you pose as a writer. This is because they think that you look down on them as illiterate. So, I myself must pretend to be a person on their side. ... Edo people, on the other hand, have a very strong sense of pride. Their independence comes from that foundation. ... Nevertheless, I think that the masses that I see and the masses that you assume are different. I tried to address this difference through [reflecting on] your concept of independence but it was kind of unbearable. ... Ultimately, I decided that seeking a common foundation in our images of the masses will not help in overcoming our difference. I am thinking of [things] such as how my mother or those who are very close to me see and build their relationships with others.[40]

The passage demonstrates that for Nakagami, Yoshimoto's image of *taishū* is an illusion constructed through a simple binary relation between the intellectual and the masses without any geopolitical

---

38. Tanigawa 1985, 40.

39. Nakagami and Yoshimoto 2005, 66. Edo is an old name for Tokyo in the era of Tokugawa shogunate (1603–1867).

40. Nakagami and Yoshimoto 2005, 66–67.

consideration. Although he, too, was one of the New Left students who enthusiastically read Yoshimoto's essays in search of independence from entrenched ideologies and authorities, Nakagami felt a sense of discomfort toward the image of the "universal" *taishū*. This discomfort arose from Nakagami's frustration at the binarism practiced by intellectuals from the hegemonic center and their ignorance of the geopolitical context. Nakagami, on the other hand, sought to invalidate the difference-erasing nature of the collective *taishū* identity by producing narratives about society's Others who are the subalterns whose social identity lies precisely in their difference.

The Transgressor Nagayama Norio

Rather than feeling any sense of affinity with the New Left students from the *gebaruto* conflicts in which he had participated, Nakagami strongly empathized with a nineteen-year-old serial killer Nagayama Norio (1949–1997). Between October 11 and November 5, 1968, Nagayama killed four people with a stolen handgun.[41] Immediately after this young man's arrest in April 1969, Nakagami wrote an essay titled "Hanzaisha Nagayama Norio kara no hōkoku" ("Statement by the transgressor, Nagayama Norio," 1969), which included recollections of Nakagami's own life and a fictional monologue by Nagayama. This essay demonstrates Nakagami's insights into the inner self of violent and socially stigmatized transgressive youth. Before discussing Nakagami's essay, background information is provided on Nagayama who also "went up" to Tokyo in 1965 from a peripheral area of Japan.

Nagayama Norio was born in 1949 in Abashiri, Hokkaido, the seventh of eight children. Abashiri was notorious for the prison that opened in 1890, which functioned effectively as an internment

---

41. Nagayama's victims were two security guards, one in Tokyo and one in Kyoto, and two taxi drivers, one in Hakodate and one in Nagoya.

camp for recidivist criminals and political prisoners.[42] In his auto-biographical novel titled *Naze ka Abashiri* (*For some reason, it was Abashiri*, 1984), Nagayama wrote of the shock he experienced at the age of seventeen when he saw "Abashiri Yobito-mura Bangaichi" (literally meaning "outside Abashiri Yobito village") as his legal address in his family registry (*koseki*).[43] This stigmatized image of Abashiri is an important element when considering Nagayama's case. Ishikawa Yoshihiro, who conducted a psychiatric examination of Nagayama while the young man was in prison, notes that it is also important to consider Nagayama's childhood when examining his crimes.[44] After his father became addicted to gambling, Nagayama's mother returned to her hometown in Aomori, leaving four children, including the five-year-old Nagayama, in Abashiri. Although the children reunited with their mother in 1955, Nagayama's childhood was spent in extreme poverty and dysfunctional family circumstances. He was neglected by his parents and abused by his siblings and later become a batterer of his younger sister and niece. He was also frequently absent from school.[45]

In 1965, after graduating from junior high school, Nagayama came to work in Tokyo through a middle school/high school leaver group employment system known as *shūdan shūshoku*. This was a mass employment policy that had been instituted by the postwar government and saw the employment of groups of junior high school or high school graduates to facilitate the nation's rapid economic growth. In the late 1950s and early 1960s, graduates of junior high schools were especially popular as employees for the many small-scale factories and stores whose business output had dramatically increased with the mass production and consumption that characterized the postwar economy. Such young people arrived in

---

42. The latter included the first chairman of the Japanese Communist Party, Tokuda Kyūichi (1894–1953), and the former longtime leader of the JCP, Miyamoto Kenji (1908–2007).

43. See Nagayama 1990, 192–94.

44. See Ishikawa's comment in *ETV tokushū Nagayama Norio*.

45. See Ishikawa's comment in *ETV tokushū Nagayama Norio*.

industrial centers throughout the country on specially designated trains carrying "baby-faced fifteen-year-old boys and girls … from farm villages in Northern Japan."[46] These images, which were reported every spring "during cherry blossom season" throughout the era of economic growth, made a strong impact on the consciousness of the Japanese public and normalized notions of group immigration and youth employment "immediately after graduation."[47] In "Hanzaisha Nagayama Norio kara no hōkoku," Nakagami refers to Nagayama as the "banished" son of "a matrilineal family."[48] This is the same expression used by the writer in his account of Ikuhei's separation from his siblings following his exile from his mother's home by her creation of a new patriarchal family. Unlike Ikuhei, however, Nagayama's exile was the result of *shūdan shūshoku*.

There is an important difference in Nagayama's experience of *shūdan shūshoku* compared to that of graduates before the mid-1960s. From 1965, the year Nagayama started working in a small fruit market in Tokyo, more than 60 percent of middle school students continued on to high school education. As a result, the labor market began to draw on high school rather than junior high school graduates. While initially lionized by the media as "golden eggs," the fifteen-year-old *shūdan shūshoku* graduates were soon regarded as symbols of poverty and underachievement (both of which were often closely related to the financial circumstance of their families). In other words, they represented the gap in society between rich and poor.[49] In the discourses of Japan's economic superiority, such middle school leavers became pariahs to be erased from view or blamed for their own misfortunes.

The negative connotations of Abashiri became even more evident following the release, also in 1965, of the hit movie *Abashiri bangaichi* (literally meaning "outside of Abashiri district," translated

46. Katayama 2010, 12–14.
47. Sugayama 2000, 34–38.
48. NKZ 14:238.
49. Tsuchida 2005, 6–15.

as *Abashiri Prison*). Starring Takakura Ken (1931–2014), this film became the first in the hugely popular yakuza film genre with a number of sequels released between 1965 and 1972. Because the address in his family register was similar to that of the prison, Nagayama was misunderstood and humiliated by his employer and coworkers as if he himself had a criminal record. As a result of this harassment, he eventually quit the fruit market and drifted from one job to another in Tokyo.[50] Nagayama's murder of four victims occurred in this economic and cultural context. In spite of his limited education, once in prison Nagayama became an enthusiastic reader of literature and philosophy and wrote many autobiographical essays and novels. His first and best-selling autobiographical work, *Muchi no namida* (*Tears of ignorance*) was published in 1971. In 1983, he was awarded the Shin Nihon bungaku shō (New Japanese Literature Prize) for the novel *Kibashi* (*Wooden bridge*). In the same year, the Supreme Court of Japan handed down the death penalty, and Nagayama was executed on August 1, 1997, at the age of forty-eight.

In a 1978 public lecture, Nakagami outlined his reasons for feeling a close affinity with Nagayama. Both came to Tokyo in 1965, where Nagayama coincidentally worked in a jazz bar that was frequented by Nakagami. Both were born into poor families on the periphery of Japanese society.[51] However, there were also significant differences. While Nagayama's mother remained alone after her husband left, Nakagami's mother remarried and entered a new family (*ie*) headed by a patriarch. Despite being neglected by his biological father, Nakagami was well cared for and educated by his stepfather. It was, in fact, this man's generous financial support that permitted Nakagami's idle life in Tokyo. The almost illiterate Nagayama, on the other hand, was rejected by his father, who became addicted to gambling. When considering the criminal actions of Nagayama, Nakagami realized that, as was the case with Ikuhei, literacy—that is, education—was a significant difference between

---

50. See Nagayama 1990, 191–93, and *ETV tokushū Nagayama Norio*.
51. Nakagami 2000, 61–62.

himself and the young transgressor of his own generation. Acknowledging this, Nakagami felt strongly drawn to Nagayama. In "Hanzaisha Nagayama Norio kara no hōkoku," Nakagami regarded himself as "one of many (boys like) Nagayama Norio." Haunted by the question "Why wasn't I the transgressor Nagayama Norio?,"[52] Nakagami sought to understand why he became a writer who chose a "fountain pen" over a "pistol."[53]

While repeatedly acknowledging that it was impossible for him to ever know the inner landscape of the *shūdan shūshoku* boy (Nagayama), Nakagami tried to understand the young man's crime as an attempt to overcome "the pain of the self-identification principle" (*jidōritsu no fukaisa*).[54] To clarify this key phrase, I cite a passage by Nakagami that probes the difference between himself and Nagayama. Here, Nakagami refers to another young murderer, the eighteen-year-old Ri Chin-u (1940–1962). A so-called Zainichi Korean, Ri was convicted of killing two young girls in 1958 and executed in 1962. In the late 1960s, this young murderer often featured in cultural productions such as the film *Kōshikei* (*Death by Hanging*, 1968) directed by Ōshima Nagisa (1932–2013). A 1967 essay collection titled *Naibu no ningen* (*Humanity and the inner self*) by Akiyama Shun, discussed in greater detail below, also addresses Ri's inner self. Rather than identifying with Ri, however, Nakagami was drawn to Nagayama's experiences as similar in some way to his own.

> For Nagayama, there was never any *naibu* [inner self] (that is, language). Why did he lack this? To provide an answer, rather than draw on the one known as Ri Chin-u, perhaps I should refer to the experiences of my own self who stands face-to-face before Nagayama Norio. By doing this, perhaps I can understand why I regard him as a person who could only express himself externally through actions such as crime, a person who lacked an inner self. Perhaps in this way I can begin to understand how he tried to

---

52. NKZ 14:230.
53. NKZ 14:224.
54. NKZ 14:223.

claim that self and came to identify with that self. I feel this will help me know more about Nagayama.

Why do I write?

Why do I commit the crime of writing rather than an actual crime when writing is a crime that denies—we might say "*non*" [the French word is used in the original]—consciousness, denies imagination and denies the other who refuses eternal salvation?

Why do I use a fountain pen and not a pistol?

Why do I not push myself ahead in the world but retreat instead into the infinite depths of my own self? What can my writing achieve?

I feel I have discovered that writing is a way of survival. Nagayama Norio thought that through action (crime) he could overcome his own pain of the self-identification principle.

And at that moment he did grasp his own identity. But once Nagayama had fulfilled his inner self and ceased acting, this self was overwhelmed by anxiety, dissociation and boredom. ... He had no language by means of which he could express these.[55]

The term *naibu* comes from Akiyama's *Naibu no ningen*. This word literally means "inner part," but here more precisely "inner self" or "inner landscape." This latter is the sense adopted by Nakagami in his essay. Akiyama's book discussed the inner self of the individual by examining Ri's background and writing. Before examining Akiyama's view, I should confirm that Nakagami's "Hanzaisha Nagayama Norio kara no hōkoku" appeared *before* Nagayama began publishing his writing. Therefore, Nakagami's view of Nagayama as a person who "never" has an "inner self (that is, language)," and who therefore "can only express himself externally through action such as crime" is restricted to before the late 1960s. Unlike Nagayama at that time, Ri had already written extensively about his background and crime. To Nakagami, Ri, who had demonstrated the ability to express himself in writing, was a "*naibu no ningen*," or person with an inner self (language).

---

55. NKZ 14:224.

Nakagami also notes that Nagayama's inner self was character-ized by the pain of the self-identification principle, *jidōritsu no fu-kaisa*. This absence of *naibu* suggests that there was a sense of loss (*sōshitsu*) in Nagayama's inner self, a sense that derived from the "anxiety, dissociation and boredom" that attacked young people generally at the time and resulted in frustration and uncertainty re-garding the future. The term *jidōritsu no fukaisa* was frequently dis-cussed in Japanese literary material during the 1960s. In the forego-ing passage, I understand the concept as suggested in the writing of Haniya Yutaka (1909–1997). In Haniya's novel, *Shirei* (*Dead spirits*), which was written intermittently between 1946 and 1995, the young male protagonist questions his self-identity: "He murmured 'I ...' but he could not continue to form the words 'am me.' To voice this would definitely have been indescribably painful."[56] Morikawa Tat-suya notes that "the pain of the self-identification principle" has a close parallel to the idea proposed by Jean-Paul Sartre (1905–1980) of "being in itself,"[57] and the fact that "Man is all the time outside of himself: it is in projecting and losing himself beyond himself that he makes man to exist; and, on the other hand, it is by pursuing transcendent aims that he himself is able to exist."[58] In 1960s Japan, Sartre's theory of existentialism was widely read as another "new" theory that to some extent provided a set of ideas New Left students would refer to in their attempts to overcome social alienation. In Sartrean terms, this was *angājuman*, that is, engagement.

As Hasumi and Karatani note, Nakagami's depiction of violent male protagonists is heavily influenced by Akiyama's perspective of Ri's inner self.[59] Akiyama wrote:

We cannot deny the relationship between the crimes of individu-als who have withdrawn into themselves and psychoanalytic

---

56. Haniya 1998–2001, 3:125.

57. See Morikawa 1968.

58. Sartre 1948, 55.

59. See comments by Hasumi and Karatani in Asada, Karatani, Hasumi, and Miura 2002, 185–89.

thinking. It seems to me, however, that, in their need to assert themselves, these individuals committed crimes that drew on points that psychoanalysis has had no option but to abandon. While psychoanalytic ideas have been instrumental in establishing and developing views of the interior world that are accepted by the wider society, in that process they destroyed the tiny insect which has lived in this inner world for so long. This insect is the "self" that each person has—no matter who they are. This is not the ego of everyday language. This is the I which tries to mean only I and which, refusing to be categorized, refusing to be analyzed and refusing to be defined, is the most meaningless and the most uncertain existence in the world.[60]

Through referring to Ri's self-writing, Akiyama demonstrates the existence of a "self" that refuses to be categorized, analyzed, or defined by universal principles. In developing these ideas, Akiyama cites an excerpt from "Bad Blood (Mauvais Sang)," a work in the collection *A Season in Hell* (1873) by Arthur Rimbaud (1854–1891): "They won't kill you any more than if you were a corpse." The critic argues that Ri committed a crime to defend his self in the sense that, in the same way a corpse can no longer be damaged, there was no need to further suffer rejection by the *gaibu* (exterior world).[61] Because of this, Akiyama regards Ri as a *naibu no ningen* who can only fulfill his inner world through acts of his imagination, that is, killing girls and then writing narratives of these crimes and himself.

Drawing on Akiyama's interpretation of Ri, Nakagami argued that at least until he committed his crimes, Nagayama had never had a *naibu*, that is, language. Nagayama, the young, illiterate criminal, could not rely on writing as "a way to survive." In this sense, there was a parallel between Nagayama and Ikuhei. There were also, as noted, significant differences between these men. For Nakagami, Ikuhei was an uneducated Burakumin man caught in the double oppression of the mainstream society and the matrilineal family.

---

60. Akiyama 1991, 122–23.
61. Akiyama 1991, 128.

Like the burned Indian widow, Ikuhei was a perfect "absent" as a "subaltern." While Ikuhei had no chance to "speak up," Nagayama eventually found a voice by publishing autobiographical essays and novels written in prison. Thus, like Nakagami, Nagayama eventually found writing as "a way to survive." Interestingly, once Nagayama began to express himself in written language, Nakagami no longer felt an affinity with him. In fact, in his 1975 essay titled "Toki wa nagareru ..." ("Time goes by ..."), Nakagami severely criticized material by Nagayama, including *Muchi no namida* and *Jinmin o wasureta kanaria tachi* (*Canaries that forget the people*, 1971), as the latter's exploitation of language to justify his crimes on the grounds of social problems such as poverty and a dysfunctional family. Nakagami writes that Nagayama's justification by logic places the young man in the same category as the police, bourgeoisie, citizen society, and the nation that the latter regards as his enemies.[62] In other words, Nakagami's identification with Nagayama ceased once the latter began to express himself in writing.

Although his approach to the inner self resonated with existentialism, Akiyama investigated the issue of "self" without resorting to any hegemonic interpretation or psychoanalytic study of identity. His ideas are also distinct from the Sartrean engagement favored by New Left activists. In fact, Akiyama's attitude closely parallels Nakagami's criticism of hegemonic perspectives, such as the collective *warera* identity of elite New Left students and Yoshimoto's *taishū*, both of which inevitably exclude his socially and geopolitically marginalized half-brother. Akiyama's essay on Ri inspired Nakagami to realize that Nagayama's crime was enacted to overcome a sense of loss in his inner self. The crime, however, paradoxically heightened the young man's anxiety, producing pain at the uncertainty of self. While acknowledging that writing is a crime of negation against "consciousness, imagination and the other who rejects eternal salvation," Nakagami nevertheless turned to writing as an act that permitted the representation of his inner landscape. This was his

---

62. NKZ 14:239–42.

strategy for remaining alive—surviving—without the need to kill himself or the other.

In "Hanzaisha Nagayama Norio kara no hōkoku," Nakagami confirmed his will to represent Ikuhei's voice through writing.

> Gradually, I'm getting closer to the age (twenty-four years old) at which my brother died. Without understanding the reason for his death, I will turn thirty, then forty and start declining. I want to write about this point of time. I want to let people who live one hundred years later know that Kinoshita Ikuhei lived like this and died by hanging himself.[63]

As noted, Ikuhei's death gave Nakagami a very important motivation for writing. As elaborated on in later chapters that discuss the Aki-yuki trilogy, Nakagami often draws on the mythic motives of matricide, patricide, and fratricide when depicting Ikuhei's violence and suicide. In a stanza of his 1967 poetry titled "Umi e" ("To the sea"), for example, Nakagami interprets Ikuhei's death as a cyclic repetition of mythic tragedy: "My elder brother is dead … Greek tragedies keep playing in the whole world."[64] In the following section I explore "Ra-kudo," a short story published before "Misaki," that depicts the voice of a young husband whose memory of his half-brother's suicide is a key factor in his violence toward his wife and daughters. This narrative, I argue, evolved from the writer's 1960s writing about the inner landscape of alienated youth as discussed above.

The Narrative of an Ill-Tempered Husband and a Battered Wife

Notwithstanding Nakagami's unique peripheral background and the radical impact it had on his narratives, many critics have stressed

---

63. NKZ 14:234.
64. NKZ 1:61.

his late 1960s participation in the literary coterie magazine *Bungei shuto* as evidence of the writer's apprenticeship as an exponent of literary Naturalism. This style is regarded as "the most traditional mainstream path" of modern Japanese literature.[65] The founder of *Bungei shuto*, Yasutaka Tokuzō (1889–1971), was a writer from the Waseda School, which was arguably the most active stronghold of Naturalist literature and its derivative novelistic genre, the "I-novel" (*watakushi shōsetsu*).[66] Noriko Mizuta Lippit explains that the I-novel is a Japanese literary genre that encompasses a type of "confessional literature" in which the private affairs and experiences of the protagonist often correspond with those of the author.[67] Edward Fowler notes that the I-novel is a form of novelistic expression that fundamentally sets out to portray what exponents of Naturalism regarded as a "realistic" view of the world.[68] Arguing that the I-novel is better understood as a Japanese "literary and ideological paradigm," Tomi Suzuki considers this "paradigm" to be a mode of reading a narrative as a "direct" representation of the writer's "self."[69] According to Takayama Fumihiko's biography of Nakagami, "Rakudo" is largely based on an incident from Nakagami's life,[70] but this is unrelated to my textual analysis of that work. This is because I do not wish to approach "Rakudo" as an I-novel, that is, as a representation of the author's "confession," "realistic view," or "self." Rather, I discuss the narrative as the writer's attempt to "give [literary] expression" (*hyōgen o ataeru*)[71] to a young man who can only express his inner self through violence.

"Rakudo" is one of sixteen narratives in Nakagami's collection *Keshō* (*Makeup*, 1978) and one of seven sequential narratives that

---

65. Karlsson 2001, 11.

66. Karlsson 2001, 11.

67. Mizuta Lippit 1980, 13.

68. Fowler 1988, 3–42.

69. Suzuki 1996, 6. In *Narrating the Self: Fictions of Japanese Modernity*, Suzuki asserts that the I-novel is, like all fiction, pure fabrication.

70. Takayama 2007, 338–39.

71. Nakagami 2012, 175.

depict repeated acts of domestic violence committed by a man against his wife. Later stories in the sequence give an account of the man's subsequent separation from and reunion with this wife and their two young daughters. As noted, the man's violence is often invoked by his ambivalent feeling toward his dead half-brother. Like Nakagami's family, the family of the protagonist works in fields associated with manual labor and transport. Rather than laboring, the protagonist works as an administrator in the company office.[72] In this sense, the protagonist can be regarded as one of an increasing number of white-collar workers, known as *sararī man* (literally, salary man), who came to attention in 1970s Japan. The story narrates the fragmentation of a family that consists of the late twenties protagonist, his wife, their two daughters, and the wife's parents. The family lives together in a new *tateuri* (ready-built house) with a cramped (*neko no hitai hodo no*—no bigger than a cat's forehead) garden in the suburbs of Tokyo.[73] With urban areas sprawling outward from central Tokyo between the mid-1950s and the early 1970s, during Japan's rapid economic growth, there was large-scale construction of *tateuri*. For most families at that time, buying a *tateuri* meant acquiring the "dream" of "my home." This was in contrast to "our home," the "traditional house" that had previously been passed down from father to son.[74] "Rakudo" depicts a young husband's sense of isolation from the other family members of a "my home" that he partly owns with his in-laws. He feels especially frustrated with his wife who, in his eyes, is more of a daughter to his parents-in-law than his wife.

On March 3, Girls' Day or Hina matsuri (Doll Festival) in Japan, the man's sense of isolation from his family heightens. That morning his wife asks him to come home in time for the family feast to celebrate the day, but he replies that because of "the *hina* dolls," he feels like going out for a drink. Explaining that "when-

---

72. NKZ 3:106.
73. NKZ 3:105.
74. See Someya 2009.

ever I see them I can only feel pain," the man declares that "after
all, they are dolls, that is, a substitute for a human. My brother
hanged himself on the third of March at the age of twenty-four."[75]
Although reluctant to take part in the family's celebration, the man
fully understands that this is a special day for his daughters and
promises his wife that he will return home early. Aware that he was
letting his daughters down, once he began drinking he was nonetheless unable to stop and did not return home until late at night. As
she served his meal, his wife said accusingly, "We were waiting for
you."[76] At these words, he felt a rush of anger, particularly at the
fact that the wife does not seem to have commemorated his brother's death in any way.

> "There is not even a single flower here," said he. "You never listen
> to what I say." The wife dropped her head. She thought that he
> might calm down if she pretended that she was the one at blame.
> Everyone who knew him, however, was aware that he wanted to
> fight once he had had a drink. It got on his nerves that everyone
> thought this way. I don't like the food I'm eating, he thought. I
> don't like these chopsticks, I don't like this table or chairs. ...
> There is nothing I like here. Suddenly he turned the table over. His
> wife quickly leaped back. Her husband had broken a pendant light
> and pulled the refrigerator over many times in the past, so she was
> used to this kind of outburst. She huddled near the gas stove. ...
>   Without a word, he broke the four table legs. Couldn't she at
> least have offered a single flower for my brother? She could have
> used anything to make a Buddhist altar. It could have been in the
> corner of the kitchen or even in the toilet.[77]

It is not surprising that among feminist scholars such as Livia
Monnet, Nina Cornyetz, and Eve Zimmerman, Nakagami's frequent depiction of this kind of male violence against women is often

---

75. NKZ 3:109.
76. NKZ 3:108.
77. NKZ 3:109–10.

condemned as a masculinist and highly gendered—phallocentric—representation of heterosexual relations.[78] Although I certainly accept the position of feminist scholars, I am nonetheless interested in the argument presented by Japanese male scholars that Nakagami's depiction of violence does in fact permit insights into the brutality of modern hegemonies against those who lack power.[79] I wish to state unequivocally that there can be no justification on any grounds for masculinist violence against women and children. Making a categorical stand against a cultural representation of violence, however, is less straightforward. In my view, the depiction of male violence against women in literature is problematic when it justifies or reproduces social oppression against women. Narratives that expose the cause of such violence falls, I argue, into a different cate-

---

78. For example, see Monnet 1996a and 1996b, Cornyetz 1999, and Zimmerman 2007. Also see Zimmerman's comment in her 1993 round-table discussion with Karatani, Suga, Yomota, and Watanabe (Karatani, Zimmerman, Suga, Yomota, and Watanabe 2000, 197 and 199) and Karlsson's commentary on the body of Nakagami analysis in the West (Karlsson 2014). Japanese male scholars such as Asada and Watanabe, on the other hand, dismiss as a "feminist misreading" (*feminisuto no gokai*) the critique that regards Nakagami's phallocentric writing as contributing to gender oppression (Asada, Okuizumi, Karatani, and Watanabe 2000, 235).

79. In his conversation with Asada, Watanabe, and Karatani, Hasumi for example, argues that the phallocentrism of Nakagami's work demonstrates *ryōgi sei* (ambivalence) in that it draws on narratives of "physical violence" in an attempt to reveal systems of "ideological violence" (Hasumi, Watanabe, Asada, and Karatani 1994, 235). In this way, much Japanese scholarship—inevitably by male commentators—has focused on what might be regarded as a questionable way of legitimating Nakagami's depiction of gendered violence against society's Other. This "Other" is often the woman but can also be Burakumin or members of other socially marginalized groups. These critics argue that Nakagami's depiction of violence by individuals is a representation of the cruelty enacted by modern hegemonic society and ideology against those who lack power. They have thus declined to overtly critique the presence of phallocentrism in the writer's work. Although my reading of Nakagami is to some extent informed by the interpretations of Japanese male scholars, I reject their notion of a feminist "misreading." I return to these issues in greater detail in chapter 4.

gory. In my understanding, "Rakudo" is an example of the latter. As noted, I also see a certain conditional value in the poststructuralist reading presented by Japanese male scholars who understand Nakagami's texts as a critical representation of the violent base that underlies the hegemonic concepts driving social relations in Japan. This viewpoint in no way prevents me from condemning violence against real-life women.

For my analysis of male violence in "Rakudo," I introduce the idea of Japanese scholar Mizuta Noriko. In her 1993 book, *Monogatari to han monogatari no fūkei: Bungaku to josei no sōzōryoku* (*The landscape of narrative and anti-narrative: Literature and the imagination of women*), she comments as follows:

> Although criticizing male writers for the fact that they have never understood women, never precisely depicted women or never represented women as human beings is [undoubtedly] very correct, it is irrelevant as a critique of male writers. This is because male writers probably depict their own inner landscape in which they search for a dream woman as a result of their disappointment with real women.

Although Mizuta does not identify the title, she apparently criticizes the book *Natsume Sōseki to iu hito: Wagahai wa wagahai de aru* (*A person called Natsume Sōseki: I am me*, 1987) by a pioneer of feminist reading in Japan, Komashaku Kimi (1952–2007). In this book, Komashaku reads the patriarch in Sōseki's *Kōjin* (translated as *The Wayfarer*, 1912), who always worries what his wife thinks, as a nonpatriarchal feminist who tries to have a deep and meaningful relationship with his wife.[80] For Mizuta, this point of view is "inappropriate."[81] She argues that it is incorrect to explain men's romantic fantasy, their abandonment of the family by drowning themselves in the women

---

80. See Komashaku 1987.
81. Mizuta 1993, 76.

of red-light district (as in Yoshiyuki Jun'nosuke's novels), or their monomaniac fetishism in which there are no real women (as in Tanizaki Jun'ichiro's narratives), as all about woman-hating.[82] Mizuta apparently criticizes Tomioka Taeko, Ueno Chizuko, and Ogura Chikako's 1992 round-table discussion published as *Danryū bungaku ron* (*A critique of literature by Japanese male writers*), which profiles the misogyny of Japanese male writers.[83]

According to Ueno, from the mid-1980s to the early 1990s, Mizuta's *Monogatari to han monogatari no fūkei* was regarded as the *terminus ad quem* of Japanese feminist literary criticism.[84] As Saitō Minako notes, Mizuta's publication was one example of the new discourses of Japanese academism of the time.[85] Referring to Saitō's discussion of the difference between "[second-wave] feminist critique" and "gender critique," I define Mizuta's perspective as a "gender critique." Discussing Elaine Showalter's collection, *New Feminist Criticism: Essays on Women, Literature, and Theory* (1985), Saitō explains that the purpose of this work is to analyze representations of women through a "women's viewpoint," or "gynocriticism," and thereby reevaluate the works of women writers who were marginalized by male writers in the genealogy of modern literature. "Gender critique," on the other hand, focuses on analyzing the "gender ideologies" that appear in texts without necessarily providing an essentialist articulation of any "women's viewpoint" on the part of either the writer or readers of a text.[86]

Referring to Mizuta's gender critique of the masculine basis of modern Japanese literature, I interpret the following passage from Nakagami's "Rakudo." This is an especially difficult to read scene in which the man commits an act of extreme violence against his

---

82. Mizuta 1993, 76, and Ueno 2013, 145.

83. See Tomioka, Ueno, and Ogura 1992.

84. Ueno 2013, 126.

85. Saitō 2009, 13.

86. Saitō 2009, 14.

wife and daughters. This violence becomes the direct reason for his
wife's decision to leave the marriage.

> That morning, too, he returned home after drinking heavily. He
> had not seen his daughters for three days. After stumbling as he
> climbed the stairs, he went into his wife's room where she was
> sleeping with their two girls. He asked his wife to let him into her
> futon. The embers of the quarrel with the fellows with whom he
> had been drinking were still in his head. It was always like that. ...
> He still felt bad because of last night's argument. He wanted to
> sleep being held by a woman—actually, not by any woman but by
> his wife and daughters. He wanted to feel the warmth of their
> touch. He thought that if he could just do that, the tension and
> dissatisfaction that never went away might be dispelled.
>
> "No," replied his wife.
>
> That was all that started it. He hit his wife. He was a terrible
> man. ... He picked up the oil heater which stood in the corner of
> the room and threw it at her. For a split second, he felt like killing
> his wife and his children along with himself. Oil spread all over
> the futon. It was on himself, his wife, and daughters. His two
> daughters, their sleep suddenly broken, were crying and scream-
> ing. He could smell the rancid odor of the oil. He looked for
> matches. There were none in the room.[87]

The man's anger and violence are interrupted by his father-in-law
crying out that the mother seems to be having a heart attack. The
wife shoves him aside to run down the stairs and call an ambulance.
Two days later, the man leaves for a week-long business trip. When
he returns, the house is empty. Left alone, he thinks:

> It would have been better if we had all been burned. The four of
> us should have gone up in flames. This is a man's heart, he
> thought. His two daughters would have embraced each other and

---

87. NKZ 3:111–12.

gone up in flames. His wife would have embraced the daughters. He would have embraced them all. The flames would have become one and burned the room, then burned up the house.[88]

In my analysis of this confronting scene, I focus on the writer's depiction of the inner landscape of the patriarch and his wife's rejection of the "man's heart" (*otoko no kokoro*), or, to borrow from Mizuta, the "discourse of men."[89]

Mizuta notes that many Japanese male novelists become writers to absorb themselves in their inner landscapes. She explains the nature of this inner landscape.

> It is a realm into which they can neither see nor enter, unless they pass through "a dream, i.e., through women." Their inner landscape is inlaid in the mosaic of modern social structures. Therefore, any critique must analyse the structure of the "dream," i.e., of "women" constructed by male writers who tessellate a pattern of their inner landscape [with images of the ideal woman]. Male writers often selfishly impose their dream onto women, or interpret women arbitrarily, and it is the distance between their imagined dream women and real women that makes their inner landscape so gorgeous. ... What we can see in the work of the male writer is the inner landscape of the man that can be clearly articulated only through his concocted "discourse of women." [The male fantasy of women] is, thus, a "discourse of men."[90]

Mizuta further argues that modern Japanese literature often depicts a man who seeks refuge from the "public" (*ōyake*) space in the "private (*watakushi*) realm" in which women reside. In contrast to the public sphere, Mizuta explains that the home was considered the most private space in modern Japanese society. The red-light dis-

---

88. NKZ 3:114.
89. Mizuta 1993, 76.
90. Mizuta 1993, 76.

trict was also a very private space where "amorous men" (*iro gonomi*)[91] went to see women who lived "outside" the home. Like the home, this space was totally detached from society and the public principles of that society.[92] Mizuta expands on the social significance of the public/private divide and how this divide affected literary production:

> The more that "public" spaces exclude women ... the more the "private" world and "woman" connect with each other to form the private space of "women" and "sex," which is out of touch with society and the world controlled by politics, laws and economics. For men, the private realm of women and sex is not only an induction into their inner landscape but often, in fact, an induction to the inner self. ... In the structure of modern Japanese society which considered literature as a useless practice that deviated from the focus of [productive] social activities, it was no wonder that the I-novel [*watakushi shōsetsu*], which provided a literary presentation that was grounded in a "private" [*watakushi*] realm, became the mainstream genre in Japanese modern literature and that men who were dependent on women became its protagonists.[93]

For women, however, home and the red-light district were never private realms. In fact, the home was the only public space available for women to become an *ichinin mae*—a respectable wife and mother who would bear an heir for the family. Childbearing, moreover, was acknowledged as the social activity by means of which a wife ful-

---

91. *Iro gonomi* has been a key theme in the Japanese literary tradition and is evident in classics such as *Ise monogatari* (*The Tale of Ise*, a collection of poems and associated narratives dating from the Heian era) and *Kōshoku ichidai otoko* (*The Life of an Amorous Man*, 1682) by Ihara Saikaku (1642–1693). This type of man is also evident in modern works such as *Bokutō kitan* (*A Strange Tale from East of the River*, 1937) by Nagai Kafū (1879–1959) and "Shū'u" ("Sudden Shower," 1954) by Yoshiyuki Jun'nosuke.

92. Mizuta 1993, 63–65.

93. Mizuta 1993, 65.

filled her role as producer of the labor force for the nation. Although the red-light district was the target of social stigma, it was also a public space for women whose economic activity using their bodies and sexuality was legally protected.[94]

I previously noted that the I-novel is regarded as a confessional, yet fictional literature genre/paradigm of sincere introspection that draws at least partially on events experienced in the life of the author to write the private life of the protagonist. Citing the works of feminist scholar Komashaku Kimi and dramatist Yamazaki Masakazu, Ueno redefines the I-novel as the narrative of the "impotent patriarch" (*fugainai kachō*) or "ill-tempered patriarch" (*fukigen na kachō*) who feels strongly pressured by his role in the family.[95] The ill-tempered patriarch's antisocial behaviors, such as adultery and violence, are depicted as occurring in the realm of the private life that makes a strong contrast to the patriarch's public image as a respectable man (*ichinin mae*) who dutifully supports a family. This contrast can be seen in I-novels such as "Ōtō" ("Cherries," 1948) by Dazai Osamu (1909–1948) and *Shi no toge* (*The Sting of Death*, 1960) by Shimao Toshio (1917–1986). As noted, I am not arguing for "Rakudo" to be considered an autobiographical I novel. I do, however, argue that given Nakagami's *Bungei shuto* experiences and the "autobiographical" elements of his writing, it was impossible for the writer not to be influenced by this genre early in his career while he was developing his writing style. I conclude that the scene depicting the "Rakudo" protagonist's violence against his family qualifies this protagonist, in Ueno's words, as an ill-tempered patriarch.[96]

---

94. Mizuta 1993, 64.

95. Ueno 2013, 242.

96. About a decade before Nakagami wrote "Rakudo," male authors such as Kojima Nobuo (*Hōyō kazoku*, translated as *Embracing Family*, 1965) and Ōe Kenzaburō (*Man'en gan'nen no futtobōru*, translated as *The Silent Cry*, 1967) began to present the wife as "the sexed Other" who, through asserting her own self and sexuality, is able to refuse her husband's discourse. These were two contemporary writers whose work had a great influence on Nakagami. See Nakagami and Ogawa 1981 and Nakagami and Ōe 1980. As seen in Etō Jun's essay collection

According to Mizuta, modern Japanese literature often depicts men who "depend on" women in their expectation of "regressing" into a private realm in which they will be able to fantasize that there is a pure inner self.[97] Like the protagonist of "Rakudo," these patriarchs return home in the hope of relieving their lonely and wounded inner selves through their wives' sexuality. This sexuality is not the *iro gonomi*-style sexuality of the licensed quarters. Rather, it is the passivity of hegemonic maternity. For this kind of "patriarch" protagonist, the ideal home is an embodiment of the perfect unity of his inner self and "his" woman's sexuality, which he expects will embrace his ego like a "selfless," "pure," and "comforting" mother.[98] The patriarch who assumes this motherhood myth as the woman's true nature, however, is merely a child who desires a mother's unconditional love without the need to fulfill adult obligations toward his partner.

Any "perfect fantasy" of the woman that is constructed by the man must inevitably be flawed, given the unrealistic masculinist assumptions that feed this dream. As Mizuta explains:

Seijuku to sōshitsu: "Haha" no hōkai (Maturity and loss: The fall of the "Mother," 1965; Etō 1995), Kojima's *Hōyō kazoku* is often discussed as a typical depiction of the transformation of family relationships in Japanese society in the "my home" era. As Barbara Hartley explains, Etō's critique of modern Japanese male writers actually reveals his own "penchant for absolutist and exclusionary binary thinking" (Hartley 2003, 50), in other words, his penchant for the dogmatic "man's heart." Mizuta explains that the wife in *Hōyō kazoku* is aware that "the return home of her man from the outside world is actually the acquisition of power by the patriarch." What the wife rejects in this narrative is being involved in the man's "act of self-salvation," which relies on sacrificing herself as a woman (Mizuta 1993, 80). *Hōyō kazoku* revealed that patriarchal family discourse, which up until that time had been based on the man's fantasized view of female sexuality, had collapsed and been invalidated by the woman who rejected her impotent patriarch. "Rakudo" can also be seen in this genealogy of writing that represents the impotent patriarch as one whose inner landscape is exposed as empty by the woman who departs to leave him alone.

97. Mizuta 1993, 63–64.
98. Mizuta 1993, 71.

In spite of these expectations and fantasies, rather than finding happiness or relief through loving a woman, men who flee from the public to the private space i.e. to the "woman," become single-mindedly dependent on that woman and agonize over themselves. This is because, rather than the "woman," what they find in the private space is no less than the sexed Other.[99]

Informed by Mizuta's view, we can interpret the violent young patriarch in Nakagami's "Rakudo" as a man who is confronted by his wife as the sexed Other, that is, as a woman who rejects the fantastic image the man has created of her. By saying "no" to her husband's request to sleep in her embrace, she rejects her husband's desire to "regress" and to become her child. For the agonized "ill-tempered" patriarch, his wife's sexuality can only be understood in terms of "motherhood," which he fantasizes as a pure and comforting self-less love. When he cannot find a home, that is, his inner landscape, in which he is perfectly unified with his wife in terms of fantasized motherhood, he becomes a furious batterer who resorts—since he has departed the public sphere and no longer has an image to uphold—to brutally violating his family. In Nakagami's text, perfect unification and unthinkably extreme violence overlap in the protagonist's fantasy of his family being consumed by flames. In "Rakudo," Nakagami depicts "a man's heart" through the image of the family unified in the house on fire. The words, "It would have been better if we had all been burned. The four of us should have gone up in flames," are a prime example of Mizuta's typical protagonist patriarch who constructs his inner landscape as the ultimate unity of "home = woman = interiority."[100] Nakagami's protagonist imagines a collective family suicide through (self)-immolation, which can further be understood as a thirst for the eternal unification of his family. More important, it can simultaneously be regarded as fear and rejection of the women—his wife and his daughters—as

---

99. Mizuta 1993, 67.
100. Mizuta 1993, 70.

the Other who challenge him. This sense of fear toward the Other, the very Other about whom he fantasizes, is at the core of the "man's heart" of the ill-tempered patriarch.

We might read "Rakudo" as the narrative of a man who became metaphorically dead when rejected by his wife. In this reading, the wife becomes a bereaved widow. In actuality, the man's dream of self-immolation with his family is a dream of his wife's self-immolation, that is, the fantasized woman's sacrifice for the patriarch. Given this perspective, Nakagami's depiction of the patriarch's desire to burn his wife and daughters can be read through the lens of the Hindu practice of sati, as discussed in chapter 1. Although suicide was generally forbidden in Hindu law, Spivak explains that sati was understood as an exceptional suicide that did not violate Hindu precepts because it was "sanctioned" as a woman's self-sacrifice for the sake of the man to whom she was bound in marriage. Commenting on European expressions of shock and outrage at the notion of sati, and with a clear tone of disdain for the enthusiasm among Western scholars for condemning sati while being blind to the gendered workings of their own society, Spivak explains the ideological underpinnings of the rite as follows:

> That this was an alternative ideology of the graded sanctioning of varieties of suicide as exception, rather than its inscription as "sin," was of course not understood [among Europeans]. Sati could not, of course, be read with Christian female martyrdom, with the defunct husband standing in for the transcendental One; or with war, with the husband standing in for sovereign or state, for whose sake an intoxicating ideology of self-sacrifice can be mobilized.[101]

Drawing on Spivak's view, the man in "Rakudo" can be read as acting as the self-constructed "transcendental One" who fantasizes about guiding his wife—and in this case his daughters as well—to

---

101. Spivak 1999, 297–98.

the other world. Furthermore, the dogmatic "man's heart" of this failed patriarch demonstrates his penchant for and willing subjection to the authority of the "state," which institutionalizes his position as the unquestioned head of the family. In this context, the man's actual and imagined violence against his family reveals that his interiority is nothing more than an insubstantial self-justification that draws authority from the hegemonic ideology of the state.

Following the violence enacted against her, his wife takes their daughters and, with her parents, leaves the marital home. Toward the end of the novel, the man receives a letter from his wife that arrives a week after her departure. Given that Nakagami inscribes the real names of his two daughters, Nori and Naho, we might note the autobiographical resonances in this section of the letter.

"I am writing because I feel sorry for leaving home without talking to you properly." This is how the letter began. "I feel very sad that our marriage has finally fallen apart. I had thought that your drunken frenzies would someday be cured or that I could give you a medicine to make you dislike alcohol, but now I realize your outbursts are probably part of your nature. ... You will never get better with medicine or anything else. But I think you are okay as you are." As he read through the letter, his eyes dimmed with tears. The shapes on the page were swaying and he was unable to make out the words. He briskly mopped the tears with his palm. "Nori already knows what happened. She is old enough to know. It seems she secretly went to see [her friend] Tomo to say farewell. Because she could not go to kindergarten, I took her to the park. All the children were there with their fathers and I could sense Nori gazing at them. Naho seems to have made new friends already. Our children are strong, aren't they? At night, Nori and Naho always talk with each other about Daddy. Nori only tells Naho about fun memories such as when we visited the zoo together or the time we swam together in the sea of the Kii Peninsula."[102]

---

102. NKZ 3:114.

I have noted that in modern Japanese literature, the home is a metaphor for a private realm, the realm of the woman. The emptiness of the house in which the young patriarch is left alone is thus a metaphor for his empty inner landscape in which the voice of his absent wife echoes.

If "Rakudo" is a representation of the "discourse of men" that projects the patriarch's inner landscape, which can be expressed only through his concocted "discourse of women," to what extent does the wife's letter disclose her inner landscape? Some aspects indicate her feelings. For example, there is a description of her disappointment and resignation at her husband's violence and the fact that the marriage has come to an end. The letter gives details of the children's situation after the separation. These elements, however, do not clearly reveal the wife's inner landscape. On the contrary, her inner self is disguised by writing about her children's resilience and love for their father. In the text, on only one occasion do we catch a glimpse of the wife's inner landscape. This is when she responds with the single word *no* to her husband's request to enter her futon after three days of drinking. By depicting the wife's letter as one that keeps silent about her inner self, and by confining the wife's voice and only direct rejection of her husband's fantasy to the articulation of the word *no*, "Rakudo" demonstrates the unavoidable constraints that operate on a woman's voice in her relationship with the violent patriarch. We can recall Spivak's insistence on the impossibility of the voice of the gendered subject speaking to or being heard by the other.

In spite of the unavoidable limits that act on the woman's expression of her interiority, her silence can be thought of as an act of resistance. It is true that the letter barely describes her inner self. Her act of writing and sending this letter, nonetheless, implies a speech act on her part intended to keep her inner self isolated from the violence of her husband. In other words, by writing the letter—even a letter in which she declines to express her inner self—the woman's self becomes independent from her husband's discourse for the first time. This strategy recalls Mizuta's view of writing by modern Japanese women writers. Referring to the works of Tamura Toshiko (1884–1945), Miyamoto Yuriko (1899–1951), and Hayashi Fumiko (1903–1951), Mizuta explains the significance of "writing" for these modern Japanese women.

> Works by modern [Japanese] women writers displayed their rejection and their various forms of resistance against the "discourse of woman" that was concocted by men. While male [writers] developed their interiority through their own fantasized "woman," women [writers] discovered their own interiority through separating themselves from men. ...
>
> Only through "writing" did women writers attempt to find the "private" realm to display their own inner landscape. For them, a trigger for their "writing" was often their disappointment with men.[103]

Although the letter in "Rakudo" does not go so far as to reveal the wife's private realm, her "disappointment" with her husband triggers this text.[104] As Mizuta goes on to explain, the above does not mean there are no men in the inner landscape of women. In fact, the inner self of the woman was established through conflict with men within the confines of the hegemonic masculine society in which a woman's self was constrained. Only by separating from these men and the hegemony that operated in their favor could women access their own inner selves. A wife who empowers herself after separating from her husband in a manner similar to "Rakudo" is seen in two other Nakagami short stories, "Keshō" ("Makeup," 1976) and "Sangatsu" ("March," 1977), which also appeared in the *Keshō* collection. The conclusion of "Sangatsu" depicts the reconciliation of the couple by the wife's compromise.

The genealogy of the "Rakudo" narrative has continued in the writing of Nakagami's eldest daughter, Nakagami Nori. Her 2017

---

103. Mizuta 1993, 76–77.

104. Although it is not relevant to my textual analysis of "Rakudo," Nakagami's wife is also a novelist, Kiwa Kyō.

novel, *Tengu no kairo* (*The circuit of a long-nosed goblin*) reveals the hidden voice of a heroine who remains traumatized by the childhood experience of being battered by her father while her mother watched helplessly. The ill-tempered, violent father and the silent mother in this work can be read as a representation from the child's point of view of the "Rakudo" husband and wife. In a scene from *Tengu no kairo* that depicts this kind of domestic violence, the battered child shudders at the voice of her mother, who comments nonchalantly, "You're half asleep, aren't you?"[105] Discussions of the narratives of Nakagami Kenji have given little attention to the voice of the child. However, Spivak's injunction to intellectuals to create the conditions that will enable the subaltern to speak surely also refers to children. From this perspective, Nakagami Nori's text gives a valuable contemporary insight into her father's narratives.

A Writer Who Never Escapes from Discrimination

While "Hanzaisha Nagayama Norio kara no hōkoku" and "Rakudo" are texts set in Tokyo, novellas such as "Shugen" ("The Mountain Ascetic," 1974) and "Jain" ("Snakelust," 1975) are third-person narratives with settings that often hover between urban areas and their peripheries. This was the space Nakagami referred to as the *roji*. The term *roji* articulates the site of Nakagami's subaltern narratives that are underlain by the geopolitical objective of "writing back to the centre."[106] His Akiyuki trilogy depicts the

---

105. Nakagami N. 2017, 115.

106. Ishikawa 2011, 1. Borrowing the postcolonial concept of "writing back" to the hegemonic center from the work of Ashcroft, Griffiths, and Tiffin (1989), Ishikawa 2011 analyzes Nakagami's "Misaki" and its sequel, *Kareki nada*. Drawing on a statement by Salman Rushdie (b. 1947), a writer Nakagami regarded as a peer, to the effect that "the Empire writes back to the Centre," Ashcroft, Griffiths, and Tiffin argue that "writing back" is the way postcolonial—that is, subaltern—writers and texts respond to and engage with mainstream literature. Also see Ashcroft, Griffiths, and Tiffin 1989, 2. Concerning Naka-

Kishū Kumano *roji* as the narrative site of a transgressive young man's sense of loss in his inner self. This aspect is further discussed in the next chapter.

Following his *jōkyō*, however, Tokyo became Nakagami's stronghold. Although he frequently visited his parents, relatives, and friends in Shingū, and even tried to make his home in Atashika on the Kii Peninsula, he never returned to the area to settle. Moreover, he spent considerable time overseas. In other words, he never lived as an adult in Kasuga, the *roji* of his Kumano narratives. In this sense, the claim by Zainichi Korean writer Yang Sok-il (b. 1936) that Nakagami is a writer who "escaped from the *roji*" and "never lived his life in the *roji*" is literally accurate. According to Yang, to escape from the *roji* is to escape from life in the *hisabetsu buraku*. To him, therefore, Nakagami was a writer who "never tried to grasp the depths of Buraku issues or discriminatory matters."[107] Noguchi Michihiko, however, reads Nakagami's *jōkyō* very differently. Recalling the writer's assertion that "the *roji* was the world in which there was nothing related to liberalism,"[108] Noguchi asserts that what the young Nakagami escaped from was this "*roji* world."[109] For Nakagami, this was the world in which there was no one who understood his sensibility or love for art and nature, that is, for things such as classical music and flowers. To his parents, classical music was nothing but "crap," and loving flowers was "merely something that women and children do."[110] Nakagami recalled: "As a boy who was always interested in utterly impractical things, I was excluded not only from the Buraku community but also from my parents." In fact, he "felt suffocated by the very contractor's sensibility of my

---

gami's statement about Rushdie, see Nakagami and Subraminian 1993, 215. (Note that the correct spelling is Subramanian, but Nakagami adopts "Subraminian" in English in his text.)

107. Yang 1995, 101–2.

108. NKZ 5:432, cited in Noguchi 2001, 76.

109. Noguchi 2001, 76.

110. NKZ 15:305–6.

father and as far as possible always wanted to escape this."[111] As
Noguchi points out, the main reason for Nakagami's *jōkyō* was not
to enroll at university but to leave the "suffocating" *roji* world.[112]

Noguchi rejects Yang's criticism of Nakagami as a writer who
"never tried to grasp the depths of Buraku issues or discriminatory
matters." In arguing against Yang, Noguchi focused on Nakagami's
1969 short story "Ichiban hajime no dekigoto" ("The very first hap-
pening"). This narrative, Nakagami's first work published in a major
literary magazine, *Bungei* (*Fiction*), depicts the life of a young boy
apparently based to some extent on the writer's own boyhood. Although there is no reference to the *roji*, this "debut" work includes
proper place names such as Wakayama, Shingū, Noda, and Kasuga.
In the narrative, Kasuga is where the boy once lived with his mother
and siblings, while Noda is where he lived with his mother and sister in the house of his mother's new husband. The protagonist's alcoholic half-brother frequently visits the home of his mother and
her new husband in Noda. Although he threatened to kill them, this
half-brother eventually killed himself alone in Kasuga. Given the
writer's unambivalent description of Noda and Kasuga, Noguchi
asserts that Nakagami had "no intention to hide the Buraku" in his
writing. This is because "for people who know Shingū, it is obvious
that these two towns are the *hisabetsu buraku*."[113] Noguchi further
discusses how the protagonist's occasional derogatory words against
his close Korean friend, whose community is near these towns, also
signifies Nakagami's "original intention" to be a writer who "directly confronts discrimination."[114] By depicting the childish quar-
rels of a Korean boy who says, "I'm not Korean," "I don't like Koreans,"[115] and the protagonist who retorts that the former is "a
liar,"[116] Nakagami overtly depicts the discrimination lodged in the

---

111. NKZ 5:432.
112. Noguchi 2001, 76.
113. Noguchi 2001, 76.
114. Noguchi 2001, 76.
115. NKZ 1:252.
116. NKZ 1:260.

psyches of these boys and the pain they involuntarily caused each other in this exchange.

Although at the time of publication, "Ichiban hajime no deki-goto" did not particularly attract notice in the Japanese literary community, or *bundan*, the narrative was reevaluated by Hasumi Shigehiko in his 1978 essay collection *Shōsetsu ron = Hihyō ron (Theory of the novel = Theory of critique)*. Here, Hasumi argues that as early as this "Ichiban hajime no dekigoto," Nakagami's writing featured the "absolute cruelty" of narrative that became a distinct feature of later works such as the Akiyuki trilogy.[117] Hasumi points out that unlike most novelists who first produce a bildungsroman narrative that focuses on the protagonist's process of development of their self-identity, Nakagami was "the first writer" who aimed from the start to represent the violent nature of "narrative" itself.[118] In his essay collection "Monogatari no keifu" ("Genealogy of narratives," 1979–1985), Nakagami discusses "narrative as discrimination."[119] As will be discussed in the following chapter, his work can thus be read as a critique of both narrative and discrimination.

---

117. Hasumi 1984, 173.
118. Hasumi 1984, 171–82.
119. NKZ 15:166 and 173.

CHAPTER 3

The Voice of an Illegitimate Son

Family Tragedy in Kumano

This chapter builds on the previous discussion of Nakagami's earlier writing to focus on the writer's most well-known work, the Akiyuki trilogy, as the representation of a transgressive young man and his fragmented family in the peripheral community of Kishū Kumano. As previously noted, this trilogy consists of "Misaki" ("The Cape," 1976), *Kareki nada* (*The sea of withered trees*, 1977), and *Chi no hate shijō no toki* (*The end of the earth, supreme time*, 1983, hereafter *Chi no hate*). This trilogy is modeled to some extent on Nakagami's own experiences, with the hero, Akiyuki, regarded by scholars such as Kobayashi Toshiaki and Alan Tansman as the alter ego of the writer.[1] Like "Rakudo," however, the Akiyuki trilogy cannot be regarded as an autobiographical I-novel. Rather, I argue that the work hosts the emergence of a set of new writing practices derived from overlaying the Western-influenced naturalist literature mode and the more traditional Japanese narrative (*monogatari*) mode. Between the 1970s and 1980s, while writing the Akiyuki trilogy, Nakagami developed the theory of *monogatari* that informed his production of

---

1. Kobayashi 2009, 110–12, and Tansman 1998, 257.

a series of *shōsetsu* (novels) that provided various representations of the socially marginalized.

Because terms related to the Burakumin context never appear in "Misaki" or *Kareki nada*, many readers of these works were unaware that the protagonist's birthplace Kasuga—the *roji*—depicted in these narratives was in fact a *hisabetsu buraku*.[2] Nevertheless, use of the term *roji* successfully conveyed the geopolitically marginalized circumstances of the people of Kishū Kumano, the "hidden country" of ancient texts. In *Chi no hate*, on the other hand, when referring to Burakumin the writer makes overt use of derogatory labels, such as *eta* and *yotsu*, that remain in use today. This work unambiguously depicts Akiyuki's background and therefore the *roji* as associated with the outcaste context. In addition to being a concrete expression of Nakagami's theory of *monogatari*, *Chi no hate* stands apart from the first two works in the trilogy in that it was written after Nakagami's identification of himself as the first and only novelist who chose to "become a Burakumin."[3] In this sense, *Chi no hate* is more useful than the earlier works in the trilogy for my particular focus on Nakagami's representation of the voice of the Burakumin and the writer's theory of becoming a Burakumin. My analysis of *Chi no hate* focuses on the recurring theme of the dismantlement of the Kasuga *roji* that occurred under the pretext of improving the *hisabetsu buraku* environment as part of the 1969–1979 Special Measures for Assimilation Projects legislative reforms. This work also presents the remnants of the preurbanized outcaste community.

Reminding us of Noguchi's argument relating to Nakagami's *jōkyō* as a means of fleeing his personal circumstances in Shingū, the ambivalence of the young male protagonist toward his complicated family relationships is a driving force behind the tragedy of the Akiyuki trilogy. In each volume, traumatic past events are repeatedly narrated to demonstrate the conflict that besets Akiyuki's family and display the significance of the past for the present.

---

2. Hirano 1982, 285.

3. Nakagami and Yasuoka 1980, 365.

Akiyuki's Family Tree

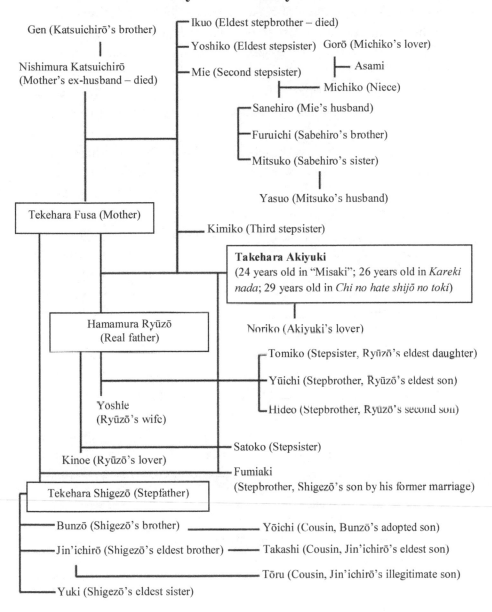

Gen (Katsuichirō's brother)

Nishimura Katsuichirō
(Mother's ex-husband – died)

Ikuo (Eldest stepbrother – died)

Yoshiko (Eldest stepsister) Gorō (Michiko's lover)

Mie (Second stepsister)

Asami

Michiko (Niece)

Sanehiro (Mie's husband)

Furuichi (Sabehiro's brother)

Mitsuko (Sabehiro's sister)

Yasuo (Mitsuko's husband)

Tekehara Fusa (Mother)

Kimiko (Third stepsister)

Takehara Akiyuki
(24 years old in "Misaki"; 26 years old in *Kareki
nada*; 29 years old in *Chi no hate shijō no toki*)

Hamamura Ryūzō
(Real father)

Noriko (Akiyuki's lover)

Tomiko (Stepsister, Ryūzō's eldest daughter)

Yūichi (Stepbrother, Ryūzō's eldest son)

Hideo (Stepbrother, Ryūzō's second son)

Yoshie
(Ryūzō's wife)

Satoko (Stepsister)

Kinoe (Ryūzō's lover)

Fumiaki
(Stepbrother, Shigezō's son by his former marriage)

Tekehara Shigezō (Stepfather)

Bunzō (Shigezō's brother) ———— Yōichi (Cousin, Bunzō's adopted son)

Jin'ichirō (Shigezō's eldest brother) ——— Takashi (Cousin, Jin'ichirō's eldest son)

Tōru (Cousin, Jin'ichirō's illegitimate son)

Yuki (Shigezō's eldest sister)

Akiyuki's mother, Fusa,[4] had five children with her first husband, who was a resident of Kasuga, the *roji*. Following the death of
her husband and one of her sons, she met Hamamura Ryūzō, who
drifted into the *roji* after the war. Members of the Kasuga community condemned Ryūzō as an *uma no hone* (bone of a horse).[5] Fusa
became pregnant by him with Akiyuki. He was eventually arrested
and jailed for gambling. Fusa left Ryūzō after discovering he had
made two other women pregnant. Akiyuki—and his two half-
sisters, Satoko[6] and Tomiko, who were the children of these other
two women—were born while Ryūzō was in prison. When Ryūzō
returned to meet his three-year-old son for the first time, Akiyuki
refused to acknowledge his father. After leaving Ryūzō, Fusa met a
man named Takehara Shigezō. When Akiyuki, her youngest son,
was seven years old, he and Fusa relocated to a neighboring town to
live with Shigezō and his son. Akiyuki's elder half-brother, Ikuo,
and half-sister Mie remained in the *roji*.[7] Ryūzō also returned to the
roji where, through the dishonest exploitation of land, he established
a highly profitable lumber business. Although *roji* residents scornfully referred to him as *hae no kuso nō* (the king of fly shit), Ryūzō
married and established a legitimate family (*ie*) with a wife, a daughter (Tomiko), and two sons (Yūichi and Hideo) in a home on the
heights overlooking the *roji*. When Akiyuki was twelve, Ikuo became violent and often threatened to kill Fusa and Akiyuki. Amid
rumors that Ikuo and Mie were having an incestuous relationship,

---

4. In "Misaki," Akiyuki's mother is called Toki. Nakagami renamed her
Fusa in *Kareki nada* and *Chi no hate*.

5. *Uma no hone* (the bone of a horse) is a derogatory expression for a person
of unknown background or parentage. See "Uma no hone," in *Kōjien* 1983, 228.

6. In "Misaki," Satoko is called Kumi and Akiyuki is unsure whether she is
his real half-sister. Nakagami renamed her Satoko in *Kareki nada* and *Chi no hate*.

7. Akiyuki's eldest half-sister, Yoshiko, and the third sister, Kimiko, migrated to Nagoya and Osaka, respectively, to work after graduating from junior
high school. In *Kareki nada* and *Chi no hate*, each already has her own family in the
area to which she migrated. In "Misaki," because Kimiko was not depicted as
one of Fusa's children, Akiyuki has only two half-sisters, Yoshiko and Mie.

Mie eloped with a close friend of Ikuo, who took his own life at the age of twenty-four. Following her brother's death, Mie hovered between sanity and insanity.

"Misaki" opens during the postwar building boom. Akiyuki is twenty-four years old—the same age, significantly, at which Ikuo took his own life—and working in a road construction gang run by Mie's husband. Every once in a while, Akiyuki runs into his biological father (Ryūzō), whom he calls *ano otoko* (that man). Although the man initiates conversation, Akiyuki responds only in monosyllables. Akiyuki feels the presence of the man because he is constantly the object of his father's gaze. He reflects to himself: "You've been watching me all the time. Even when I was a child, I could feel your eyes on me. I'll burn them out of their sockets, destroy your gaze."[8] Nakagami's depiction of the father's gaze invokes the theory of the "male gaze." Laura Mulvey argues that the gaze of men within film narrative constructs women as vulnerable objects for male viewers.[9] Although male himself, the young Akiyuki is nevertheless vulnerable to the power inherent in the gaze of his father.

Ryūzō's attitude to Akiyuki is evident from the fact that the older man requests Mon,[10] who owns a bar in the red-light district, to welcome Akiyuki but absolutely refuse entry to his legitimate sons, Yūichi and Hideo. Ryūzō's motive for strictly forbidding his sons from visiting the red-light district is because his common-law daughter, Satoko, works there as a prostitute. Mon later realizes that this direction was nothing but Ryūzō's "snare"[11] to ensure that his illegitimate son and daughter met and engaged in incest. As early as "Misaki," Akiyuki had heard a rumor that Ryūzō kept a young

---

8. Nakagami 1999b, 80.

9. See Mulvey 1975, 6–9.

10. Although *Kareki nada* does not describe Mon's background, readers are told in *Hōsenka* and *Chi no hate* that she has a sibling-like relationship with Ryūzō, who is a half-brother of Mon's father.

11. NKZ 6:128.

woman in the red-light district.[12] Mie told Akiyuki that the woman concerned was probably his half-sister by a different mother.

Akiyuki went to the red-light district to try to talk with this woman, who may have been his half-sister. Realizing that her customer (Akiyuki) had no interest in sex, however, she sent him away. Walking the long path back home, he was haunted by questions:

> Was she the man's latest mistress? Or was she his child by a whore? Could she also be his younger sister? ... Had the sister fondled her own brother's penis without knowing it, and had she made her own brother touch her breasts? Mentally he asked her: Why are you working in that kind of place? Why the thinly disguised prostitution? He, the man's son, was getting along fine. The man's other daughter, born to the proper young woman, was now a coddled girl herself. But you alone, the child of the whore, how did you end up this way? Or, if the rumors are true, why are you now the man's mistress?[13]

Akiyuki feels indignation at his father's lustfulness and mistreatment of Satoko. At this point Akiyuki has not had sexual relations. His reluctance to engage in relations with a woman is often expressed as a fear of becoming like his lustful father. It is the fear that "if he did it [sexual intercourse with a woman] just once, he'd become obsessed with it and end up with his mind in the sewer just like that man, who couldn't keep his hands to himself."[14]

Akiyuki's view of his father comes not only from tragic memories of his family but also from the *roji* people's endless rumors. For Akiyuki, the *roji* is a place in which he is oppressed by the echoing voices of the inhabitants who "laughed, celebrated and groaned, violating and heaping abuse on one another."[15] Through his 1984 and 1985 readings of William Faulkner's Yoknapatawpha cycle,

---

12. Nakagami 1999b, 7.
13. Nakagami 1999b, 70.
14. Nakagami 1999b, 24.
15. Nakagami 1999b, 16.

published as "Faulkner, hanmo suru minami" (Faulkner, the luxuriant South), Nakagami theorizes rumor as a "violent" factor deployed "to reinforce the community, to produce narratives in the community and also to dismantle the community."[16] He sees himself as one of several writers, including Gabriel García Márquez, Toni Morrison (1931–2019), and Salman Rushdie (b. 1947), influenced by Faulkner's literature to write of a marginalized "South."[17] These writers—including Nakagami—come from areas that, in common with "the South" in Faulkner's novels, has been marginalized by the mainstream. Evoking Spivak's view of rumor as the "subaltern means of communication,"[18] each writer deploys rumor as a consistent narrative strategy, with blood relationships and the enclosed subaltern community commonly depicted through the rumors people spread. Subaltern "communication," furthermore, can be related to the silences that people keep or are forced to keep. Nakagami and Spivak focus on the structureless structure of rumor that contains no definite origin or end. In the writing of Homi K. Bhabha, this structureless aspect of rumor is referred to as "indeterminacy."[19] For Bhabha, "the chain of communication"[20] in rumor is "intersubjugative, communal," with an "iterative" power of "circulation" and "contagion" that links with "panic" and "insurgency."[21] Nakagami expresses a similar position:

> Because rumor belongs to the community, its perspective is not singular but complicated, that is polyphonic. I think that there are even larger numbers of speakers of the narrative than polyphony.
> … Rumor is voice; voice as violence that shrouds the whole of a

---

16. NKZ 15:539. It can be associated with Nakagami's view of the community in Sayama and the Sayama incident, as discussed above in the introduction.

17. NKZ 15:542–43.

18. Spivak 1988b, 21.

19. Bhabha 2012, 286.

20. Bhabha uses Mikhail M. Bakhtin's metaphor of "the chain of communication." See Bhabha 2012, 270.

21. Bhabha 2012, 286.

narrative and thus activates it. We might say that rumor keeps on being reproduced through the violent device of the voice.[22]

At the close of "Misaki," with his desire to "commit one terrible crime and get revenge on the man,"[23] Akiyuki goes to the red-light district to have incestuous sex with Satoko. Even though he is unsure whether she is his real half-sister, he is impelled by the community's rumor of a sexual relationship between Ryūzō and Satoko, and also between Ikuo and Mie, to have sex with the woman who may be his sibling.[24] Akiyuki's uncontrollable anger—or "panic" to use Bhabha's term—and his wildly impulsive violation of family taboos, including incest and fratricide as depicted in *Kareki nada*, can be seen to result from the power of rumor.

It is not merely the lust of the father and the rumors that circulate throughout the *roji* community that affect Akiyuki. Akiyuki constantly feels oppressed also by the gaze of his half-sisters, especially Mie. For the latter, Akiyuki is nothing but the image of her dead brother. Mie's insanity also causes Akiyuki to hate his parents, whose lustfulness created the whole family tragedy. As his eldest half-sister, Yoshiko, tells Akiyuki, "Mie kept calling, 'Akiyuki, Akiyuki,' as if you were her lover or something."[25] Mie is the half-sister to whom Akiyuki feels closest. This relationship is rooted in the childhood memory of Mie lying beside him when their mother left to meet her lover. For Akiyuki, there was also a memory of the awakening of his erotic impulse. Akiyuki's hidden desire for Mie is revealed in a scene from *Kareki nada* in which he realizes that "the woman [he slept with] was like Mie."[26] According to Zimmerman,

---

22. NKZ 15:539.

23. Nakagami 1999b, 87.

24. The *roji* rumor of incest between Ikuo and Mie is not depicted in "Misaki," but in *Kareki nada*, it is depicted that Akiyuki heard about it after Ikuo's death.

25. Nakagami 1999b, 70.

26. NKZ 3:364.

this implicates the "difference between incest along the father's line (playful self-creation) and incest along the mothers' line (abhorrent repetition)."[27] This suggestion is confirmed in one of a number of autobiographical essays published in *Kumano shū* (*A collection of Kumano stories*, 1984). The author explains that although in the matrilineal *roji* community, Akiyuki's incest with his half-sister by a different mother "does not really violate [the community's] taboo," incest between brother and sister by the same mother is a "dreadful" transgression.[28] For Akiyuki, who knew the "rumor of Ikuo and Mie"[29] and internalized the incestuous narrative of that pair, incest with Mie is a means to violate the matrilineal code that also risks repeating Ikuo's madness and consequent suicide. As Zimmerman points out, "Akiyuki chooses survival by pursuing Satoko."[30] Here, Akiyuki also realizes that Mie "forbade him"[31] to have sexual intercourse with any woman until the age of twenty-four. This silent manipulation of Akiyuki's sexual status is the result of Mie's fear of lust as the cause of her elder brother's death.

As a number of critics note, it is possible to read Akiyuki's incest as a substitute for patricide.[32] Yomota Inuhiko points out that Akiyuki justifies his incest with Satoko as an offense against his father. This is because, for Akiyuki, committing incest implies a violation of his father's biological order and a negation of Ryūzō as the paternal origin.[33] The son furthermore expects to be reproached by his father for violating the incest taboo. In other words, Akiyuki wants Ryūzō to be a father who condemns the act of incest that the son performs as a means of negating the authority of the father.

---

27. Zimmerman 2007, 99.

28. NKZ 3:238.

29. NKZ 3:364.

30. Zimmerman 2007, 100.

31. NKZ 3:364.

32. For example, see Yomota 1996, 196; Watanabe 1996, 19–26; Iguchi 2004, 85–89; and Karatani 2006, 254.

33. Yomota 1996, 169.

"I slept with Satoko." Akiyuki [said]. Even after he spoke the words, other words he wanted to speak were like a whirlpool inside Akiyuki; he thought that he wanted to beg forgiveness. To beg forgiveness, he should humbly scrape the floor with his bowed head. But Akiyuki knew too that a voice in his heart was saying to the man he faced, I have violated you with my penis, which is just like your penis, the one that made me. I will never cease to be your bitter seed for as long as I live. Akiyuki spoke as though he were delirious, "I fucked Satoko," he waited for the man's head to smash and bleed against the wall, and to rip, cut off, and cast away his penis; the penis that made Akiyuki and Satoko in different stomachs; for the man to put out both eyes, slice off his ears. Akiyuki waited for the man let out a raging moan of pain. … This was, after all, his father. As the father, he should whip Akiyuki, knock Satoko down.[34]

Cornyetz discusses the way this scene expresses the "homosexual" desire of the son Akiyuki to "fuck" his father, through Satoko, in an act that wields the penis as an agent of rape and power.[35] If we accept that this is the case, then for Akiyuki the father's expected censure of the act of incest also signifies censure of homosexuality. In other words, Akiyuki desperately seeks the father's hegemonic law to prohibit incest and homosexuality. According to Sigmund Freud (1856–1939), regulation by the law of the father is essential for the son, who can only dissolve his Oedipal complex after internalizing that law.[36] Judith Butler asserts that resolution of the Oedipal complex largely affects gender identification. She argues that the consolidation of discrete gender identity (masculinity and femininity) and the law of heterosexual desire are affirmed by internalization of the incest taboo. She notes, however, that prior to this there is an internalization of the taboo against homosexuality.[37] From this

---

34. This excerpt from Nakagami's *Kareki nada* was translated by Nina Cornyetz. See Cornyetz 1999, 217–18. For the Japanese text, see NKZ 3:362.

35. Cornyetz 1999, 218.

36. See Freud 1976.

37. Butler 1990, 63.

perspective, we might note that the unsettled and paradoxical gender identification of Akiyuki, the son possessed with patricidal desire, was depicted in "Misaki" as that of a young, virile man with a strong physique who was simultaneously a sexually inexperienced object of the father's desiring gaze.

In contrast, *Kareki nada* depicts the sexually confident twenty-six-year-old Akiyuki in a passionate relationship with his lover, Noriko, the daughter of a wealthy timber merchant. Noriko's parents oppose marriage between their daughter and Akiyuki, who comes from the slum-like *roji* community and is the biological son of the notorious timber dealer Ryūzō. For Akiyuki, a showdown confrontation with Ryūzō is crucial for his reputation and future identity. This is because he unconsciously knows that provoking the father's rage against the son's commission of incest and the young man's fantasy of homosexuality with the father is essential for him to become a hegemonically mature adult man who can enter into a heterosexual marriage. That is, Akiyuki expects his Ryūzō to initiate him into the institutions of the patriarchal hegemony so that in the near future Akiyuki can become a father, that is, the patriarch of a conventional Japanese *ie* family.

Ryūzō's answer, however, betrays Akiyuki's desperate desire to be reproached for breaking the incest taboo.

> "It can't be helped. It happens all the time," the man said. He laughed in a low voice. "Don't worry about such things. Even if you two made a baby, even if it were an idiot child, it can't be helped. Although, if you have an idiot child, it's not easy for the mother."
>
> "I'll give birth to the idiot," Satoko said.
>
> "Do it, do it. It doesn't worry me if you have an idiot. I own land in Arima. One or two idiot grandchildren will be no trouble."[38]

---

38. The first four lines of this excerpt from *Kareki nada* were translated by Nina Cornyetz and the remainder by myself. See Cornyetz 1999, 217–18. For Japanese text, see NKZ 3:362–63.

Akiyuki realizes, when he sees his father laughing at the son's relationship with the half-sister, that his transgression of the incest taboo can never invoke the ire of the perverted patriarch, Ryūzō. Like the outside world, the wider *roji* community most certainly does reproach acts of incest, as is evident in the words of a local dance ballad, "Kyōdai shinjū" ("A brother-sister double suicide"), the words of which appear in full in the *Kareki nada* narrative. The ballad, which is frequently referenced in the Akiyuki trilogy as the hidden voice of the marginalized community, tells of a young man's desperate love for his sister. When the brother expresses his love, the girl replies: "People who heard this would call us beasts, if our parents heard of this they would kill us."[39] When Ryūzō, however, hears of his children's incest, he merely laughs, observing that he doesn't even care if the pair has an "idiot" child.

As McKnight notes, critics such as Yomota, Cornyetz, and Zimmerman focus on interpreting Akiyuki's family narrative as a "psychodrama to fuel the 'irrational' course of Nakagami's narratives."[40] My interpretation of this scene can also be explained as an example of psychoanalytically inclined literary criticism. In her investigation of Nakagami's writing in the framework of the "linguistic turn" in the domain of "the *Buraku* activist movement,"[41] McKnight provides a unique interpretation of Akiyuki's "confession." "In this scene, Akiyuki, like Ushimatsu, contemplates prostrating himself abjectly with his head on the tatami floor in deference to authority. And like Ushimatsu's flight to Texas, the solution

---

39. NKZ 3:415–17. While a full text of "Kyōdai shinjū" appears in *Kareki nad*a, some elements in this version of the ballad are different from those in essays written by Nakagami, such as "Fūkei no mukō e: Kankoku no tabi," and "Monogatari no keifu." See NKZ 15:210–12. The version of the ballad cited in those essays was recorded around 1978 by Nakagami who, after publishing *Kareki nada*, recorded a local Kasuga woman singing the text. To articulate the actual folkloric value of the ballad, my analysis in chapter 4 draws on the version Nakagami recorded.

40. McKnight 2011, 96.

41. McKnight 2011, 31.

presented by the judge, Akiyuki's father, is provided by a land grab."[42] Referring here to Ushimatsu, the Burakumin protagonist of Shimazaki Tōson's 1906 novel *Hakai* (the canonical Japanese text relating to Buraku issues and a classic of the Naturalist "confessional" tradition), McKnight discusses Akiyuki's words as presenting a "radical break in confessional narrative."[43] This is because, unlike that of Ushimatsu, Akiyuki's confession produces no effect of "high melodrama" or "tragic enlightenment"[44] related to the father-son conflict that is presented in literary canons such as *Oedipus Rex* or *Hakai*. In *Kareki nada*, the father invalidates the son's advance and attempts to replace the son's narrative with an invented narrative of land and capital. While Cornyetz, Yomota, McKnight, and I focus on the Oedipal conflict between Ryūzō and Akiyuki, in chapter 4 I probe the father and son's relationship as a homosocial bond between men mediated through the sexed subject of the daughter/half-sister, Satoko. For that analysis of Nakagami's depiction of the incestuous sister's oppressed voice, I closely read the "Kyōdai shinjū" ballad.

Ryūzō's failure to condemn Akiyuki's incest demonstrates his refusal to count Akiyuki and Satoko as members of his conventional patriarchal family. After he became a successful timber dealer, Ryūzō established a legitimate family (*ie*) with his wife, a daughter, and two sons. In addition to being the patriarch of a conventional family, Ryūzō leads an underworld group, the Hamamura gang. The conventional family and the gang are necessary for him to demonstrate his superior capacity to rule both mainstream society and the hoodlum-like groups in the local area. As articulated more clearly in the last volume of the Akiyuki trilogy, Ryūzō considers his "legitimate" son Yūichi as the heir to the patriarchal family. He regards Akiyuki as the future head of the Hamamura gang. While Akiyuki desires a conventionally Oedipal and hidden homosexual

---

42. McKnight 2011, 94.
43. McKnight 2011, 96.
44. McKnight 2011, 96.

kinship bond with Ryūzō, Ryūzō consigns Akiyuki to the gangster world that the older man also seeks to dominate.

Akiyuki's desire to bring paternal ire down on himself can also be read as implying a penchant for patriarchy that results from his ambivalence—longing yet hatred—toward Fusa as the promiscuous "matriarch" of his family. Listening to Mie's ambivalent cries to Fusa, which ranged from "I want my mother"[45] to "Murderer, I hate you!"[46] Akiyuki unconsciously internalized Mie's yearning for the lost family, the patriarch of which was her own father. Her voice condemned Fusa's relationship with Ryūzō and Shigezō. Although Mie repeatedly claims that she cherishes Akiyuki, he cannot help feeling oppressed by his half-sister's "speech act."[47] When depicting the conflict in Akiyuki's family, Nakagami draws on forms he regards as providing narrative archetypes of family tragedy, including Western myths and Japanese myths and folk tales from Kishū. In "Misaki," for example, Nakagami references the tragic Greek tale of Electra, who helped her brother, Orestes, kill their mother and their mother's lover, who had murdered their father. Nakagami explained that he wanted to depict Mie as a Japanese Electra and the brother, Ikuo, who kills himself rather than seeking revenge, as an "inverted" Orestes.[48] If Ikuo is an inverted Orestes, Mie can be interpreted as the sister who unconsciously manipulates her brothers (Ikuo and Akiyuki) to subvert and metaphorically kill her mother. We might note that in the Akiyuki trilogy, Mie's matricidal tendencies are overshadowed to some extent by the protagonist's Oedipal desire for patricide.

By creating a new family with Shigezō and his son, Fusa effectively rejected three patriarchs. These were her common-law husband, Ryūzō; her eldest son, Ikuo; and her youngest son, Akiyuki. After Ikuo's death, Akiyuki was the only and therefore eldest son in

45. Nakagami 1999b, 66.

46. Nakagami 1999b, 67.

47. See Spivak 1999, 273, and Austin 1962, 45–52.

48. NKZ 15:60–61.

the "matrilineal" family. However, his privileged position was invalidated when Fusa married Shigezō to create a new family headed by her legitimate husband outside the *roji*. If we accept that the *roji* is a "maternal realm,"[49] this rejection by the matriarch suggests the exile of these three men from the *roji*. Affiliation with the mother would suggest affiliation with the hegemony of the *roji* (i.e., the mother) and thus signifies an attempt to appropriate the "fertility" and associated power of "production" of that site. Each of these three men has a strong connection with the *roji*: Ikuo as a son of an indigenous man from the community, Ryūzō who was once an *uma no hone* despised by the *roji* community who is now "the king of fly shit" who has risen to the "heights" overlooking the whole city,[50] and Akiyuki who identifies as "an illegitimate child of the *roji*."[51] The urgent longing by these men for the "mother" *roji* implies a simultaneous desire for matricide as retaliation for being rejected by Fusa and her attempt to exile them from the position of supreme patriarch. Severed as he is from the mother, paternity, which usually suggests creation, becomes a symbol of destruction and unproductiveness for Akiyuki. Ryūzō's destructive capacity is suggested, for example, by the rumor that he set a fire that razed parts of the *roji*. In *Chi no hate*, his intention to leave the *roji* empty implies the unproductive element in his nature. Ikuo, who destroys himself after failed attempts at matricide and fratricide, shared a similar inherent flaw of perverted "paternity." The rumor concerning incest between Ikuo and Mie also implies a sense of unproductiveness. Furthermore, Ikuo dies before creating his own family.

To challenge the paternal pattern of destruction and unproductiveness, Akiyuki needs to be based in the *roji*, which contains the maternal power of "production" and "fertility."[52] In *Kareki nada*, he clearly identifies himself as "an illegitimate child of the *roji*." "In a

---

49. Nakagami and Abe 1995, 63.

50. NKZ 3:299.

51. NKZ 3:446.

52. Asada 1996, 26.

sense, Akiyuki grew up as a child that the *roji* conceived and gave birth to. Akiyuki had no father. He was not the illegitimate child of Fusa but of the *roji*. The illegitimate child had no father, no mother, nor a single sibling. That's what Akiyuki thought."[53]

In the last part of *Kareki nada*, feeling strong affection for the *roji* that is his motherland, Akiyuki accuses Ryūzō of various atrocities in the area, including theft, murder, and arson. This son's challenge against the father takes place by the river in front of Ryūzō's wife and the couple's three children. It is the night of the *bon*[54] festival, at which time the *roji* people dance to the tune of the "Kyōdai shinjū" ballad. Ryūzō justifies himself by saying, "It's nothing more than rumor, that's all," before telling Akiyuki, "You don't need to care about the *roji*."[55] In the following confrontation with Ryūzō, who displays toward his family "an affinity which leaves no room for anyone else to join in,"[56] Akiyuki cannot conceal his hatred and anger.

> "You have no right to call me Akiyuki," Akiyuki lashed out. That was when it happened. "You bastard," cried Hideo, making as if to attack Akiyuki. ... "Let me go!" shouted Hideo violently twisting his body as Yūichi restrained him from behind. ... Burying her face in her mother's back, Tomiko began to weep. Akiyuki knew that Tomiko, Yūichi and Hideo belonged to Ryūzō. And although he could only refer to Ryūzō as "that/the man" and never as "father," there was no doubt that Ryūzō was the legitimate father of the other three.[57]

Feeling defeated, Akiyuki walks away from Ryūzō's family, and he is chased by Hideo. In the struggle that ensues, Akiyuki pins Hideo

---

53. NKZ 3:446.

54. Bon is a Japanese Buddhist festival held in August. During this festival, people pay respect to the dead. See *Kōjien* 1983, 2224.

55. NKZ 3:451.

56. NKZ 3:449.

57. NKZ 3:451–52.

down "as if he was raping a struggling woman."[58] Seized with a
murderous impulse, Akiyuki eventually beats Hideo to death. Like
the triangular relationship between Ryūzō, Akiyuki, and Satoko,
the triangle between Ryūzō, Akiyuki, and Hideo reveals the homosexual desires of these conflicting men. I return to examine this
point in greater detail through a discussion of "homosociality" in
the following chapter.

Many critics have noted various aspects of Akiyuki's sensibility
for "the repetition of family tragedy."[59] In "Misaki," when a cousin,
Yasuo, murders his brother-in-law, Furuichi, Akiyuki instinctively
links the mortal relationship between the pair to his own relationship with the now-dead Ikuo. In *Kareki nada*, the inevitable repetition of this narrative is depicted through Akiyuki's identification
with Ikuo and his murder of his younger half-brother, Hideo. Akiyuki realizes that by this act, he has repeated Ikuo's intent toward
himself. He reflects:

> Ikuo was his half-brother. When he thought of this fact, he was
> astonished to realize that at that time [when this elder half-brother
> was trying to kill him] Ikuo must have felt the same feelings that
> he now felt and must have been in the same circumstances in
> which he now found himself. Standing in the dusk and soaking in
> the sunlight which still remained in the sky, he felt his eyes shining
> gold.
>
> I will kill you [Hideo], Akiyuki thought. Ikuo had thought
> [the same thing] at that time. Ikuo's eyes at that time were Akiyu-
> ki's eyes now.[60]

Akiyuki's murder of Hideo occurs abruptly (*toppatsu-teki ni*).[61] After
killing his half-brother, Akiyuki identifies himself with Ikuo, who

---

58. NKZ 3:453.

59. For example, see Yomota 1996, 154–55; Watanabe 1996, 21–27; Iguchi
2004, 85–89; and Karatani 2006, 263–67.

60. NKZ 3:331.

61. NKZ 3:452.

wanted to kill Akiyuki, and Hideo, whom Akiyuki kills. Ultimately, however, by murdering Hideo, Akiyuki realizes that rather than being murdered by Ikuo, he has killed himself (Ikuo no kawari ni Akiyuki wa, Akiyuki o koroshita).[62]

Akiyuki's fratricidal challenge to his father's authority is once more in vain, as is evident from Ryūzō's thoughts.

> Akiyuki should have killed Yūichi instead of Hideo. Irresolute Yūichi is not very dear to me. … Hideo was different. He was more similar to the man than Akiyuki because of his heed-lessness and bad temper. Akiyuki, however, had suffered more pain. … Akiyuki, who would be thirty-two by the time he had served six years in prison for murder, was good value, the man thought.[63]

Although Akiyuki wishes to break away from and deny his family genealogy, it is clear that Ryūzō, in spite of Akiyuki's role in Hideo's death, continues to regard the former as a successor, at least of the underworld Hamamura gang. *Kareki nada* concludes by foreshadowing Ryūzō's role in the dismantling of the *roji*. This suggests that Akiyuki's status as an "illegitimate child" of the *roji* will be effaced and replaced by the status that will come as his father's preferred successor. For Akiyuki, who now realizes the impotence of the narratives of incest and fratricide, only one strategy remains as a challenge to the power of the father. Ryūzō has constructed a fantasy narrative of past family glory and it dawns on Akiyuki that he must seize this enigmatic narrative of a fabled past. As *Kareki nada* draws to a close, the conflict between father and son clearly has the "capacity"[64] to continue into the last volume of the trilogy, *Chi no hate*.

---

62. NKZ 3:457.

63. NKZ 3:477.

64. Asada 1996, 27.

Discourse of Narrative as Law/System

Following the success of *Kareki nada*, Nakagami compared himself to a "Russian formalist,"[65] as he publicly discussed his view of narrative from the Burakumin perspective. In Japan, the late 1970s and early 1980s was a time of "new academism" (*nyū akademizumu*), a trend to the study of Western theories such as poststructuralism. This was accompanied by the publication of translated works from many Western scholars. Nakagami was one of several thinkers whose ideas on narrative closely paralleled those of theorists such as Mikhail Bakhtin, Roland Barthes, and Jacques Derrida.[66] However, he also saw the trend to embrace these thinkers as Japanese Eurocentrism.[67] He therefore sought exchange, too, with Japanese scholars such as Yoshimoto, Hasumi, Karatani, and Asada.[68] In this context, Nakagami mounted a critique of traditional Japanese written narrative (*monogatari*) that he regarded as an embodiment of the "law/system" (*hō/seido*) that scaffolded the ascendency of exclusionist mainstream thought.

A number of English-language scholars have discussed Nakagami's approach to narrative theory, but generally, little attention outside Japan has been given to the role of prominent scholar of French theory and film studies, Hasumi Shigehiko in Nakagami's working through his ideas on this issue. I begin my discussion of Nakagami's view of *monogatari* by examining the interpretation of

---

65. NKZ 15:426.

66. This can be seen in Nakagami's interviews with various Japanese writers and scholars included in *Nakagami Kenji zenhatsugen* volumes 1 and 2 (1978 and 1980, *Complete discourse of Nakagami Kenji*) and *Nakagami Kenji hatsugen shūsei* volumes 1–6 (1995–1999, *A collection of discourse of Nakagami Kenji*, edited by Karatani and Suga).

67. Nakagami 2004, 36.

68. Asada's first book, *Kōzō to chikara: Kigō ron o koete* (*Structure and power: Beyond semiotics*, 1984), sold 150,000 copies and led to a boom of Japan's new academism.

monogatari in the *Kareki nada* text given in Hasumi's essay "Monogatari toshite no hō: Céline, Nakagami Kenji, Gotō Meisei" ("Law as
narrative: Louis-Ferdinand Céline, Nakagami Kenji and Gotō Meisei," 1977). Since its publication, this work has strongly influenced
academic interpretations of Nakagami's narratives.[69] In an interview
with Hasumi, Nakagami moreover noted that the essay paralleled
his own view of the *monogatari* structure that he developed while
writing *Kareki nada*.[70]

Hasumi assesses *Kareki nada* as an epoch-making "work"
(*sakuhin*) that illustrates the operation of the *monogatari* form in a
contemporary narrative structure.[71] The term *work* contrasts with
the term *novel* (*shōsetsu*), used by Etō when declaring *Kareki nada* to be
the culmination of seventy years of the Japanese Naturalist literary
tradition of expression that depicts "the real life [the lived experi-
ence]" of the people.[72] Rather than the character representation
that impressed Etō, however, Hasumi is interested in *Kareki nada* as
a "narrative" that reveals "law as narrative"[73] and affirms the inev-
itability of the *monogatari* structure conforming to a set pattern.
"'Narrative' is an absolute duty demanded at every level of our lives,
so that anyone who disobeys must inevitably expect to be punished
harshly by the 'narrative.'"[74] Noting that *Kareki nada* displays the
violent nature of "narrative" through the depiction of the hero's
defeat and punishment, in a second essay Hasumi proclaims Nakagami as a writer who proves that literature is, in fact, a dynamic attempt to resist "narrative."[75]

As we have seen, the plot of *Kareki nada* details the many trans-
gressions of family taboos—such as incest and fratricide—committed by Akiyuki, who was born as an illegitimate child from the

---

69. Nagashima 1996, 301.
70. Nakagami and Hasumi 1980, 181–82.
71. Hasumi 1984, 292–93.
72. Etō 1996, 144.
73. Hasumi 1984, 305.
74. Hasumi 1984, 286.
75. Hasumi 1984, 182.

closed, peripheral community of the Kasuga *roji*. Furthermore, the hero's incest with his half-sister and his murder of his half-brother are committed as substitutes for patricide, and both are triggered by frustration toward the father. The archetype of the patricidal narrative can be found in biblical tales and in Japanese and Greek mythologies. As read in Nakagami's 1989 interview with Zimmerman, Akiyuki's murder of his half-brother has a close parallel to the biblical tale of Cain and Abel in terms of one brother killing another to win the father's love.[76] In his essays on *monogatari*, Nakagami often refers to narratives from the *Kojiki* and local Kumano oral folklore as Japanese versions of archetypal global narratives that demonstrate (recalling Hasumi), "an absolute duty demanded at every level of our lives."[77]

Like the ancient Greek tragic hero Oedipus, the protagonist in *Kareki nada* "unconsciously" constructs himself as the successor to his father by killing his half-brother, even though he does not necessarily wish to emulate his father. Rather, he wants to become a conventional patriarch. Hasumi remarks that the fratricide is forced on Akiyuki so he might comply with the archetype of the son. In the closing section of *Kareki nada*, the exiled (imprisoned) hero only appears in rumors spread by people in his community. In other words, he is deprived of his voice and confined in "narrative" as punishment for resisting his narratological "duty" to be a successor.[78] Thus, Hasumi reads *Kareki nada* as a "work" that foregrounds the discourse of narrative as an invincible "law" ordering our view of the world. Referencing Japanese and French sources, Hasumi's essay also demonstrates that "law as narrative" is a principle independent from the other laws that govern the world.

Inspired by Hasumi's argument, Nakagami developed his own view of "narrative" as a "law/system" from the perspective of *monogatari*, that is, the tradition of Japanese writing. In "Monogatari no

---

76. Zimmerman 1999a, 133–34.
77. Hasumi 1984, 286.
78. Hasumi 1984, 296–303.

keifu" ("Genealogy of narratives," 1979–1985) and "Monogatari no teikei" ("The archetypal pattern of narratives"), Nakagami inverts Hasumi's notion of law as narrative, arguing instead for "narrative as law/system," a phenomenon that can be seen in any art form. Between 1979 and 1985, "Monogatari no keifu" was intermittently serialized in the prestigious academic journal *Kokubungaku* (*Japanese literary studies*). Publishing an essay in *Kokubungaku* signified Nakagami's challenge to the literary authorities, both critics and novelists, who made up the *bundan*, the "authoritative" literary community in Japan. Reflecting on the influence of the "new academism" that sought to "deconstruct" preceding paradigms, Nakagami's essay features citations from Derrida's critiques of logocentrism while also invoking Deleuze and Guattari's idea of the rhizome.

In these essays, Nakagami presented a Burakumin writer's critique of five of Japan's most respected writers: Satō Haruo (1892–1964),[79] Tanizaki Jun'ichirō (1886–1965), Ueda Akinari (1734–1809), Orikuchi Shinobu (1887–1953), and Enchi Fumiko (1905–1986).[80] Nakagami identified each as a writer of *monogatari* who invokes (alludes to) "*monogatari* as law/system." By reading selected works by these five writers, Nakagami probes the negative social impact of hegemonic *monogatari* while seeking strategies to write against what he regards as this oppressive tradition. On one hand, because their fiction addresses narrative principle rather than "humanity," Nakagami appreciates these writers as "detached from a humanist perspective."[81] Although he severely criticizes Tanizaki as a writer who never resists the exclusionist "archetype" of narrative, Nakagami regards all five writers as aware of *monogatari* as law/system and therefore as unhesitatingly depicting its violent nature in their writ-

---

79. Satō Haruo also came from Shingū. He was not a Burakumin but the son of a prominent local doctor. His novel *Wanpaku jidai* (*A naughty boy's childhood*, 1958) includes a description of Shingū Burakumin areas, including Kasuga, as residential districts where people are discriminated against by the mainstream because of "foolish convention." See Satō H. 1958, 156–57.

80. The chapter "Enchi Fumiko" (1985) is unfinished.

81. NKZ 15:256.

ings. Although "Monogatari no keifu" is a lengthy and heavily theoretical—but unfinished—discursive series of essays published in a prestigious journal, "Monogatari no teikei" presents a concise and clear argument for what was mostly an audience of literary studies students. Since a detailed examination of the essay on Enchi Fumiko appears in chapter 5, I confine my commentary here to Nakagami's view of *monogatari* given in the public lecture.

Monogatari is a compound of two words, *mono* (things) and *katari* (talk), and the word originally describes the act of people talking about things (*mono o kataru*). As its derivation suggests, *monogatari* is closely tied to oral traditions passed down from generation to generation. In Nakagami's view, furthermore, *mono* is "soul" and *katari* is "not only the activity of telling but also the passing down of religious precepts and historical memories."[82] The repetition of this "passing down" leads to the formation of archetypal (*teikei*) *monogatari* codes. These codes, which according to Nakagami include haiku forms based on the use of *kigo* (seasonal words)[83] and *kachō fūgetsu* (flower, bird, wind, and moon) expressions,[84] created stereotypical rhetorical forms that characterize the Japanese literary tradition. Once the oral language of the people, the literary tradition gradually became the province of an exclusive elite. In this way, established stereotypes came to operate in a way that excluded difference. The corollary is that only writing that conforms to these stereotypes is regarded as legitimate.

Noting that archetypes of *monogatari* work to "rob novels of freedom" in terms of providing representations outside fixed boundaries, Nakagami explains his attempt to "shift" his fiction from these accepted narrative codes as a way to resist the exclusion of difference that is a marker of "*monogatari* as the law/system."[85] The trace of Nakagami's resistance to the archetype can be seen in

---

82. Nakagami 1999c, 225.

83. Nakagami 1999c, 224.

84. For further detail see Nakagami's discussion on Tanizaki Jun'ichirō in "Monogatari no keifu." See NKZ 15:140–56.

85. Nakagami 1999c, 232.

Kareki nada. Although this narrative depicts Oedipal conflict between son and father, for example, the pivotal narrative of patricide
is "shifted to" (replaced by) a narrative of incest and fratricide.
Through this process of shifting, *Kareki nada* creates a mode of de-
centralization that contests and ultimately disrupts the exclusionist
idea of *monogatari* as law/system.

When Hasumi's essay was first published, Nakagami was traveling around the Kii Peninsula gathering material for the serialization
of the travel journal *Kishū*. This text was read in chapter 1 as the
writer's investigation of the roots of discrimination. Here I read
Kishū, or an excerpt from this work, as an investigation of "the roots
of *monogatari*" in literature and oral folklore.[86] This was the role
Nakagami attributed to that text.

One of the later chapters of the *Kishū* collection, titled "Yoshino,"
gives an account of the writer arriving after dark by car at a town in
that famous cherry blossom–viewing mountain site. The car head-
lights illuminate the stalks and flowers of goldenrod, the ubiquitous
roadside weed. Nakagami observes that this sacred remote area of
Japan is an "ideal"[87] site of narratives about mysterious origins.
These narratives include Tanizaki Jun'ichirō's novella *Yoshinokuzu*
(*Arrowroot*, 1931), in addition to the oral folklore of wandering nobles of the Heike clan. Nakagami draws a parallel between these
narratives and the goldenrod plant.

> In the light of the car, the shadow of the florescent yellow flow-
> ers stirred lightly. I got out of the car. Bringing the flowers close
> to my nose and breathing in the hay fever–inducing pollen, I
> squeezed the blossoms in this land of narrative, "Yoshino." ...
>
> I realised that *monogatari* is similar to this tall goldenrod flower.
> ...
>
> These flowers, the poisonous roots of which kill other plants,
> are a symbol of *monogatari*, and I found them in the place that was
> the setting of *Yoshinokuzu*.

---

86. NKZ 14:628–29.
87. NKZ 14: 632.

> Visiting ... the Yoshino region to search for *monogatari*, I see
> myself as if struck by the poison of *monogatari*. What is *monogatari*?
> My hunch is that it is like the tall goldenrod. It has roots of dis-
> crimination and flowers that lightly wave in the night and blaze
> golden during the daytime.[88]

To many Japanese people, goldenrod represents the invasive nature
of foreign influences in Japan. As Long notes, in this passage, the
foreign weed is seen to prevail in the Yoshino region, a key site in
the Japanese narrative tradition, and becomes, in Nakagami's eyes,
a metaphor for the violent nature of *monogatari*.[89] For Nakagami,
dynamic *monogatari* (the waving goldenrod flower) has discrimination (poison) in its roots.

In the *Kishū* essay series, Nakagami writes that *monogatari* only
exists within the bounds of *shakai kiyaku*,[90] that is, within the confines of social convention. The term *convention* here is ultimately a
synonym for law/system (*hō/seido*), a term that appears in "Monogatari no keifu." To Nakagami, furthermore, the term *convention* or *law*,
and the exclusionary processes implied, is a synonym for language
and the official systems that language supports. The writer illustrates this idea by relating an exchange with a young Burakumin
man who has been unable to get a driver's license because he has
struggled to understand the formal Japanese language used in the
traffic regulation handbook.

> In order to gain a driver's license, the young man was studying
> [the traffic handbook]. Two men of about the same age were en-
> couraging him all the while. At first, he did not understand the
> sense of words such as "immediately" and "prevent," but, through
> studying, his literacy gradually improved and he passed the test
> for the learner's license. However, he could not pass the provi-
> sional license test. He failed seven times. Actually, what he failed
> was [not the driving test but] a test of language.

88. NKZ 14:629.
89. Long 2006, 18.
90. NKZ 14:631.

For example, he was confused by a sentence in the regulations that read "you must not reverse along a highway." The boy
claimed that he could not understand this, muttering "just revers-
ing a little [should not be a problem]."[91]

For Nakagami, this episode demonstrates how the roots of discrimination he encountered metaphorically in the form of the goldenrod
with its poisonous roots affected on the Burakumin man's ability to
accommodate himself to the law of language, that is, to understand
language as the production of convention that does not necessarily
express lived experience.[92] The young man in "Yoshino" can be
seen as one archetype of the unconventional men depicted in Nakagami's narrative. The "Yoshino" essay particularly displays Nakagami's emphasis on the paradox created by his desire to write against
convention, that is, against the law of language, while being required
to use this same language to write those *monogatari* that give voice to
the narratives of the oppressed.

A Narrative of the Last Days of the Outcaste Community

Chi no hate is an account of the last days of the *roji*—the fictional site
of the *hisabetsu buraku* of Kasuga—that was "erased" in the early
1980s. At the outset of the novel, the twenty-nine-year-old Akiyuki
returns from prison to find that the *roji* has disappeared "as if erased
by an eraser"[93] and transformed into grassland. Most former residents have been forced to move to other areas or moved into
purpose-built apartment complexes constructed on the original *roji*
site. Some homeless people continue to live in a camp in the grassland that remains after the effacement of the *roji*. Actively partici-
pating in the erasure of the community of the *roji* and the eviction

---

91. NKZ 14:630.
92. NKZ 14:630–32.
93. NKZ 6:153.

of neighbors to make way for land clearance, Akiyuki's family has made an excessive profit and become local upstarts. Although there is a focus on patricide and Akiyuki's relationship with father, *Chi no hate* also interrogates the maternal. The self-implosion of the maternal society of the *roji* signifies the end of the matrilineal narrative that supports "Misaki" and *Kareki nada*. Akiyuki's mother, Fusa, long ago abandoned the *roji*. Mie, who once refused to live outside the *roji*, now repeats Fusa's narrative of abandonment and, having married a successful businessman, unhesitatingly accepts a position of status in mainstream society. Although she remains nostalgic for the *roji*, given her desire for social success, Akiyuki regards her nostalgia as mere "irony." While he thinks of asking Mie, "how can you live with yourself after trampling over the lives of [*roji*] people?" he stops himself when the traces of her fragility are revealed by her sentimental "weepy" (*nakimushi*) behavior. After visiting the grassland *roji* camp, Akiyuki decisively isolates himself from his family on the grounds that "blood relationships must disappear with the *roji*."[94]

In *Chi no hate*, a millenarian water cult, drawing followers from the *roji* and mainstream community, grows in concurrence with the start of the urbanization project. The founders of the cult, a brother and sister who were Akiyuki's schoolmates, eventually kill their mother during a ritual ceremony of purification that is intended to "remove pollution from inside the body."[95] Most followers, including the mother, are elderly women who voluntarily accept cruel acts of penance, such as drinking large amounts of water and being whipped. As the rumor of the murder spreads throughout Shingū, it is accompanied by a stench that suggests the mother's decayed body, a stench that in fact comes from sewers severed during land "reform." This matricidal narrative resonates with the overwhelming anxiety that grips the small provincial city in which, by implementing urbanization policies, the authorities have effaced the city's

---

94. NKZ 6:153–58.
95. NKZ 6:85.

most subaltern community, a community that was the "origin"—
the "mother"—of marginality in the area. The cultic brother and
sister can be seen as variants of Akiyuki and Satoko. Satoko, who
regards herself as indelibly polluted with *kegare*, becomes an enthusiastic water cult follower and willingly undertakes extreme penance. Although Ryūzō has little interest in the fanaticism of the
water cult, he surprisingly feels a great sense of "defeat" at the
founder brother and sister's matricide.[96] This feeling is in marked
contrast to his indifferent attitude toward the incestuous act between Akiyuki and Satoko, which never disturbs this father's equa-
nimity.

Following Akiyuki's release from prison, the father and son re-
unite. On this occasion, the son takes the initiative before the father, demonstrating the possibility of an inversion of the relationship between the pair.

> "Hey, Ryūzō," Akiyuki called Hamamura Ryūzō just as if the man
> was his son. Looking at Ryūzō smile like an innocent child, Aki-
> yuki related a vision he had had to the older man, "In prison,
> Hamamura Magoichi appeared in my dream again and again.
> When our honourable ancestor told me, 'Akiyuki, you are my in-
> carnation and Ryūzō is your son,' I told him not to talk rubbish.
> But Magoichi replied that he didn't mind having one inverted ge-
> nealogy during our long family line."
>
> Ryūzō looked taken aback ... but said merrily, "You always
> take everything away from me."[97]

This scene demonstrates how the novel's narrative of this father and
son proceeds on the premise of the interchangeability of their relationship—the son can be the father and the father can be the son.
Furthermore, although it is Akiyuki who initiates the exchange,
Ryūzō voluntarily accepts an inversion of their genealogical order
by referring to his son as "father" and "brother." In depicting the

---

96. NKZ 6:280–85
97. NKZ 6:30.

Ryūzō's unconventional paternity, Nakagami invokes the legend, based on historical fact, of the rebellious samurai Magoichi. Ryūzō's alleged ancestor Magoichi is associated with the *kishu ryūritan* (legend of exiled nobles)[98] of the legendary figure Suzuki Magoichi (dates unknown), the leader of the sixteenth-century Saika shū (Saika group of warriors), who were renowned for their gunsmiths, foundries, and arquebus expertise. This group initiated the Saika ikki (Saika riots, 1577–1585), a Kii Peninsula uprising ruthlessly subjugated by Oda Nobunaga (1534–1582).[99] Ryūzō's birthplace, Arima, is known as the legendary site of Magoichi's death. Although the family name of the historical Magoichi is Suzuki, in *Kareki nada* and *Chi no hate*, Nakagami gives Magoichi the family name of Hamamura. This allows the character to have a direct connection to Ryūzō, whose family name is Hamamura. Both *Kareki nada* and *Chi no hate* portray Ryūzō's obsession with establishing a legitimate origin for himself as Magoichi's descendant and with leading a gang of men known as the Hamamura shū, the name of which recalls the Saika shū. Ryūzō's declaration of Magoichi as his ancestor is scornfully dismissed by the community as "a laughingstock."[100] For Akiyuki, however, Ryūzō's reinvention of this origin initially suggests the triumph of the father by making the older man unbeatable. Yet

---

98. *Kishu ryūritan* is the genre of folktale narrative about wandering (often exiled) gods, nobles, criminals, and pilgrims. The term was firstly applied by Orikuchi Shinobu (1887–1953) in *Nihon bungaku no hassei josetsu* (*An introduction to the emergence of Japanese literature*, 1947), in reference to narratives of gods who were wandering in an *utsuho bune* (a hollow ship). See Orikuchi 2017. In *Kōjien*, the term is defined as stories about wandering noble heroes who overcome difficulty with help from animals or women. Examples of the genre include the *Kojiki* narratives of Ōkuninushi no mikoto, Yamato takeru no mikoto, the Hikaru Genji stories in the "Suma" and "Akashi" chapters of *Genji monogatari* (*A Tale of Genji*) by Murasaki Shikibu (eleventh century), in addition to the story of Odysseus in *The Odyssey*. See "Kishu ryūritan" in *Kōjien* 1983, 575.

99. *Daijisen* 1995, 1033, and Teraki 1991, 66–67. Moriyasu Toshiji argues that Nakagami's depiction of Magoichi was based on the local Arima narrative of legendary figure Suzuki Shigeyuki. See Moriyasu 2003, 266–85.

100. NKZ 3:370.

as the *Kareki nada* narrative progresses, Akiyuki realizes that he can overcome his father by appropriating the Magoichi narrative for himself. The scene from *Chi no hate* suggests that by the third book in the trilogy, Akiyuki's intentions have been realized. Given that Ryūzō voluntarily inverts the genealogical order by agreeing to refer to his son as "father," "brother," and "Magoichi," we might argue that Akiyuki's overthrow of Ryūzō is as yet only partial.

Following the encounter with Akiyuki, Ryūzō has an exchange with Fusa. When Fusa refers to Akiyuki as "your child," Ryūzō explains his interchangeable relationship with his son.

> "Hey Ryūzō, you traitor," Fusa shouted. "Come on here and tell me that you want your child!"
>
> "No, no, Fusa, Akiyuki's not my child. He's my father. You should know that, Fusa. Because Akiyuki's my father, I've mended my ways and no longer corrupt myself with gambling."
>
> "Don't talk nonsense," Fusa retorted as if she herself was the gambler.[101]

This exchange is a declaration, announced by Ryūzō who has previously been exiled from his common-law wife's matrilineal family, of Akiyuki's isolation from Fusa. For Ryūzō, the *roji* matriarchy must be overthrown because it is incompatible with his ambition to be the hegemon ruling over both the conventional society and the underworld. Ryūzō consolidates this hegemony by naming the illegitimate son, Akiyuki, as the successor to the leadership of the underworld Hamamura gang while the remaining legitimate son, Yūichi, is the heir to the patriarchal Hamamura family. Although they are a regular presence in the first two volumes of the trilogy, Fusa and Mie appear infrequently in *Chi no hate*. Ultimately, with the dismantlement of their narrative ground (the *roji*) by the husbands with whom each has established a conventional patriarchal family, the power of the matriarch and her daughter successor is lost.

---

101. NKZ 6:56.

With the emergence of the inverted father–son relationship, the meaning of patricide is invalidated. Karatani defines patricide as the modern desire to overcome the older generation to advance. Having a father to overcome is to become a "subject" who internalizes "repression by the father." Karatani further argues that modernity is "the world which is dominated by the Oedipal theme" and that *kindai shōsetsu* (modern novels) must necessarily deal with that theme.[102] While the concept of patricide in "Misaki" and *Kareki nada* is clearly Oedipal, the invalidation of the patricidal narrative in *Chi no hate* can be considered as the "deconstruction" of the grand patriarchal narrative of modernity. Asada supports Karatani's reading of *Chi no hate* as a representation of the postmodern world that invalidates (deconstructs) the modern narratives of patricidal conflict that underpin "Misaki" and *Kareki nada*.[103]

I would argue that *Chi no hate* is a novel that operates by means of (to borrow from Spivak) the "deconstructive figure,"[104] which I understand to be the strategy of deconstruction. Referring to Barthes's 1968 essay, "Death of the Author," as being characterized by this deconstructive strategy, Spivak cites the closing passage from the essay: "It is derisory to condemn the new writing in the name of a humanism hypocritically turned champion of the reader's right. ... The birth of the reader must be at the cost of the death of Author."[105] Spivak notes that this deconstructive strategy is one of "complicity as well as (and therefore fully neither/nor) deicide-parricide," that is, the elimination of neither god nor the father. Although Barthes's passage apparently carries the conviction of deicide-parricide, Spivak argues that rather than heralding the literal death of any given author, the expression "the death of the Author" is the former's deliberate "choice" of a metaphor that evokes Nietzsche's notion of the death of God.[106] Hasumi concurs with

---

102. Karatani 2006, 175.
103. See Asada 1996, 30, and Karatani 2006, 174–76.
104. Spivak 1999, 98.
105. Quoted in Spivak 1999, 98. For the original text see Barthes 1977, 148.
106. Spivak 1999, 98.

Spivak in that he also regards the notion of "the death of the Author" as Barthes's attempt to "thwart any hypocritical plots" that are produced by the "in-vogue" discourse of the death of God. Hasumi reads "The Death of the Author" as Barthes's criticism of this "anachronistic" ideological trend that randomly "inflames" the perspective that we have no choice but to accept the narrative of the end of modernity.[107] Rather than overly focusing on the deicide-parricide metaphor evoked by the expression "the death of Author"—as other critics have done—Spivak and Hasumi read Barthes in a manner that emphasizes his contestation of attributing a single meaning to a text. From this perspective, a notion such as deicide-parricide can have a range of possible meanings. For Spivak, in fact, "No possible reading is a *mis*-reading." This is because the "challenge of deconstruction" is not to justify but "to suspend accusation to examine with painstaking care if the protocols of the text contains [*sic*] a moment that can produce something that will generate a new and useful reading."[108]

Drawing on Spivak's passage, I read *Chi no hate* not as a narrative of patricide but as a narrative of the (im)possibility of (a narrative of) patricide. Unlike his abrupt desire to commit incest and fratricide as a substitute for patricide in the first two volumes of the trilogy, in *Chi no hate* Akiyuki's desire is clearly focused on the destruction of the father, Ryūzō. The conventional father–son relationship, however, is invalidated by the scene in which Ryūzō positively accepts Akiyuki's inversion of their bond. Borrowing from Spivak, Akiyuki can be seen as a son who "suspends accusation" of his father's immoral paternal pattern of disruption and unproductiveness to consider whether patricide—that is, the destruction of Ryūzō—"can produce something that will generate a new and useful reading" of the emptiness of his homeland, the *roji*.[109] Ultimately, however, this suspension of accusation is temporary and Akiyuki is

---

107. Hasumi 1985, 265.
108. Spivak 1999, 98.
109. Spivak 1999, 98.

unable to prevent himself from unleashing the full force of his rage against his father and even wanting to kill him.

> Living no better than a beggar, his [Ryūzō's] grandfather had raged against the Arima villagers. This made Hamamura Ryūzō, who committed fraud and who manipulated financial records, cold and heartless [and so he was able to] dismantle the *roji* and strip clear the land. Akiyuki was aware of this. For Ryūzō there was no reason to do this—he was merely an ant building a nest. The one who thought about meaning was Akiyuki. Like a ghost of meaning, he thought that they should make the *roji* into own-erless, common land and share it with the people who lived there in the huts that they had built for themselves. Akiyuki wanted to tell Satoko that this was his reason for wanting to kill Ryūzō, but he kept quiet, thinking that Satoko would never understand his wildly abstract idea.[110]

Akiyuki's "wildly abstract" idea of wanting to kill Ryūzō arises from the fact that the *roji* community, the motherland in which he once found his identity as "an illegitimate child," no longer exists. The agonized prolongation and indeterminacy of Akiyuki's "patri-cide" results from the invalidation of his identity that is the result of severing connections with the *roji*.

Chi no hate suggests that the end of the Father is—paradoxi-cally—concurrent with the end of the *roji* and the motherland com-munity. What is the end of community in modern society? In a work titled *Community: Seeking Safety in an Insecure World*, Zygmunt Bauman observes:

> Since "community" means shared understanding of the "natural" and "tacit" kind, it won't survive the moment in which under-standing turns self-conscious, and so loud and vociferous; when, to use Heidegger's terminology again, understanding passes from the state of being "zuhanden" to being "vorhanden" and be-

---

110. NKZ 6:375.

comes an object for contemplation and scrutiny. Community can only be numb—or dead. Once it starts to praise its unique valour, wax lyrical about its pristine beauty and stick on nearby fences wordy manifestoes calling its members to appreciate its wonders and telling all the others to admire them or shut up—one can be sure that the community is no more (or not yet, as the case may be).[111]

Bauman's view can explain Nakagami's attachment to his homeland community expressed in the autobiographical essay "Shakkyō"[112] ("Stone bridge," 1980), included in *Kumano shū*. "Shakkyō" demonstrates that the "author" (who is written as "I"—*watashi*—apparently Nakagami) views the *roji* as a "text" of the "Dark Continent of language."[113] This essay also displays Nakagami's isolation from the community because of his need to articulate the significance of the *roji*. His assertion/celebration of, yet mixed feeling of hatred toward, the *roji* is never understood or accepted by his family or peers in Kumano, who see him as too self-conscious because of his own "inferiority complex."[114] Feeling irritated by the capitalist influenced views of the members of his community who never doubt that the effacement of the *roji* benefits their peripheral society, the "author" tries to "discover the *roji*" and become (to use a phrase given by Faulkner in his map of Yoknapatawpha County), the "sole owner and proprietor"[115] of that site.

  Chi no hate, published three years after "Shakkyō," can be interpreted as a novel that demonstrates the "birth of the Author." A reader of the *roji*, Nakagami became an author of the *roji* by writing *Chi no hate*. In his 1983 interview with novelist Kojima Nobuo (1915–2006), Nakagami commented, "Having finished writing *Chi*

---

111. Bauman 2001, 11–12.

112. The essay title, "Shakkyō," is from the title of a well-known *nō* play.

113. NKZ 5:282–83.

114. NKZ 5:274.

115. Faulkner 1991, 313–14.

no hate shijō no toki, I feel for the first time that I have written a *shōsetsu*."[116] Although Yomota argues that *Chi no hate* was written because the *roji* was effaced, Watanabe reverses this view. According to Watanabe, *Chi no hate* was written through Nakagami's establishment and possession of the *roji* as the last topos of narratives of the marginalized that have been passed down from generation to generation since ancient times.[117] As discussed in the previous section, after the effacement of the *roji,* Akiyuki "discovers" new meaning in this community. At the same time, he is aware of the ambiguity of that community. While the *roji* can be a place of "warmth" for subalterns, who include "dispirited and ghostly" men with no pride or confidence and lustful women with their illegitimate children, members of this community only welcome outsiders on the condition that newcomers are more "useless" than themselves. For Akiyuki the *roji* is a place of the "mother," but for the outsider Ryūzō, who was excluded because he was "[more] clever and [more] vigorous [than *roji* people]," it is a hated place.[118] Drawing on Bauman's view of "the Other" in a community of "sameness," Ryūzō can be seen as the alien who gives the community "the fear of uncertainty."[119] Akiyuki does attempt to understand his father's view of the *roji* community by seeking to understand the differing nature of the relationships of both himself and his father to the *roji*. Akiyuki's insight into his father's view could come only after invalidating their father-and-son conflict that resulted when this conflict lost its origin, the *roji*. It was here that the son once based himself to challenge his father.

Bauman discusses the relationship between community and identity, citing Jock Young's observation, "Just as community col-

116. Nakagami and Kojima 1995, 265.

117. See Watanabe's comment in his 1994 round-table discussion with Karatani, Asada, and Hasumi (Hasumi, Watanabe, Asada, and Karatani 1994, 24).

118. NKZ 6:313.

119. Bauman 2001, 115–16.

lapses, identity is inverted."[120] *Chi no hate* demonstrates how Akiyuki shifts his view of identity after the *roji* dismantlement, that is, after the invalidation of his self-identification as "an illegitimate child of the *roji*." Akiyuki's ideas are clearly presented to the reader in a passage that is significant for its references to the historical circumstances of *hisabetsu* people who were brutalized by the mainstream as a result of "impure" occupations like tanning leather:

> Although their voices were naturally alike, Akiyuki intentionally lowered his tone to sound even more like Ryūzō and said: "When I returned to this place from prison, I walked round the *roji* crying. At that time, I thought I could become anything. Walking and crying, I thought how, even though I would derogatorily be called *eta* [great filth] or *yotsu* [four]—I could become a man who tanned leather for a living in the muddy water of the lotus pond … or I could be a man who was crippled after being brutally beaten by a gang of lumbermen on New Year's day, only because when mingling with the crowd of visitors of Hayatama Shrine he accepted one of the rice cake pieces that those lumbermen were handing out. … So, I can even become Hamamura Magoichi," …
>
> "Ryūzō, Akiyuki, whom you thought of as your blood son, … died at the same time that the *roji* was effaced. Of course, I am alive, and I am certainly a son of Hamamura Ryūzō who has inherited the blood of Hamamura Magoichi, but, I am more suitable to be a *yotsu*—nothing less than a beast—or a *jūichi* [eleven] which is one level below the Jews."[121]

As noted in the introduction, the term *eta* and *yotsu* are known as derogatory names for Burakumin. Since the English word *Jew* is a homophone for the Japanese term *jū* (十), meaning ten, *jūichi* (十一, eleven) implies, as Akiyuki says, one (*ichi*, 一) level "below the Jews." According to Yasuoka Shōtarō, the term was pronounced *to-ichi*[122] and used by Japanese Americans in Hawaii to refer to Burakumin

---

120. Bauman 2001, 15.

121. NKZ 6:176–77.

122. The Japanese word *to* is *tō*, which also means *jū* (ten).

there.[123] By using these offensive terms, Nakagami unambiguously depicts Akiyuki's Burakumin background for the first time in the trilogy. In other words, Akiyuki's awareness of the context of the discrimination against the Burakumin is finally expressed when he witnesses the dismantlement of the Burakumin community and becomes involved in the issue of "land ownership." Nakagami regarded land ownership as the crux of *buraku mondai*.

In their readings of Tōson's *Hakai*, Nakagami and Karatani argue that Ushimatsu will meet new discrimination in Texas, the place to which he flees to escape discrimination in Japan. The foreign association of the pejorative term *jūichi*, which draws on a culture of denigration of people with a Jewish background, supports this view. In the same way that Jewish people were subjected to centuries of pogroms and other brutal assaults that culminated in the Holocaust, the Burakumin will become a target of discrimination by the mainstream in the United States. Commenting on Karatani's observation that "Japanese people are thoroughly discriminated against in America and the Burakumin [in America] are discriminated against by those same Japanese people," Nakagami notes that this is because *hisabetsu sha* (people who are discriminated against) are also *sabetsu sha* (people who themselves discriminate).[124] Based on Nakagami's view, I interpret Akiyuki's claim that he "[can] become anything" as his desire to become nothing, that is, neither *hisabetsu sha* nor *sabetsu sha*. This paradoxical perspective subverts the entrenched practice of discrimination against the Burakumin. Nakagami voluntarily committed to "becoming a Burakumin." Only as a Burakumin could he represent the voices of the *mukoku* (voiceless) Buraku people. This he did by making every effort to avoid becoming a *sabetsu sha* who endorses the discriminatory mainstream thought that re-creates the oppressed subject. To borrow wording from Spivak, Nakagami sought in every way to avoid becoming a "self-marginalizing" or "self-consolidating" *hisabetsu sha* informant.

---

123. Nakagami, Minakami, and Yasuoka 1999, 105.
124. Nakagami and Karatani 2011, 49–51.

Ryūzō, on the other hand, who identifies with the great ancestor Magoichi and who insists that both he and his son are descendants of Magoichi, is both *hisabetsu sha* and *sabetsu sha*. After the effacement of the *roji* community, Ryūzō becomes "productive" in terms of establishing a male community called the Hamamura gang. For him, the gang is a counterpart of the *roji* community in that it is a group made up of people who have been driven asunder by the hegemonic center. Ryūzō responds to Akiyuki's words with the claim that "You're not *jūichi*, but the head of the Hamamura gang."[125] Ryūzō needs his son to become Magoichi so he can belong to a single unbroken line of Magoichi genealogy. Above all, Ryūzō desires an identity, which Bauman explains as "a surrogate of community," a "surrogate" of the "natural home" that people imagine and desire as the "cosy shelter of security and confidence."[126] Asserting that such a "warm circle"[127] is "never available in our rapidly privatized and individualized, fast globalizing world," Bauman explains that a life dedicated to a search for identity is "full of sound and fury."[128] Those who seek a fixed identity must struggle day in and day out to "keep aliens off the gates and to spy out and hunt down the turncoats in their own midst."[129] This is the struggle Ryūzō faces in establishing a fixed—single—Magoichi genealogy and forming the Hamamura gang.

---

125. NKZ 6:177.

126. Bauman 2001, 14–15.

127. Bauman cites Göran Rosenberg's concept of the "warm circle" to explain what Bauman regards as "the naïve immersion in human togetherness": "Human loyalties, offered and matter-of-factly expected inside the 'warm circle,' are not derived from external social logic, or from any economic cost-benefit analysis. This is exactly what makes that circle 'warm': it has no room for cold calculation and rote-learning of whatever society around, frostily and humourlessly, presents as 'standing to reason.'" See Bauman 2001, 10.

128. Bauman 2001, 14–15. In his interview with Takahashi Toshio, Nakagami also uses Faulkner's (originally Shakespeare's) word "full of sound and fury" to express Ryūzō's feeling for the *roji*. See Nakagami and Takahashi 1996, 92–93.

129. Bauman 2001, 16–17.

To establish his own "circle," Ryūzō welcomes Akiyuki, who killed his favorite son as "another similarly afraid and anxious individual." Ryūzō, however, does not trust Akiyuki. Yoshi, an old friend of Ryūzō and the leader of the homeless "nomads" who have made their homes in the grassland *roji*, tells Akiyuki that Ryūzō "always hates men who are similar to him so that, although he would feel lonelier than anybody else if he didn't have you or me, he hates us."[130] This is because his alleged Magoichi line and the Hamamura gang are, after all, the result of his strong obsession with and aspiration to achieve patriarchal dominance. Moreover, Ryūzō displays his position as patriarch by exacerbating the tensions that exist between legitimate son Yūichi, heir to Ryūzō's patriarchal family, and illegitimate son Akiyuki, successor of the underworld Hamamura gang. In spite of his desires for the future of these young men, Ryūzō actually remains as the father and the object of patricidal desire by both sons. Invalidating his own position as the father by identifying himself as Akiyuki's son or brother is nothing more than Ryūzō's strategy to establish himself as unbeatable by his son. Ultimately, Akiyuki indeed remains as the son. Karatani argues that Akiyuki is the son of "inertia,"[131] who is locked into an Oedipal challenge against the father even though the significance of that conflict has already been effaced.

What is the patricide of "inertia" depicted in *Chi no hate*—the world after the invalidation of the Oedipal concept? In the last chapter of the novel, Ryūzō commits suicide after Yoshi is shot dead by his son, who had intended to kill Ryūzō. The passage below is the scene in which Ryūzō, having waited to make a spectacle of his death before Akiyuki, hangs himself in the full view of his son. It dramatically conveys Akiyuki's panic in the face of his awareness that his father is about to take his own life and the conflict that grips him regarding whether he should intervene.

---

130. NKZ 6:198.
131. Karatani 2006, 175.

Morning had broken and from the glare outside, the shadow
[Ryūzō] could see Akiyuki standing in his work clothes in the reception room. Realizing this, Akiyuki became flustered. I don't
want to call him, I mustn't call him, but, I must stop him, I must
keep him back here where I am. In his distress Akiyuki thought,
what on Earth am I for the shadow, what is the shadow for me?
At that point, he found his voice and shouted. At the same time,
the shadow, which stretched as if suspended in air, shook violently and, as the chair fell, dropped with a thud. "It's wrong,"
Akiyuki shouted as if it was the only word he knew.[132]

This suicide is an enigma for Akiyuki. Yomota reads Akiyuki's
words "It's wrong" (*chigau*) as the son's ultimate demonstration of a
refusal to repeat the father's narrative.[133] Karatani, on the other
hand, interprets this as an outward show of Akiyuki's confusion
and anger toward the enigmatic self-destruction of the unbeatable
father. Karatani further argues that this shout is Nakagami's representation of the end of modernity.[134] Akiyuki's exclamation can be
read as a cry of anguish toward the postmodern world in which we
can no longer rely on modern grand narratives, such as the father,
family, community, or history.

With the deaths of Ryūzō and Yoshi, the leader of the nomads
who tried to disrupt the urban planning of the area by camping in
the grassland *roji*, Akiyuki thinks that "the *roji* has now clearly disappeared. The bond between parents and children has also been
broken, as well as the bond between the mother, the sisters and
their only surviving boy."[135] Akiyuki clearly sees that the project to
build a shopping center, which his own family has largely driven,
will completely efface the grassland *roji*. At the end of *Chi no hate*, the
grassland goes up in flames. It is rumored that the fire was set by
Akiyuki, who leaves the area without telling anyone. His departure

---

132. NKZ 6:415–16.
133. Yomota 1996, 159–85.
134. Karatani 2006, 169–70 and 175.
135. NKZ 6:449.

from the lost origin suggests that he will find a new life as an originless nomad. Prior to his death, Yoshi had welcomed Akiyuki as
"Genghis Khan," a reference to the leader of the Mongol nomad
tribes. Yoshi goes on to explain the nomad life: "We're easy-going,"
he notes. "We don't need a house or anything. We even collected all
the wood ourselves for these camps we recently built. If we're told
to get out, we'll just go somewhere else."[136] Asada notes that Nakagami's depiction of the nomad recalls the postmodern concepts of
nomadism and deterritorialization in Deleuze and Guattari's *A
Thousand Plateaus* (1980).[137] This reworked concept of the nomad is
particularly relevant for Akiyuki, who chooses to "become anything" to overcome the oppressiveness of the modern patriarchal
ideology of family and community. Setting the fire was not motivated by an obsessive concern with identity or territorial boundaries
similar to that of his father. Rather, setting the fire implies that
Akiyuki cuts his connection with the cyclic repetition of subaltern
narratives through which the *roji* had been established. In this sense,
he does not repeat his father's narrative.

From another perspective, Akiyuki's departure from the *roji* implies the unavoidable repetition of his father's narrative in terms of
separation from the son. Like the young Ryūzō, in *Chi no hate* Akiyuki becomes sexually promiscuous. In "Misaki" the protagonist
was a virgin, and in *Kareki nada* Akiyuki had a steady lover, Noriko.
By the time of *Chi no hate*, however, Noriko has married the man
who takes over her father's business. She is the mother of a three-
year-old son whose father is actually Akiyuki. Taking her son,
Noriko leaves her husband for Akiyuki. Although Akiyuki loves
Noriko, he continues to live alone, occasionally visiting the apartment where she lives with their son. In his relationship with Noriko,
Akiyuki cannot avoid repeating the narrative of the fatherless son
of the matrilineal family. This implies his desire to remain as a "man

136. NKZ 6:48.
137. Asada 1996, 31. Also see the discussion of the concepts of nomadism
and deterritorialization in Deleuze and Guattari 2004.

who refuses to be a patriarch." Such an attitude is in contrast to Ryūzō, who retains a patriarchal family and an underworld gang. Akiyuki's departure from his hometown nevertheless can be recognized, like Ryūzō's death, as the "self-disruption of the father" toward his own son. Since the depiction of Noriko's psychology is relatively limited, we never know her thoughts about her new life as a single mother or about her lover's "nomadism." To Akiyuki, Noriko becomes merely a manifestation of feminine sexuality that reflects his *naibu* (inner landscape). She provides him a concrete identity as lover, common-law husband, and father. This role of prop for the male is the fate of many women in the Akiyuki trilogy, which is discussed in greater detail in the next two chapters.

For Akiyuki, both family and community—whether subaltern or mainstream—are exclusionist units whose members are obsessed with their origin or narrative of identity. To keep the unity of this narrative, those who deviate must be exiled. Thus, *Chi no hate* is a work that depicts the reoccurrence of the exclusionary concept of identity while demonstrating a way of overcoming this by depicting a hero who voluntarily invalidates his identity by becoming anything he can, that is, by becoming nothing.

Criticism of Nakagami's Burakumin Narratives

Accolades were heaped on the first two Akiyuki trilogy novels, but critical reception of *Chi no hate* was more subdued. For Nakagami, *Chi no hate* was a turning point in his writing career in terms of his motives for writing and his position in the Japanese literary community. Following the publication of *Kareki nada*, the sequel to "Misaki," Nakagami was hailed as "the standard-bearer" of younger, postwar era–born writers.[138] Etō even proclaimed *Kareki nada* to be a masterpiece of modern Japanese literature (*kindai shōsetsu*).[139] Yet

138. Suga 2000, 663.
139. Etō 1996, 144.

while Etō and Yoshimoto lauded "Misaki" and *Kareki nada*, they were less impressed with *Chi no hate*.[140] Many critics saw this novel as a "failure" in terms of a lack of drama and tension. In his review of Zimmerman's English translation of "Misaki," Mark Morris, while noting the greater complexity of *Chi no hate*, assessed the work as "Nakagami's most eloquent failure."[141] Kawamura Minato argued that in contrast to the strong narrative of "Misaki" and *Kareki nada*, the account of Akiyuki's challenge to the father in *Chi no hate* was indecisive and lacking in rebellious action. He further argued that the *roji*, once the mythical topos of a tragic family narrative, had become merely a backdrop to the play of current affairs and reality.[142] Asada acknowledged these flaws but concluded that *Chi no hate* was an epoch-making "great failure,"[143] a *shōsetsu* that depicted the end of *kindai shōsetsu*, the end of modern narrative.[144]

From the perspective of Buraku studies, Noguchi has criticized Nakagami's depiction of the *roji* as not representing the contemporary reality of *hisabetsu buraku* districts. Contesting any claim that the *hisabetsu buraku* of Kasuga was obliterated, Noguchi points out that although the environment was dramatically changed through the Assimilation Projects, people continued to live there. Nakagami, however, selectively chooses various aspects of the history of Kasuga to fictionalize the disruption of the "maternal" *roji*. This also permits him to write the project of Ryūzō, whose patriarchal status was synchronously disrupted. Given that the writer's narratives "greatly differ from the circumstances of the *roji* today," Noguchi

---

140. See Yoshimoto's comment on the Akiyuki trilogy in Nakagami and Yoshimoto 2005, 49–70.

141. Morris 1999.

142. Kawamura 1983, 200–209.

143. Asada 1996, 29.

144. This is a concept that was extensively discussed during the late 1960s and 1970s by French philosophers such as Barthes, Derrida, and Deleuze. Karatani, Yomota, and Watanabe who, with Asada, are the coeditors of NKZ, agree with Asada's reading of *Chi no hate*. For example, see Karatani 1996, Yomota 1996, and Watanabe 1996.

concludes that "Nakagami took his eyes off the actual *buraku mon-dai.*"[145] This, Noguchi explains, is the reason for the severe criticism of Nakagami's work by Burakumin writer Kawamoto Yoshikazu. Kawamoto notes, "While Nakagami Kenji may be an admirable writer, in the context of the *buraku mondai* his novels amount to say-ing nothing."[146] For nonfictional essay writers such as Noguchi and Kawamoto, who take an empirical and fieldwork-based approach to *buraku mondai* research, Nakagami's literary representation of the *roji* as a *hisabetsu buraku* precinct in *Chi no hate* must inevitably be re-garded as "insufficient" in terms of the "real" history of the early 1980s life of the Burakumin residents of Shingū, Wakayama. Naka-gami believed that the most important element of *buraku mondai* was the issue of land ownership in the *hisabetsu buraku*. Given this view, we can say that *Chi no hate*, with its Burakumin characters who seek hegemonic control and ownership of the *roji*, gives "literary repre-sentation" to the *buraku mondai* associated with the Kasuga reform project. This was a project in which many of Nakagami's relatives were actually involved.

My analysis of *Chi no hate*, grounded in an understanding of the first two narratives of the Akiyuki trilogy and an investigation of Nakagami's representation of the end of the city's most subaltern community, focused on the depiction of Ryūzō and Akiyuki as a Burakumin father and son whose interchangeable relationship marks the invalidation of hegemonic patriarchal norms. Nakagami's Burakumin male protagonist was ambiguously characterized as in-trospective yet thoughtless, composed yet nervous, and individual yet communal. By representing both the resilience and vulnerability of the Burakumin man and giving voice to this man's declaration to become "nothing," Nakagami provides a radical means of identifi-cation without entrenching discrimination against the Burakumin or creating new subalterns. In this sense, he attempted to transcend the hegemonic structures of the literary and social worlds.

---

145. Noguchi 2001, 91.
146. Kawamoto 2000, 60–71.

CHAPTER 4

The Voice of an Incestuous Sister

Among Nakagami's representations, one of the most powerful is that of the oppressed voice of the sister (*imōto*) who has an incestuous relationship with her older brother (*ani*). Akiyuki's patricidal activities have received a great deal of scholarly attention, but little interest has been shown in the narrative of his younger half-sister, Satoko, whose sexuality he exploits as a strategic weapon in his bitter conflict with the father. In the previous chapter, we noted how Akiyuki's rivalry with his father was marked by attributes that were both Oedipal and homosexual. This chapter draws on notions of male homosocial desire developed by Eve Kosofsky Sedgwick to discuss how Satoko is presented in the narrative as a mere object for Akiyuki to confirm and enhance his bond with Ryūzō. The incest narrative depicted in the Akiyuki trilogy echoes "Kyōdai shinjū" ("A brother-sister double suicide"), a folk song drawn from the rich oral history of the Kasuga Burakumin precinct. By reading this folk song, I analyze the sister (*imōto*) represented in the ballad as "the sexed subaltern subject" (to borrow Spivak's term) who has "no space" to speak in modern patriarchal society.

The Brother's Exploitation of a Sister's Sexuality

As discussed in chapter 2, the discourse of ambivalence constructed by influential Japanese male critics in relation to Nakagami's depiction of violence against women has been valorized as the hegemonic (male) reading of this aspect of Nakagami's work. In addition to the term *ambivalent*, expressions such as *bisexual* (*ryōsei teki*), *androgynous* (*ryōsei guyū teki*), or *bilineal* (*sōsei teki*)[1] are frequently used by these scholars when discussing the violence against women in many of Nakagami's narratives. Feminist scholars, of course, read Nakagami's writing as a highly gendered and phallocentric representation of heterosexual relations.[2] This has led to criticism from male scholars. The words of Asada Akira are typical of the backlash against feminist readings of Nakagami's work.

> [In Nakagami's narratives], sexual intercourse between a man and woman is always depicted with this ambivalence. In "Misaki," for example, although Akiyuki rapes his half-sister, he is a virgin while his half-sister is an experienced prostitute. Moreover … immediately after the couple first have sex, the woman climbs on top of the man again in an attempt to arouse him. … While some scenes are graphic depictions of what appears to be a man raping a woman, most sex scenes in Nakagami Kenji's narratives occur from initiatives taken by women. I must say that those who are critical of Nakagami's depiction of sexual violence against women demonstrate a stunning lack of interpretative ability when they fail to acknowledge this point.[3]

In a continuation of this deeply problematic statement, which can imply that there should be no condemnation for men who rape

---

1. Hasumi, Watanabe, Asada, and Karatani 1994, 30–38.

2. For example, see Zimmerman's comment in her 1993 round-table discussion with Karatani, Suga, Yomota, and Watanabe (Karatani, Zimmerman, Suga, Yomota, and Watanabe 2000, 197 and 199).

3. Hasumi, Watanabe, Asada, and Karatani 1994, 32.

women who take the initiative in sex, Asada dismisses the feminist interpretation as a misreading (*feminisuto no gokai*) which, in his interpretation, demonstrates a "stunning lack of interpretative ability" of Nakagami's depiction of sexual violence.[4] The feminists he targets are identified only vaguely but seem to include so-called radical feminists who, it is claimed, take gender alone to be the single essential and universal division of human experience. Rather than elucidating any real failure regarding the feminist approach, the excerpt cited here merely reveals Asada's limited understanding of feminist analysis, particularly the fact that a number of prominent feminists positively read various aspects of Nakagami's depiction of women and sex. Ueno Chizuko, one of Japan's leading contemporary feminist scholars, refers to the heroines of *Hōsenka* and "Sekihatsu" ("Red Hair," 1979) as typical Nakagami women characters who "always maintain their subjectivity in sex" and "make decisions through their bodies," that is, by means of their sexuality.[5]

Livia Monnet's work makes clear how the discourse of male Japanese Nakagami critics forecloses the possibility of feminist intervention in debates around the author's narratives. Monnet strongly criticizes the tendency of these men to "literally" read and conflate as one single "ambivalence" the many varied expressions of gender, sex, and sexuality found in the writer's texts. She associates this with the dogmatic "legislation" of correct readings made by these men during the "Nakagami boom" that occurred immediately after the writer's death in 1992 and saw the canonization of certain narratives. Profiling the fear of "gender trouble"[6] implicit in the readings given by these critics, Monnet provides a feminist-deconstructionist analysis of a number of Nakagami's short stories, including "Fushi" ("The Immortal," 1980) and "Jūryoku no miyako" ("The capital of gravity," 1988). Monnet reads these works as

---

4. Asada, Okuizumi, Karatani, and Watanabe 2000, 235.

5. Ueno 2006, 19.

6. Monnet 1996a, 15. Monnet references Judith Butler's *Gender Trouble: Feminism and the Subversion of Identity* (1990).

drawing on a "gender-sexuality-violence" nexus that expresses hegemonic masculinist fantasies (that are also, in her view, highly pornographic) of marginalized women as the "uncanny" and the "abject." At the same time, Monnet appreciates these stories as works that demonstrate the postmodern "parodic" technique of rewriting and subverting the grounds of masculinist textual politics.[7] Following Monnet, Cornyetz criticizes as "ambivalent masculinist politics" the way these male scholars assert that Nakagami's depiction of rape is a representation of ambivalence. "An ambivalent masculinist politics has informed the canonization of Nakagami's work, because *any* celebration of Nakagami's work must accept an assault on gender constructs and indicates a willingness on the part of the reader to undergo a breakdown of conventional gendered discourses and phallic dominance."[8] While concurring with the interpretation by male Japanese critics of Nakagami as deconstructing hegemonic constructs of gender, Monnet and Cornyetz question the masculinist reading of his work that has emerged from the homosocial processes in which these critics have engaged in their push to have their ideas accepted by other readers.[9]

Rather than developing an argument around the general question of the ambivalent masculinist politics of male Japanese scholars, I work through my own questions related to the Akiyuki trilogy that arise from Asada's statement. These questions include: can Satoko really be seen to take the "initiative" when having incestuous sex with Akiyuki? Asada's reading of "Misaki" repeatedly makes the claim that Satoko is depicted as an experienced sex worker who gives the sexual lead to the virginal Akiyuki. This critic insists that

---

7. For further detail, see Monnet 1996a and 1996b.

8. Cornyetz 1999, 208–9.

9. While they may disagree with the canon established by male Japanese scholars, the fact that Monnet and Cornyetz were invited by Karatani and Asada to publish essays in *Hihyō kūkan* (*Critical space*) was a sign that by the late 1990s male scholars were at least open to dialogue with feminist scholars and their critiques.

Satoko's power (subjectivity and initiative) confirms the "ambivalent" sense of their incestuous relationship. While Asada reads Satoko taking the initiative as her "private" pleasure, which "literally" permits her to "enjoy the young body of an inexperienced man,"[10] I interpret it as her "speech act," her "socially valid verbal action"[11] to demonstrate her social—or "public," to borrow Mizuta's term—role as a prostitute. Because Akiyuki is a newcomer to her brothel, Satoko is obligated to make the new client comfortable. Thus, rather than a strategy to seek her own pleasure, Satoko initiating sex with Akiyuki is better understood as a duty associated with her paid work. Furthermore, although she apparently voluntarily commodifies her sex to support herself and her retired prostitute mother, Satoko has no way of knowing that this new first-time client is actually her half-brother and is therefore powerless as a subject to agree to having incestuous sex. Unlike the resisting wife in "Rakudo," Satoko has no chance to say "no" to her brother's desire. Neither does she have any way of knowing that she is committing incest.

As previously noted, Akiyuki is oppressed by being an object of the father's "gaze." He is contradictorily depicted as a young, virile man of strong frame who is also a naive subject. Akiyuki's incest is motivated by his desire to gain the subjective agency necessary to break the frustrating line of his father's gaze. There is ambivalence, nonetheless, in this desire in the sense that he shifts between wishing to be an aggressor and a victim. "He would commit one terrible crime and get revenge on the man. No, he'd rather be the victim of a terrible crime himself."[12] The "terrible crime" referred to here is sex with Satoko. In this sense, Akiyuki's act of incest can be seen as rape, that is, as a young man's exploitation of a woman's sexuality to overcome the frustration he feels in the face of paternal authority.

---

10. Asada, Okuizumi, Karatani, and Watanabe 2000, 236.
11. Austin 1962, 45–52.
12. Nakagami 1999b, 87.

From this perspective, Nakagami's mode of representation and the interpretation of Akiyuki's incest given by male Japanese intellectuals appear to be deeply masculinist-colored.

In the act of incest depicted in the Akiyuki trilogy, the partner who "ambivalently" confuses duty and pleasure is not Satoko, as Asada claims. Rather, it is Akiyuki. The scene in which the couple has sex makes it very clear that for Akiyuki, incest is a way to negate and degrade the father, the parent they have in common.

> This woman was definitely his younger sister, he thought. Their hearts were beating hard. How I've longed for you [*itoshii, itoshii*],[13] their hearts were saying to each other. With his ass in the air like an animal, he didn't know what to do even though she meant so very much [*itoshii*][14] to him. He wanted to pluck out his beating heart and press it into her breast, merge their two hearts, rub them one against the other. The woman moaned. Their sweat flowed. I'm your brother. We two are the pure children of that man, the one I can now call "Father" for the first time. If only we had hearts for sex organs. Akiyuki wanted to rip open his chest, and show his sister, her eyes closing as she strained and moaned, the blood of that man running through his veins. From that day on he would smell like an animal. … Off in the distance he could hear somebody, perhaps a drunk, yelling. The woman cried out, her eyes tightly shut, as if she couldn't take any more. Beads of sweat stuck to her eyelids like tears. Now, he thought, that man's blood will spill over.[15]

This scene depicts three different but intertwined unities that Akiyuki imagines: first, the unity of the half-siblings; second, the unity of the children and their father; and finally, the unity of the father and son. In Akiyuki's fantasized unity with Satoko, the significance of incestuous sex, that is, the physical unity that results through the

---

13. NKZ 3:242.

14. NKZ 3:242.

15. Nakagami 1999b, 90–91.

couple merging their sex organs, becomes the emotional integration symbolized by the merging of their two hearts, which feel longing (*itoshisa*) for each other. Feeling a strong sense of affection for the woman he embraces, Akiyuki also senses the blood relations that tie the father and his children and is thus able to recognize "the man" as his father for the first time. At the climax of the sex act, recalling the merging identity of the father and son discussed in the previous chapter, Akiyuki envisions that he ejaculates his father's blood.

In terms of Nakagami's depiction of this scene, I agree with Japanese woman writer Matsuura Eriko (b. 1958), who celebrates Nakagami as a writer giving a "graceful" depiction of the sex act and sexual desire that is inseparable from a surge of feelings, including affection and fear. Matsuura's insightful interpretation of Akiyuki's sex organ as a penis that both "ejaculates with *itoshisa*" and "transforms into a heart" is a much more effective means of explaining the ambivalence inherent in this sex scene than the assumption of Satoko's lust made by male critics. I concur with Matsuura's remark that Nakagami's "honest" and "fair-minded" depiction can be seen even in his "scenes of self-centred, violent sex by males against women."[16] I would argue that Matsuura's view, which sees an effective gender critique in the writer's "honest" depiction of the inner landscape of violent men, closely parallels Mizuta's reading of modern novels by Japanese male writers. Matsuura argues that there is no representation in any of Nakagami's narratives that justifies male violence against women. Her view supports a reading of the Akiyuki trilogy as revealing the ideological and physical violence that prevails in a phallocentric society. This view, however, must not be rationalized simply by Asada's claim of Nakagami's depiction of brother–sister sex as ambivalence by emphasizing Satoko taking the initiative. As previously noted, although Satoko may have been able to choose to have sex, she lacked the knowledge as a subjective subject to choose to engage in incest. I read this incest narrative as Nakagami's representation of a Akiyuki's justification for exploiting

16. Matsuura 1995, 4–5.

his prostitute sister's sexuality to support an Oedipal challenge concealing a homosocial desire to confirm and cement his bond with the father.

As noted in chapter 3, while Akiyuki desires both an Oedipal and hidden homosexual kinship bond with Ryūzō, Ryūzō seeks to have Akiyuki bond with gangsters. Nevertheless, the desire of both men can be seen as homosocial. I begin by exploring the perspective of homosociality with reference to *Between Men: English Literature and Male Homosocial Desire* (1985) and *Epistemology of the Closet* (1990), both written by Eve Kosofsky Sedgwick, who is recognized as a groundbreaking theorist in the field of queer studies. In these essays, Sedgwick provides a powerful lens for viewing patriarchal society as a sphere controlled by male homosociality. Unlike homosexual relationships, which are characterized by sexual attraction and activities between people of the same sex, *homosocial relationships* refer to the bond between members of the same sex, typically men, based on their desire to establish (apparently) nonsexual friendship and brotherhood. We should note that homosociality also involves antagonism between male rivals.

For her interpretation of the male homosocial triangle in English literature, Sedgwick refers to René Girard's discussion on "erotic triangles." Girard argues that an erotic triangle in which two men contend for a woman's love may actually disguise the rivalry that operates in an attraction between the men. In such a triangle, the woman is merely an object mediating male desire. Each man confirms himself as a desiring subject by desiring, that is, objectifying, a woman who is in turn desired—objectified—by his rival. The bond between rivals in an erotic triangle is "even stronger, more heavily determinant of actions and choices, than anything in the bond between either of the [competing] lovers and the beloved."[17] Also referring to Gayle Rubin's criticism of patriarchal heterosexuality and Claude Lévi-Strauss's view of marriage, Sedgwick sees the bond between such men as based on what she calls the "traffic in

---

17. Sedgwick 1992, 21.

women." She defines the traffic in women as the "use of women as changeable, perhaps symbolic, property for the primary purpose of cementing the bonds of men with men."[18] She further observes that the structure of the "bonds of men with men" consists of three aspects: homosocial desire, misogyny, and homophobia. Homosocial desire is exercised by an individual man to establish a bond with other men to identify and demonstrate himself as a "man," that is, as an active member in a male-dominated society. In the male bond, women become the object of men's desire and are alienated as the other through the traffic in women. This is the process of misogyny. This traffic in women is necessary to maintain and demonstrate that heterosexual desire is essential in the homosocial circle. These homosocial men therefore internalize homophobia and strictly forbid themselves any involvement in a homosexual act.

Nakagami's depiction of Satoko is a classic representation of a female subject who becomes the object of rivalry between two men in the manner of Sedgwick's male-male-female homosocial triangle. For Ryūzō, Satoko is a daughter. According to community rumor, she is also her father's mistress. For Akiyuki, she is the half-sister with whom he has actual incestuous sex. The Oedipal conflict is played out as two men fighting over a woman's sexuality. The relationship of this father and son is characterized by a misogyny that alienates Satoko as the sexed Other. This is apparent in Ryūzō's private dialogue with Akiyuki, which judges Satoko as "useless" because "women are just for men to sleep with." While admitting that he is helplessly attracted to women, in his mind Akiyuki agrees with Ryūzō, thinking that "women are merely sexual organs."[19] As the target of Ryūzō's and Akiyuki's misogynistic desires, Satoko is an essential medium for the father and son to confirm and enhance their bond. Drawing on Mizuta's view (discussed in chapter 2) the homosocial desire shared by Ryūzō and Akiyuki can be explained as a "discourse of men" represented through the woman's sexuality.

---

18. Sedgwick 1992, 25–26.
19. NKZ 3:393.

In *Between Men* and *Epistemology of the Closet*, Sedgwick hypothesizes that homosocial desire is "potentially erotic" and accordingly investigates "the potential unbrokenness of a continuum between homosocial and homosexual."[20] In the previous chapter, we discussed Akiyuki's hidden homosexual desire for Ryūzō in the context of the Oedipal complex that (to borrow Butler's explanation) affects gender identification not only through the incest taboo but, prior to that, through the taboo against homosexuality. Akiyuki's vision of unity with his father during sex with Satoko can accordingly be read as an expression of the homosexual desire embedded in the male bond. The "continuum between homosocial and homosexual" can also be seen in Akiyuki's fratricide of his younger half-brother, Hideo. "It [Akiyuki's murder of Hideo] happened abruptly. In the distance that separated them, there were only two possibilities—a caress or violence. Even from a meter away, the outline of each body was ambiguous in the dusk."[21] As noted in chapter 3, this murder is depicted with an image of the violent sexual assault of a woman, that is, incest committed by the older brother against the younger brother. In this scene, Hideo's depiction as a feminized object also implies his position as a woman whose role is to project Akiyuki's hidden homosocial/homosexual desire for Ryūzō. Like his incest does, Akiyuki's fratricide consequently brings him and his father closer together. This is confirmed in the last volume of the trilogy, when Akiyuki voluntarily approaches Ryūzō to take part in the latter's business ventures and underworld gangs.

Satoko, on the other hand, becomes "useless" as the female party in the homosocial triangle. She is initially an essential medium in the construction of the bond between her father and brother. However, once she is judged as "useless" by these men, her position in the triangle is filled by Hideo. Satoko and Hideo are (incestuously) raped by Akiyuki. Hideo dies during this metaphoric rape, but Satoko survives. In other words, while the younger brother

20. Sedgwick 1992, 1.
21. NKZ 3:452.

(*otōto*) is erased from the Oedipal/homosocial narrative of his father and brother, Satoko (the *imōto*) remains alive to tell her own narrative, in spite of being stigmatized as "useless."

A Ballad of Brother-Sister Double Suicide

What is the difference that sees Satoko live while Hideo dies? I consider the answer by reading the oral narrative of "Kyōdai shinjū," a ballad sung in the Kasuga Burakumin precinct. The family tragedies and the characters in the Akiyuki trilogy echo local folklore that tells of the riotous subversion of morality (*ikki*) by the rebellious samurai Magoichi and of the double suicide (*kyōdai shinjū*) of an incestuous brother and sister. For my analysis of Nakagami's depiction of the Burakumin woman's voice, it is useful to investigate the historical context of the "Kyōdai shinjū" ballad in addition to the author's unique interpretation of this work. I present my own interpretation of the ballad to illustrate the significance of the *imōto* in modern Japanese society.

Until the 1970s, the "Kyōdai shinju" folk song was sung and led mostly by local Kasuga women during the *bon* festival.[22] In his essay "Fūkei no mukō e: Kankoku no tabi" ("Beyond scenery: A trip to Korea," 1983), Nakagami explains his use of the ballad in *Kareki nada*: "Although I was unaware while I was writing, I regard *Kareki nada* as a novel that breaks the secret code of the 'Kyōdai shinjū' dance ballad. I myself probably comprehend the *Kareki nada* narrative through interpreting the 'Kyōdai shinjū' text."[23] In summary, the folk song gives an account of a brother, Monten, who lives in Kyoto and falls in love with and wastes away pining for his sister, Okiyo. Although initially shocked when she learns of her brother's love, Okiyo eventually agrees to sleep with him on the condition that he kills her husband who, she tells him, is a *komonso* (formally

---

22. Zimmerman 2007, 86.
23. NKZ 15:60.

komusō), a mendicant monk. As revealed at the end of the ballad, the monk husband is Okiyo's fictive creation. Monten actually murders Okiyo, who is dressed in *komonso* attire. The death occurs in Gōshū (the traditional name of Shiga prefecture) on the Seta Bridge, which Nakagami sees as a metonym for the border between the center or life and the periphery or death.[24] The song concludes with Monten committing suicide in Kyoto.[25]

A full text of "Kyōdai shinjū" appears in *Kareki nada*, but some elements in this version are different from those in essays written by Nakagami, such as "Fūkei no mukō e: Kankoku no tabi" and "Monogatari no keifu." The version of the ballad cited in those essays was recorded around 1978 by Nakagami who, after publishing *Kareki nada*, recorded a local Kasuga woman singing the text. To articulate the actual folkloric value of the ballad, my analysis draws on the version that was recorded.[26] The words of the song are as follows:

We do not often hear of a brother-sister suicide	さても珍し　兄妹心中
The brother is twenty-one, the sister twenty	兄は二十一　妹は二十
Brother Monten adores his sister	兄のもんてん　妹にほれて
Pining for her, he then falls ill	それがつもりてご病気になりて
He eats only two of three daily meals	三度の食事も二度となる
Then two becomes one	二度の食事も一度となりて
So the mother visits her son	そこで母上見舞いに上る
How do you feel, my son?	これさ兄さんご病気はいかが

---

24. NKZ 15:216.

25. As noted in chapter 1, Kyoto was the ancient capital, where the emperor, who was the symbol of *hare* (purity or glory) once lived. In this context, "the hidden country," Kumano, is juxtaposed against the center of Japan, the political entity that operated under the brilliant auspices of the sun goddess.

26. The recorded version of "Kyōdai shinjū" is published in NKZ 15:210–12. My English translation of "Kyōdai shinjū" from *Kareki nada* is published in Ishikawa 2011, 13–14.

Should I call a doctor? Should I bring medicine?	医者を迎おか介抱しよか
I need no doctor, nor medicine nor remedy	医者も薬も介抱もいらぬ
But I long to once see Okiyo, my sister	一度会いたい妹のおきよ
So Okiyo comes to her brother's sick bed	そこでおきよが見舞に上る
How do you feel, my brother?	これさ兄さんご病気はいかが
Should I call a doctor? Should I bring medicine?	医者を迎おか介抱しよか
I need no doctor, nor medicine nor remedy	医者も薬も介抱もいらぬ
A thousand nights with you would see me well	私の病気は千夜でなおる
If you refuse one thousand then I beg you for one	千夜いやなら一夜をたのむ
Hearing her brother, Okiyo is shocked	そこでおきよはびっくりいたし
Do you know, my brother, what it is that you ask?	これさ兄さん何言やしゃんす
You and I are brother and sister	私とあなたは兄妹なかよ
So people who heard this would call us beasts	人に聞かれちゃ犬畜生と
Our parents would disown us if they knew	親に聞かれちゃ勘当なさる
There is a woman somewhere to be your wife	兄に似合いし女房もござる
And a man to be my husband, too	私に似合いし夫もござる
My husband is a mendicant monk	私の夫はこもんそ吹きよ
Aged nineteen, his name is Masao	年は十九でその名は正夫
If you kill Masao	正夫殺してくだしゃんしたら
For one night, two nights, or even for three	一夜二夜でも三夜でも
I will lie with you, my brother	添うてあげますこれ兄さんよ
Having spoken, Okiyo goes to a different room	言うておきよはひと間にさがり

Where she dresses her hair and makes up her face	髪を結うたりお化粧したり
And then makes ready to dress	さあさこれから仕度にかかる
First a slip of white habutai silk	下に着るのは白はぶたいよ
Then a black habutai kimono	上に着るのは黒はぶたいよ
An everyday Hakata weave obi	帯は当世の筑前博多
Is wound twice around her leaving a three-shaku length[27]	二回回して三尺残る
Fastening the obi's remnant three shaku	残る三尺きちゃと締めて
She conceals her face with a monk's straw-basket hat	深い網笠面手にかぶり
Then playing her one shaku five sun shakuhachi flute[28]	一尺五寸の尺八笛を
She sets out across the Seta Bridge	瀬田の唐橋笛吹いて通る
Monten shoots at the form on the bridge	ワーとうったらうちおとしたら
As a shot rings out a woman screams	ワーと泣く声女の声
Oh, no! It's my sister, Okiyo	さあさ　しもおた妹のおきよ
I have killed my sister and can no longer live	おきよ殺しちゃ生きてはおれぬ
The brother took his life beneath a Kyoto bridge	兄は京都の唐橋の下
We do not often hear of a brother-sister suicide	さても珍し兄妹心中
I could sing other songs	私の音頭はまだまだあるが
But will leave you now.[29]	ここらあたりでおひまをもらう

"Kyōdai shinjū" is a variation of the *Gōshū ondo*, which is the generic name given to a *bon* dance ballad with a particular rhythm and melody, variations of which are still sung in many areas of Japan today.

---

27. Three *shaku* is approximately 91 centimeters.

28. One *shaku* five *sun* is approximately 45.5 centimeters. Shakuhachi is usually one *shaku* eight *sun* (about 54.5 centimeters).

29. NKZ 15:210–12.

Gōshū ondo takes its names from Gōshū, the old name for a region of Shiga, and the term *ondo* means a dance song. The words of *Gōshū ondo* vary from area to area and are generally modified to fit the local context. As Nakagami noted, however, "Kyōdai shinjū," the *Gōshū ondo* of Kasuga, is not a song about Kasuga.[30] When considering this noncharacteristic element of the Kasuga "Kyōdai shinjū" ballad, it is useful to have some knowledge of the "geopolitical" relationship between Kasuga, Shingū, Gōshū, and Kyoto. Kasuga was a *hisabetsu buraku* precinct in Shingū. Shingū is a central city of the Kumano region, isolated from the ancient capital by forests and mountains. Gōshū was a province that borders Kyoto in the north and Kumano in the south and was traditionally known as a commercial area with a good water supply from Lake Biwa. This water supply made the area a silk industry center.

Any interpretation of the "Kyōdai shinjū" ballad requires some understanding of the economic development of Meiji Japan, particularly the emergence of the silk industry. Nakagami points out that "Kyōdai shinjū" was probably brought to Kasuga by *jokō* (mill girls) who worked in silk factories in Gōshū.[31] As the principal source of Meiji-era wealth, the silk industry was a central feature of Japanese nationalism at a time when the country was struggling to achieve parity with the imperialist nations of the West.[32] A former *jokō* recalled, "We were often told (by the minister): 'You (*jokō*) are the treasure of our country; Japan would be ruined without you because the silk industry constitutes the foundation of the Japanese economy.'"[33] Initially, *jokō* were drawn from daughters of high-status families, who were proud of their contribution to the modern nation-state. However, when increasing production saw the size of factories expand, the need for *jokō* ballooned.[34] As a result, many daughters of poor families from nonindustrialized areas, including

---

30. NKZ 15:212–13.
31. NKZ 15:213.
32. Tamanoi 1998, 85–114.
33. Tamanoi 1998, 107.
34. Tamanoi 1998, 86.

Kumano, were recruited as labor in the silk factories, which, as the industry expanded, became increasingly oppressive workplaces. Production continued into the postwar era; Nakagami's eldest sister (a model for Akiyuki's eldest sister, Yoshiko) was sent to a silk industry town in the 1950s. Despite the fact that many daughters from Shingū went to work in the silk industry, "Kyōdai shinjū" did not become a community *bon* dance ballad anywhere in the city except the *hisabetsu buraku* of Kasuga. Arguing that this fact demonstrated the idiosyncrasies of Kasuga, Nakagami valued "Kyōdai shinjū" as the "silenced message" of the Kasuga women who sang the ballad without any modification to the local context.[35]

In the prewar era, mill girls were subject to the masculinist ideologies of patriarchy and nationalism. While girls from impoverished families later made up the silk factory labor force, in the early years of the industry factory girls were the daughters of the elite. This elite background can be seen in the language of "Kyōdai shinjū," which, unlike many other folk ballads, is characterized by the extensive use of *keigo*, honorific Japanese language. Nakagami seems to have been unaware of the early involvement of wealthy girls in the silk industry, and he dismisses this use of *keigo* as "bad" (*detarame*) grammar.[36] To him, the *keigo* demonstrates the transcendent viewpoint of a third-person "narrator" (*katarite*). According to his explanation, the *katarite*'s voice demonstrates the perspective of the "community which includes land, nature, and the state" that he regards as metaphorical "parents." While grieving for their children, these parents nonetheless expect tragic consequences to beset young people who deviate from the norm by violating social taboos, such as incest. In other words, Nakagami sees the *katarite* as representing the "will power" of the community, which manipulates the brother and sister as if they were "marionettes" to commit a double suicide.[37] The premodern genre *kishu ryūritan* (legends of exiled no-

---

35. NKZ 15:213.
36. NKZ 15:214.
37. NKZ 15:214–15.

bles) have long featured the extensive use of *keigo*. We might therefore read "Kyōdai shinjū" as a *kishu ryūritan* about siblings from the
Kyoto aristocracy. Given that the setting of the ballad is Gōshū, a
silk industry center, Okiyo can be regarded as one of the original
aristocratic daughters despatched to bring glory to the new Japanese
nation through her work in the mills.[38] While Monten leaves Kyoto
for Gōshū to commit murder for his love for his sister, it is Okiyo
who, having been sent to the mills, must sacrifice her life for the
family and the nation. For Kasuga women, who often left home at
a young age to go to major cities as migrant workers, "Kyōdai
shinjū" surely had personal significance from evoking separation
from the family or a lover.

Nakagami regards both the Burakumin ballad of "Kyōdai
shinjū" and the Kumano *kishu ryūritan* of Magoichi as conveying the
trace of the subalternity imposed by the center on Buraku people
and the Kumano area generally. As noted in chapter 1, the author's
view evokes Gramsci's focus on the history of subaltern groups.
The Italian theorist identified subaltern history as "necessarily fragmented and episodic" and regarded any "trace" of the historical
activity of subaltern groups as having "incalculable value."[39] For
Nakagami, Burakumin oral folklore has "incalculable value" because it is a "trace" that contains the silenced voices of Burakumin
(here Buraku women) who have been marginalized by "the activity
of the ruling groups."[40]

---

38. In support of "Kyōdai shinjū" as a narrative of elite siblings in modern
Japan, I refer to "Iyo no Matsuyama Kyōdai shinjū" ("A brother-sister double
suicide of Iyo Matsuyama"), a ballad sung until World War II in Matsuyama,
Ehime prefecture. The use of *keigo* to refer to the brother is seen in this version.
This ballad tells of the twenty-one-year-old Teruo, who is a student studying
English and his twenty-year-old sister, Okiyo, who stays at home and spends her
time sewing. Given these features, the brother and sister in this ballad can be
seen as siblings from an elite family that has the financial means to provide the
son with higher education. For further detail, see Tamai 2006, 2–21.

39. Gramsci 1971, 54–55.

40. Gramsci 1971, 55.

Nakagami's view of the value of oral narratives was confirmed after a trip to Ise, the home of Japan's principal Shinto shrine. During a visit to the shrine library, Nakagami found more than 200,000 books containing records of the activities of past royal families. Convinced that imperial authority in Japan rested on the "written word," he declared that "the emperor rules over the land by means of thousands of words and letters."[41] Since the tradition of writing literature such as *waka* (Japanese poetry) and *monogatari* (tales) has been monopolized by the nobility since ancient times, Nakagami regards the illiterate Burakumin as a people who have long been abandoned by tradition.[42] As a novelist who uses the Japanese language, Nakagami reveals his ambivalence toward the imperative on the writer to make use of the "written word," which, since the time of the *Kojiki*, has been traditionally used to justify and reinforce the hegemony of the center. Nakagami particularly considers that his role as a Burakumin novelist provided him with the paradoxical use of the written word to write against the hegemonic center. Although the act of writing naturally implies a celebration of the same hegemonic center that marginalized Burakumin, for Nakagami writing was the act of contesting that center. Furthermore, he regarded Burakumin oral culture as independent from the emperor's sovereignty over written language.[43] He asserts that the "spoken word" as seen in genres such as folklore has the "mythical function" to challenge the written word and the system the emperors of ancient times established by compiling books of mythologies.[44] The fact that "Kyōdai shinjū" was not modified to the local Kasuga context suggests an understanding among those who sang the ballad of the sociohistorical complexity of relations between the *hisabetsu buraku* and the center. While the song's *keigo* implies an elite

41. NKZ 14:606.
42. Nakagami 1999a, 340.
43. NKZ 14:610.
44. Nakagami 2000, 23.

background to the tragic couple, the brother's love for his sister strongly interrogates the hegemonic family system that is also subverted by family relations in the *roji*. To Nakagami, interpreting "Kyōdai shinjū" is to decipher the hidden voice of the subaltern members of the Kasuga community and the oppressive social penalties its members incur.

Nakagami also points out that "Kyōdai shinjū" is a song about the sexual maturity of young siblings. While the siblings are becoming mature adults, their parents are in decline. In the brother's eye, the sister's maturation occurs simultaneously with his own, so her mature body becomes a sign of his own sexual ripeness. This is also the son's displacement of the mother with the sister as the object of his erotic love. Nakagami explains that in the presence of his sister, the brother is affected by *imo no chikara*, the power of women, which the sister inevitably acquires as she becomes older.[45] *Imo* (妹) literally means younger sister. In Japanese tradition, *imo* further implies a woman in a relationship with a man.[46] For a brother, this term means sister regardless of whether she is older or younger. For a male lover, the term refers to a woman for whom he longs as if she was a loyal sister. Nakagami insists that *imo no chikara* is actually a more significant motif in "Kyōdai shinjū" than the incest taboo.[47]

Nakagami understands the power of women in the same sense as that discussed by Yanagita Kunio. In his 1925 essay "Imo no chikara," Yanagita presents his perspective on changes in the relationship between brothers and sisters during the late Taisho era, at which time the government focused on transforming Japan into a modern industrialized nation. "One thing that strikes me is the increasing intimacy between older brothers and younger sisters. As older brothers grow, they rely more and more on their younger sisters. This phenomenon, which was not known before, has now be-

---

45. NKZ 15:215–16.

46. *Daijisen* 1995, 187.

47. NKZ 15:215–16.

come quite ordinary."[48] He acknowledged this phenomenon as a phase of the liberation of women that resulted in new forms of family structure and new systems of education, but Yanagita did not probe these modern aspects. Instead, he sought to investigate the role of women in ancient myth, local ritual, and folk religion. In doing so, he identified what he regarded as women's "special physiology" (*tokushu seiri*), which gave rise to *imo no chikara*, a power specific to Japanese women.

> As it has been understood in our discipline [of Japanese native ethnology], women have controlled almost all the principal aspects of the religious festivals and prayers. In our race, shamans have always been women in principal. ... The original reason that these roles were especially suitable for women was probably in their ability of narrating mystery because their emotional nature always makes them the first in the crowd to sicken with psychosis immediately after the events. There have been many occasions for men, who fight with nature and enemies, to rely on the power of women. This is because women could always offer predictions and ideas to be used by men in their pursuit of war and peace. That people deified the power of women is a consequence of their belief in women's power. As we tend to deal with the sacred separately from the mundane, people of the past were rather afraid of touching the power of women precisely because it was regarded to be sacred.[49]

Given Yanagita's observations and leaving aside the questionable claims made regarding the tendency of women to "sicken with psychosis," Nakagami's view of "Kyōdai shinjū" as a song of *imo no*

---

48. This excerpt from Yanagita's "Imo no chikara" was translated by Mariko Asano Tamanoi and is published in Tamanoi 1998, 126. For the original text, see Yanagita 1990, 11:25.

49. Until and after the third sentence, this excerpt from Yanagita's "Imo no chikara" was translated by Tamanoi (1998, 126). The third sentence, omitted from Tamanoi's citation, is my original translation. For the original text see Yanagita 1990, 11:25–26.

chikara seems appropriate. It is also significant that the ballad is sung mostly by women and that Nakagami's depiction in *Kareki nada* of women who sang the ballad closely parallels Yanagita's view of women's ability to "narrate mystery" (*fushigi o katari eru*). Okiyo's remonstration with her brother that "people who heard this would call us beasts," and our "parents would disown us if they knew" is an expression of her fear of the authority and cruelty of the community. This she senses through her "emotional nature" (*kandō shiyasui shūsei*), which must mean, in Yanagita's theory, "sicken with psychosis" when experiencing unusual and immoral activities, such as incest. Nakagami's depiction of the nervousness, inspiration, and occasional insanity of Mie, Akiyuki's half-sister, has a close parallel to Yanagita's insistence on the "emotional nature" of women.

Yanagita argues that the increasing "intimacy between older brothers and younger sisters" (*kyōdai no shitashimi*) in the Taisho era is a revival of the traditional Japanese erotic couple paradigm known as *imose*, (妹背), literally younger sister (*imo*, 妹) and brother (*se*, 背). *Se*, which can mean brother, lover, and husband, appears in many early Japanese texts paired with *imo*, sister (both younger and older), lover, and wife. The following is a poem from the *Man'yoshu* (compiled circa late eighth century, translated as *The Ten Thousand Leaves*) featuring *imose*.

> Rather than be left behind
> longing for you,
> would that I could be
> Imo and Se Mountains
> —"husband and wife"—
> There in the land of Ki.[50]

As seen in this verse, composed by court poet Kasa no Kanamura (seventh–eighth century), since ancient times *imose* have been refer-

---

50. *The Ten Thousand Leaves*, 266–67. The land of Ki is a region also known as Kishū, Nakagami's homeland.

enced as an ideal couple who long for each other. In many novels published in the Meiji and Taisho eras, the relationship between the man and the woman was often depicted as that of an older man and a loyal, sister-like younger woman.[51] Drawing on Yanagita's *Imo no chikara* to read Meiji novels depicting a man's desire for a younger, single, middle-class woman, such as *Imōto ni okuru tegami* (*Letters to the sisters*, 1912) by Mizuno Yōshū (1883–1947) and *Futon* (*The Quilt*, 1907) by Tayama Katai (1872–1930), Ōtsuka Eiji argues that both *minzokugaku* (folklore studies) and Japanese modern literature represent women as sister-like shamans who merely reside in the "private" sphere to support and comfort men.[52] As noted in chapter 2 in the discussion on Mizuta's "discourse of men," the most "private" male spaces in Japanese society were those where women resided, including the home and the red-light district. These sites were in distinct contrast to the "public" sphere. For men, these private places were a realm in which to seek refuge from their public persona and in which, by "regressing" into the sexuality of a comforting woman, they could express their own pure, perfect selves and inner landscapes (*naibu*).[53]

In this context, although Yanagita's discussion of women initially appears to draw on the traditional view of *imo*, it is also informed by a modernist interpretation of *imōto*. Rather than the revival of an ancient concept, the increasing "intimacy between older brothers and younger sisters" can be regarded as evidence of the "formation of the modern family."[54] Yanagita devalues Taisho women's *naibu* by dismissing it as the essentialist "special physiology" of women inscribed since ancient times in Japanese religion, literature, and folklore.[55] In other words, the "Imo no chikara"

---

51. Seki 2009, 109–10.
52. Ōtsuka 2011, 204–6.
53. Mizuta 1993, 63–65.
54. Seki 2009, 110.
55. Ōtsuka 2011, 204–6.

essay offers a literature of nativism that supports the hegemonic
mode of nationalists, who sought to establish a modern Japanese
nation-state by identifying factors that define a nation, such as language, common descent, and tradition. Yanagita wrote "Imo no
chikara" as part of this tradition. This resonates with the representation by Indian nativist scholars of the sati rite as symbolic of the
"ideals of womanly conduct" and evidence of "the cool and unfaltering courage of Indian women."[56] As noted in chapter 1, in this
sense Indian women were merely used as a scapegoat to justify the
patriarchal nationalist discourse circulated by male nativists. Therefore, like the Indian sati, the *imoto* can be regarded (using Spivak's
words) as "the sexed subaltern subject" who had "no space" to
speak in the modern masculinist-oriented society.[57]

When Nakagami applies Yanagita's gendered concept of *imo no
chikara* to his interpretation of "Kyōdai shinjū," he, too, is caught in
the trap of the modernist disregard of woman's inner self, a disregard that appropriates the voices of women to fulfill nativist and
nationalist desire. This effect is also clearly apparent (as I explain
later) in his depiction of the outcaste sisters in the Akiyuki trilogy.
To understand Nakagami's attempt to reveal the "secret message"
of Burakumin women in the "Kyōdai shinjū" ballad and create a
narrative that speaks their voice, I refer to the concept of *ane* (姉,
older sister) which can also mean "working woman." In the boom
of the silk industry in the early 1900s, most mill girls were daughters
of poor peasants and were therefore outside the elite modernist
writers' concept of *imoto*, who was usually depicted as a girl student
or a young woman who lived at home, supported by her middle-
class family. A typical case of the *imoto* is found in Mizuno's *Imoto ni
okuru tegami*, which depicts three students at a girls' school in train-
ing to become the respectable *ryōsai kenbo* (good wives and wise
mothers) of the new future. On the other hand, as seen in the case

---

56. Spivak 1999, 294.
57. Spivak 1999, 307.

of Nakagami's own sister, even in the 1950s eldest sisters (*ane*) often left home for major cities around the age of fifteen to become migrant workers and remit money back to their parents and younger siblings.

In her criticism of the modernist regimentation of women as *imōto*, Seki Reiko focuses on the difference in meaning between *ane* and *imo*.

> As previously explained, "*imo*" [妹] is a term used in reference to a young woman regardless of whether she is younger or older [than the user of the term]. We should note that there is a difference—apparently subtle but actually important—between "*imo*" and "*ane*" [姉]. As a characteristic of "*ane*" which can never be found in the "*imo*," we should not forget that there is a connotation of "working woman." For instance, some dictionaries tell us that "*ane*" means "*geisha, shakufu* [barmaid], *jochū, gejo* [housemaid], *komori* [baby-sitter]" (see *Shogakukan Japanese dictionary*). Furthermore, "*ane*" [姉] also indicates "matured women" and therefore has a close parallel to "*ane*" [姐] which implies a craftswoman, vendor, yakuza's wife, prostitute or barmaid in the entertainment district.[58]

From this passage, we can conclude that in the context of women and work, *ane* particularly implies workers from "the realms of women" including the home and the entertainment district. The character Mon, known as "Mon nēsan" (姐さん), a confident, single, middle-aged woman who owns a bar in the entertainment street where Satoko works, is a good example of an *ane*. Mie, who stays at home to do housework, is never referred to as *nēsan* in the narrative. In the *roji* community, she is recognized as an *imōto* figure, that is, as the dead Ikuo's younger sister rather than Akiyuki's older sister. Even the young prostitute Satoko is not really regarded as *nēsan*, which demonstrates a lack of confidence in her occupation and her ambiguous position in the community as an "immoral" woman.

---

58. Seki 2009, 111–12.

Given that women factory workers were regarded as "nurse-maids of machines" (*kikai no komori*),[59] the silk industry can be included in the category of the women's sphere. As Seki insists, the term *ane* demonstrates that there are other more complex identifications than binary pairs, such as single/married or disreputable/respectable, in Japanese society. Her thinking contests the masculinist categorization by the influential critic Hayashi Tatsuo (1896–1984) of women into one of two categories of either *ane* or *imōto*. According to Hayashi, regardless of their sibling structure, all women could be categorized as either a typical *ane* who was "manly, active and strong," or a typical *imōto* who was "sentimental and chaste."[60] The mill girls, however, interrogated this simplistic modernist categorization in that they combined *ane* and *imōto* characteristics: they gave their "manly" all as *ane* to the arduous mill conditions because of their "sentimental" *imōto*-like affection for the families they labored to support.

The Incestuous Sister, Antigone

As a dedicated *imōto*, whose loyalty and devotion for her brother results in her death, the folklore ballad's Okiyo recalls Antigone, the daughter and younger sister of Oedipus. I accordingly discuss how Antigone is depicted in Sophocles's tragedies to profile mythical and archetypal representations of incest. Although drawn from the Western canon, Antigone's narrative can be usefully invoked in an analysis of Okiyo and the representation in Burakumin folklore of a younger sister's unspeakable incestuous love for her older brother.

In Sophocles's play *Antigone*, the eponymous heroine is a daughter of the unwittingly incestuous marriage of Oedipus, king of Thebes (her brother and father), and his mother, Jocasta (her mother). After the death of her brothers, Polyneices and Eteocles, who fight

---

59. Akamatsu 1993, 74.
60. Hayashi 1940 and quoted in Seki 2009, 110.

for succession to their dead father's throne, the kingship is assumed by Creon, Antigone's uncle, who declares Polyneices a traitor to the state. Although Creon's law decrees that mourning for Polyneices will be punishable by death, Antigone tries to secure a respectable burial for her brother. In doing so, she incurs Creon's wrath. While burying her brother alone, she is captured by Creon's guards and brought before her uncle. Declaring that she knew the law and chose to break it, Antigone expounds on the superiority of "divine law" over that made by man. Boldly defiant, she is sentenced to being entombed in an underground chamber, after which she hangs herself. The disastrous path of the narrative is complete when her cousin and Creon's son, Haemon, to whom Antigone was engaged, kills himself after finding her body. Queen Eurydice, Creon's wife, also kills herself after witnessing her husband's brutality.[61]

Hegelian and Lacanian scholars interpret the Antigone narrative as the tale of a symbolic figure of kinship and its dismantlement, in which Creon is the representative of state authority and its ethical order based on the principal of universality. Feminist scholars, such as Luce Irigaray and Carol Jacobs, refer to Antigone's defiance as an example of feminine anti-authoritarianism in the face of a political system where the state has substantially centralized social control. In feminist readings, Antigone is often regarded as a figure of feminine defiance representing kinship as the "private" domestic space, that is, the realm of women, which antagonizes the "public" phallocentric sphere.[62]

Not all feminist scholars read Antigone in precisely this way. In *Antigone's Claim: Kinship between Life and Death* (2000), Judith Butler notably sees Antigone as having a voice that represents "how kinship makes its claim within the language of the state."[63] Since Georg Hegel and Jacques Lacan focus on the support given by a sister to a kinship ideal, they make no reference to the possibility of

---

61. See Sophocles 1894, 1994, and 2000.
62. Butler 2000, 2–3. For further details, see Irigaray 1985 and Jacobs 1996.
63. Butler 2000, 6.

incestuous desire between Antigone and Polyneices. Butler insists that Antigone's devotion to her brother is "an impossible and death-bent incestuous love."[64] She argues that Antigone represents kinship in its "deformation" and "displacement."[65] As she notes, analysis of Antigone's aberrant family provides insights into the nostalgic contemporary idealization of the family, which is also evident, for example, in the Vatican's protest against homosexuality as a violation of some ideal family or the "natural" human condition. In the present day, kinship has become "fragile, porous, and expansive" through various circumstances such as divorce, remarriage, same-sex marriage, common-law marriage, migration, exile, and global displacements. For many contemporary children, the roles of father and mother are blurred and variously occupied or dispersed so that the equilibrium of "the symbolic" no longer applies.[66] Akiyuki's "matrilineal" family and his relationship with his long-separated half-sister Satoko can be seen in the context of an Antigone-style kinship displacement discussed by Butler.

As the tale of a younger sister who defends her older brother, *Antigone* presents as a narrative that demonstrates *imo no chikara*, the power of woman. Her strength to advocate for "divine law" in defiance of the king closely parallels Yanagita's view of the ability of women to narrate the *fushigi*, that is, to narrate mystery and unearthliness. Her defiance of King Creon is motivated by her grief for her dead brother, which arguably marks the "emotional nature" of the sister. It also marks the *kyōdai no shitashimi* (intimacy between older brothers and younger sisters) that is a characteristic of *imo no chikara*. Moreover, if we read an incestuous context in the narrative, *Antigone* can be interpreted as a narrative of *imose*—sister and brother—lovers.

Butler examines *Antigone* as a narrative that reveals the precariousness of idealized kinship and political sovereignty. This pre-

---

64. Butler 2000, 6.
65. Butler 2000, 24.
66. Butler 2000, 22–23.

cariousness becomes apparent through the heroine's "illocutionary act" (we might say speech act) that transgresses kinship and gender norms.[67] Antigone's transgression is to grieve for her brother and insist on her right to express this grief in "public."[68] Creon's law presumes the guilt of anyone who grieves for Polyneices (who is legally a traitor) and anyone who voices doubts about the authority of the law. Antigone is regarded as "savage"[69] by the chorus of elderly Theban men who often take Creon's side. In confronting Antigone, however, Creon attributes masculinity to her, declaring, "I am no man, she is the man, if this victory shall rest with her, and bring no penalty. No! ... she ... shall not avoid a doom most dire."[70] Antigone's "manliness" is expressed in her claim of the superiority of the "divine law" over the king's law. In Butler's explanation, this claim signifies not only defiance of the law but also the assumption of the voice of one strong law (divine) that contests a weaker one (human).[71] Antigone thus appears "to assume a certain form of masculine sovereignty, a manhood that cannot be shared, which requires that its other be both feminine and inferior."[72] Since her defiance is against King Creon, it is he rather than Antigone who is rendered feminine and inferior by her claim. To grieve her brother in public, Antigone becomes a "man," the gender of sovereignty.

Why does Antigone want to express grief for her dead brother in public even though she knows that the price of her voice will be death? For Butler, the answer lies in the heroine's monologue, recited when she approaches the hole in which she will be entombed. "O tomb, O bridal chamber, O deep-dug home, to be guarded for ever, where I go to join those who are my own."[73] Butler reads these words as an expression of her predestined incestuous love

---

67. Butler 2000, 6.

68. Butler 2000, 80.

69. See *Antigone* in Sophocles 2000, line 472.

70. See *Antigone* in Sophocles 1894, lines 484–85.

71. Butler 2000, 11.

72. Butler 2000, 9.

73. Quoted in Butler 2000, 23. See *Antigone* in Sophocles 1994, lines 891–93.

for Polyneices. For Antigone, death represents a form of marriage to her brother, who is already dead.[74] But of course, the public expression of grief for a brother who is loved incestuously must be forbidden by the law. As Butler notes, this demonstrates how kinship law (the father's law), which forbids incest between siblings, "makes its claim within the language of the state."[75] By becoming a "man," Antigone makes her unspeakable love for her brother representable as fraternal—or, so to speak, homosocial—affection. Her defiance is ambivalent in that it demonstrates antagonism toward but also affinity with state law and kinship law.

Antigone's quality of representing both the public and private spheres is the most significant difference between this narrative and the *imo no chikara* nature of women as developed by Yanagita. According to this perspective, women merely represent a "private" domestic sphere in which their role is to support and comfort men. Because it can refer to female lovers and older sisters (*ane*), the term *imo* nonetheless has a radical element in that it demonstrates both the dissolution of the barrier between kinship and the other and a chronological inversion of the relationship between sisters. Antigone, however, displays an even more radical inversion of gender.

Oedipus at Colonus, written by Sophocles several years after *Antigone*, further develops the incestuous aspect and gender inversion in the original play. In this later narrative, Antigone is told by the dying Oedipus: "From none did you have love more than from this man, without whom you will now spend the remainder of your life."[76] Butler explains this as "a demand that verges on incestuous possessiveness" by the father, who is also the brother of his daughter.[77] Oedipus's words imply his male gaze toward Antigone's sexual ripeness: he is attracted by her *imo no chikara*. The fact that Antigone

---

74. Butler 2000, 24.

75. Butler 2000, 6.

76. Quoted in Butler 2000, 60. See *Antigone* in Sophocles 1994, lines 1617–19.

77. Butler 2000, 60.

accepts her father's language implies her complicity in an incestuous relationship with him. The curse that Oedipus lays on her is "serving death" for the rest of her life; in other words, incest makes her life a "living death." The tomb as a "bridal chamber" in the earlier play suggests the deathlike nature of incest, which, hegemonically, can never be viable in a life-affirming culture.[78] If this is the case, Antigone's loyalty to (her incestuous love for) Polyneices can be seen as a transgression against but also obedience to the father's law. Butler remarks that "she both honors and disobeys this curse as she displaces her love for her [dead] father onto her [dead] brother [Polyneices]."[79] Butler calls this "promiscuous obedience," which is a strategy to disturb existing social norms, including those related to family roles.

In *Oedipus at Colonus*, Antigone's masculine gender is announced by her own father in the "private" realm of kinship. Oedipus refers to Antigone, who cares for him in exile, as a "man" and the daughter loyally accompanies her father into the wilderness. When Antigone takes the masculine initiative by saying to her father, "Follow, follow me this way with your unseeing steps, father, where I lead you!"[80] she effectively becomes his son and brother. As Butler notes, the sister/daughter has taken the place of "nearly every man in her family" and "man" is "the title that Oedipus bestows upon her, a gift or reward for her loyalty."[81] The fact that Oedipus names Antigone as a man can be also seen as concealing his incestuous desire for his daughter/sister behind a homosocial bond that is an acceptable form of affection in heteronormative kinship relations. Because she accepts her father's curse of incest as living death and gender inversion, Antigone is destined to become "promiscuously" ambivalent and transgressive in terms of both kinship and state law. She eventually kills herself because her love for her brothers (Poly-

---

78. Butler 2000, 23–24.

79. Butler 2000, 60.

80. Quoted in Butler 2000, 61. See *Oedipus at Colonus* in Sophocles 1994, lines 183–84.

81. Butler 2000, 61–62.

nices and ambiguously Oedipus) is, in Butler's words, love that "can only be consummated by its obliteration," which is "no consummation at all."[82] Based on this view, the following section discusses the sister's death-bent incestuous love for her brother in "Kyōdai shinjū."

A Sister Who Plots Double Suicide with Her Brother

One notable aspect of the "Kyōdai shinjū" ballad is the absence of the father of the siblings, Okiyo and Monten. Monten can thus be considered the heir to the family, a substitute for the father. Okiyo becomes the daughter sacrificed for the brother heir. In this context, although the mother is the father's widow, she can be seen as having the position of wife of the patriarch and "wife" of her unmarried son. Accordingly, Okiyo's relationship with her brother and mother demonstrates a close parallel to that of Antigone with Oedipus/Polyeices and Jocasta. Jocasta is dead and is seldom referred to in *Antigone*, but Okiyo's mother is alive and given a key role in the tragic "Kyōdai shinjū" narrative. This mother is a *nakatsugi*, a temporal matriarch, whose role is to relay the patrimony to the next patriarch, her twenty-year-old son, Monten, whose illness has suspended his right to succeed to the position of family head. Thus, the family inscribed in "Kyōdai shinjū" ambiguously embodies both patriarchy and matriarchy. As previously noted, the ballad depicts the tragedy of the sister's sexual ripeness, read by Nakagami as *imo no chikara*, which inevitably attracts the brother as the pair mature. In the brother's eyes, as Okiyo's sexuality rises, the mother's declines. Although the mother presumably knows of her sick son's desire for Okiyo, she does not prevent her daughter from visiting him. Given these perspectives, the mother can be seen as an enabler of brother–sister incest. To save the patriarch's life so that the *ie*

---

82. Butler 2000, 76.

(patriarchal family) will continue, the mother in effect forces her daughter to sacrifice her sexuality.

Like Oedipus, the patriarch(-to-be), Monten, is the father/brother who has an incestuous desire for his daughter/sister. For Okiyo, Monten's request of incest is the law of the "father," that is, the law of kinship and of the state because the *ie* patriarch is institutionalized by the state. "Kyōdai shinjū" can thus be regarded, to borrow Butler's view of *Antigone*, as a narrative that demonstrates "how kinship makes its claim within the language of the state."[83] In the ballad, the community voice is heard as Okiyo's words remonstrating with her brother against his desire. However, even as she voices this law, she resists. First, Okiyo declares, "people who heard this would call us beasts," and, shifting the focus from the general law to the law of the father and family, "our parents would disown us if they knew." Continuing as the voice of the law, she urges Monten: "There is a woman somewhere to be your wife, and a man to be my husband too." Having voiced this law as a good daughter should, Okiyo seems to rebel against her own chanting of the community voice by telling Monten that she has a husband and that she will lie with her brother if he kills this husband. As revealed at the end of the song, the nineteen-year-old husband, Masao, is Okiyo's fiction. Having outfitted herself in the attire of *komusō* to disguise herself, Okiyo, like Antigone, becomes a "man" who is able to defy the patriarchal law of her brother. At the same time, and in the same way Antigone advocated for divine law, Okiyo assumes the voice of the "divine" Buddhist law.

What does the assumption of the *komusō*'s voice mean for Okiyo? *Komusō* is a term that originated from an appellation for Japanese mendicant monks of the Fuke school of Zen Buddhism, which flourished during the Edo era. This school was abolished in 1871 by the Meiji government because of its strong association with the Tokugawa shogunate. Fuke monks were usually nonordained monks who did not shave their heads and went on pilgrimages

---

83. Butler 2000, 6.

from place to place. In the sense that they lived by collecting alms, the life of *komusō* monks could be traced back to that of the historical Buddha.[84] As seen in the "Kyōdai shinjū" account of Okiyo transforming herself into a monk, the *komusō* wear a hat like an inverted straw basket (*tengai*) that covers the entire face and head. These monks are renowned as players of the vertical bamboo flute or *shakuhachi*. In the *komusō* custom of Zen Buddhism, music played on the *shakuhachi* is regarded as "a vocal, though non-verbal, expression of [the] ineffable essence" of enlightenment.[85] The "Kyōdai shinjū" ballad particularly refers to the fact that Okiyo's *shakuhachi* is "one-*shaku* five-*sun*" (*i-sshaku go-sun*, approximately forty-five centimeters) in length and is thus shorter than the usual one-*shaku* and eight-*sun* (*i-sshaku-ha-ssun*, about fifty-four centimeters). This shorter *shakuhachi* implies the falsehood of the *komusō* who is, in fact, a woman. The sound of her *shakuhachi* echoing across Seta Bridge—a metonym for the border between life and death—was not the nonverbal enlightenment of the *komusō*'s Zen doctrine. Rather it was Okiyo's own "ineffable" voice, speaking her love for the brother. In the ballad, Seta Bridge is sung as a miracle realm that invalidates all law and thus opens the possibility of the violation of all varieties of taboo. For Okiyo, pretending to be a *komusō* not only substantializes her alleged husband, "Masao," whose name interestingly means "true husband," but makes her an embodiment of Buddhist law. The confrontation between Monten and Masao is a confrontation between kinship and religion or the divine. In the section of the song where Okiyo speaks the community voice, we have a sense that she believes it may be possible to change her brother's mind. In revealing that she has a husband, however, and suggesting that Monten murder her husband, she seeks to break with both kinship and divine laws.

The rhyme in the line "For one night, two nights, or even for three" (*ichiya niya demo sanya demo*) is notable within the ballad, which

---

84. Sanford 1977, 414.
85. Sanford 1977, 412.

has a rather monotonous melody sung in a low key. I read this rhyme as expressing the surge of the erotic longing of the siblings for each other. It further recalls the passage from "Misaki" in which, as Aki-yuki and Satoko have sex, their beating hearts say to each other (in Akiyuki's mind), "How I've longed for you [*itoshii, itoshii*]." In the *Kyōdai shinjū* ballad, the initiative is taken by Monten who begs his sister to provide sex. Yet if we accept that Okiyo also has desire for her brother, then the double suicide can be seen as an outcome of her will rather than Monten's. By falsely declaring to Monten that she has a *komusō* husband, Okiyo knows that she will invoke her brother's intent to kill his rival. She assumes the guise of the rival man almost certainly in the knowledge that this will result in her death. She may have sensed that, given Monten's obsessive love, he would take his own life after her death.

If we accept that the double suicide results from Okiyo's plot, then we can see the sister's strong desire for the brother. As it does in the case of Antigone, we can argue that here death means mar-riage to her brother. Furthermore, giving herself to him in this way is a means of sacrificing herself to kinship laws that prevents them from breaking the incest taboo. In other words, Okiyo allows Monten to kill her so that he might save himself from the wrath of the community. In this way, the "Kyōdai shinjū" ballad provides a paradoxical reading of the sister's voice and clearly demonstrates her capacity to achieve her will. Okiyo thus subverts the masculinist reading of *imōto*. Okiyo becoming a *komusō* monk recalls Antigone's assumption of manhood to express her unspeakable love for her brother. Butler explains that Antigone's defiance of state law is a repetition of her brother's defiant acts. Her act of defying the state situates her as the one who may be a "substitute" for the brother and hence who "replaces and territorializes him." For Butler, Anti-gone's act appears to establish her "rivalry" and "superiority" to Polyneices.[86] In this context, Okiyo's act of transforming herself into her supposed husband (Masao) demonstrates her superior sta-

---

86. Butler 2000, 11.

tus, which results in her being able to "lead" her brother to Seta Bridge. Okiyo's superiority is also evident in her understanding of the community's voice, which demands tragic consequences for those who deviate from the norm by violating strict social taboos such as incest. Like Sophocles's *Antigone*, the Burakumin ballad of "Kyōdai shinjū" confirms that in hegemonic terms, incestuous love can only be consummated through its erasure. This love, therefore, is impossible to consummate.

The Incestuous Sister's Fear of *Kegare*

Returning to an analysis of Nakagami, this section discusses the author's use of the *Kyōdai shinjū* narrative to depict Satoko's silenced voice in the Akiyuki trilogy. In *Kareki nada*, Satoko is the first person to make reference to "Kyōdai shinjū." Six months after their incest takes place, Akiyuki and Satoko meet for the first time as half-siblings. The meeting is arranged by Akiyuki's half-sister Mie, who found Satoko after asking for help from Mon. As noted, Mon is also, so to speak, a "sister" (*nēsan*) for the men of the entertainment district, including the *roji* men who frequent the street. She is a sister for the women who circulate rumors with her. Akiyuki and Satoko's reunion is realized by these "sisters" who keep an eager eye on the younger couple.

> Satoko realized who the man [Akiyuki] was. As soon as she saw Akiyuki's face, she said "I don't care who my father is. ... When you have a good life and everything is going well, it must be annoying when a whore comes to see you and says 'I'm your sister.'"
> "What are you talking about," Mie chided, worried that Satoko's words would unsettle Akiyuki. ... "You wait 'til now to tell me he's my brother, you tell me now he's my brother when it's too late," Satoko wept. Her large-framed body was hunched over, trembling. ... Seemingly feeling Satoko's sorrow as her own, Mie

stroked her half-sister's face while embracing her and soothing
her. ...

Whether she had something in mind or really needed to relieve herself, Mie left them together to go to the bathroom.

"Hey brother, why don't we do a brother-sister double suicide?" Satoko murmured as she wiped away her tears.

"Don't be stupid." Akiyuki answered. "A brother-sister double suicide" was the name of a dance ballad sung here and there
in the town during *bon*.[87]

In this passage, it is Satoko who brings the "Kyōdai shinjū" narrative into the discussion by referring to the ballad in terms of her
incestuous relationship with Akiyuki. This conversation also suggests that during their sexual exchange, without being aware that he
was her brother, she sensed Akiyuki's longing for her. Satoko's
whispered suggestion that they copy the brother and sister in the
ballad and commit double suicide reveals her desire to translate the
meaning of their incest from an exchange between a prostitute and
her customer into the forbidden erotic love between a brother and
his sister.

Although it signifies her attempt at asserting her agency, this
reference to "Kyōdai shinjū" also implies Satoko's perception of
herself as *kegare* (polluted). This is because the ballad narrates incest
as the deed of a beast, that is, of an entity polluted by *kegare*. In this
context, Satoko and Okiyo make an interesting contrast. While Satoko has become hegemonically polluted as a sexually experienced
prostitute and unknowingly breaks the incest taboo, Okiyo is a pure
sister who dies a virgin for her brother. The name Okiyo is an honorific form literally meaning pure and clean. As elaborated further
below, in *Chi no hate* Satoko becomes a fanatical follower of a local
water cult. Her involvement can be understood as her fear of being
kegare as a result of her past work as a prostitute and as a result of
having sex with Akiyuki. The brother's longing for the sister and
the sister's fear of *kegare* are key motifs of the "Kyōdai shinjū" bal-

---

87. NKZ 3:340–41.

lad. Regarding the folk song as a representation of the impossibility of a conventional marriage between the brother and sister, Naka- gami interprets the ballad as a "reversal" of the well-known *kuniumi* (birth of the country) narrative from the opening section of the *Kojiki*. This text, compiled in 712, was the "official" canon of the legitimate history of the imperial family. The *kuniumi* narrative tells of the birth of Japan following the marriage of the god Izanagi (the father of the sun goddess, Amaterasu, who is worshiped in Shinto as the founding ancestor of the imperial family) and the goddess Izanami. This couple can, in fact, be considered a brother and sister pair because they were born at the same time from Heaven. Accord- ing to Nakagami, when it is sung in the Kasuga *hisabetsu buraku*, the "Kyōdai shinjū" narrative is the Burakumin variant of the *kuniumi* narrative of the incest between the god and goddess that leads to the birth of the nation, Japan. While the divine incest produces a country, which inscribes prosperous narratives on Japanese citizens, the Burakumin incest bears "an inverted country of darkness" or a "country in reverse,"[88] where oral folklore narrates the death of those who violate taboos and render themselves *kegare*.

In the Akiyuki trilogy, the sense of failure that underpins the "Kyōdai shinjū" ballad is depicted through the insanity and conse- quent death of Ikuo. Ultimately, Ikuo dies without being able to establish his own family. We might also note that this failure is fur- ther suggested by Mie's nervous breakdown and her inability to save Ikuo or give birth to his offspring. Unlike Ikuo and Mie, Akiyuki and Satoko remain sane. I read this as a result of Ryūzō's acceptance of their incest—*kuniumi*—and his willingness to accept them hav- ing "idiot" children. As discussed in chapter 3, Ryūzō merely laughs at Akiyuki's confession. While this response stuns Akiyuki, Satoko rebelliously retorts: "I'll give birth to the idiot."[89] Ryūzō observes that because he owns a vast expanse of land in the Arima region of Kumano, he does not care if the pair have a child. Arima, a town in Kumano City in Mie prefecture, is also the setting of the *kishu ryūri-*

---

88. NKZ 15:215.
89. NKZ 3:362–63.

tan legend of Magoichi. Arima is also the location of the "under-world" in the myth of Izanagi and Izanami.[90]

> These mountains, these fields, were nothing more than stories fabricated in the fevered imagination of Hamamura Ryūzō, the King of Flies, the man with the big body and the snake eyes. Iza-nami died when her private parts were burnt as she gave birth to the god of fire. The cave in which she was interned after her death is less than five minutes by car from Ryūzō's Arima land.[91] The underworld of this myth is here. It is around this area. The man had built a monument [of the Magoichi legend] there.[92]

For Ryūzō, all the conventions of mainstream society are inverted in the "underworld" of Arima. Magoichi was a defeated hero, lame in one leg and blind in one eye.[93] Ryūzō's acceptance of "idiot" chil-dren born from incest is in opposition to the original *Kojiki* myth of *kuniumi*, in which Izanagi and Izanami refuse to accept an imperfect child called *hiruko*, meaning leech-child. This deformed child is seen as the result of the parents erring in the ritual of conjugal inter-course.[94] Unlike Akiyuki and Satoko, who would keep their "de-formed" child, the child of Izanagi and Izanami is instead aban-doned by its parents and made to float away downstream.[95]

While Ryūzō has an interest in traditional narratives, this is confined to how he can appropriate them for his own ends. He therefore laughs away those elements from texts such as the *Kojiki* that promote the conventions of the hegemonic center. The death

---

90. There is a description of Arima and the legend of Suzuki Magoichi in Nakagami's *Kishū*. See NKZ 14:572–73.

91. The cave, traditionally said to be the grave of Izanami, is in the Hana no iwaya Shrine and is dedicated to Izanami and her fire-god son, Kagutsuchi-no-mikoto. See *Hana no iwaya jinja*, http://www.hananoiwaya.jp (accessed March 19, 2019).

92. NKZ 3:372.

93. NKZ 3:267.

94. Philippi 1977, 399.

95. See *Kojiki* 1968, 48.

of the siblings in "Kyōdai shinjū" demonstrates the penalty demanded by the center for those who transgress. Ryūzō, however, rejects these hegemonic sanctions in favor of establishing his own glorious nation by affiliating in a way that removes the usual stigma of subalternity attached to Magoichi, the defeated hero of the Arima *kishu ryūritan*.

Ryūzō and Satoko resemble each other in terms of applying Burakumin folklore to create their own narratives. In Mon's view, Satoko has "inherited the good parts of Ryūzō, including his liveliness and enthusiasm." This makes her an extraordinary young woman with "a supple body with lively arms and legs just like a herbivore."[96] On the other hand, Mon compares Satoko's fanaticism regarding the water cult to Ryūzō's obsessive chauvinism regarding Magoichi. Satoko quits prostitution sometime after Akiyuki is sent to prison. Mon is the only person who understands her feeling for Akiyuki.

> "You know, Mon," said Satoko. "When I talk to you, I remember when I worked in the entertainment district. After quitting the brothel, I went and worked in a bakery. The *panpan* [prostitute] baked *pan* [bread]. It's a good joke, isn't it?"
>
> "Forget the past" said Mon. There is nothing good in the past to remember. … Satoko murmured to Mon "Because I wanted money I slept with many men but my brother was the best one." … "Satoko!" said Mon, lowering her voice as she felt her chest tighten while Satoko stuck out her tongue. [Mon continued] "What's the point of saying that? Nobody must know." The smile faded from Satoko's face and she said, "He knows. That fly shit, that beast knows." As if suddenly overwrought, Satoko stared at Mon with wild eyes. …
>
> "My brother and I both wanted him to know, but now I hate him knowing more than I would hate a million other people knowing about this."[97]

---

96. NKZ 6:212.
97. NKZ 6:212.

Satoko hates Ryūzō because she realizes that her father has exploited the secret of her incest to justify the creation of his own narrative. Satoko tried to territorialize the narrative of incest as the "Kyōdai shinjū" narrative of forbidden love between siblings and their subsequent double suicide. Her attempts are ultimately invalidated by Ryūzō's inversion of the incest taboo, a taboo supported by the *kuniumi* narrative, which abhors the birth of the deformed or "idiot" child. Ironically, Ryūzō's view leaves Satoko alive to fight against him. In her conflict with Ryūzō, Satoko tries to win Akiyuki over to her side. "Until I die, I'll keep egging my brother on by saying, 'Kill that man in the cruelest way, torture him.' Mon," said Satoko, "I told Akiyuki that his girlfriend's baby is the child of Hamamura Ryūzō."[98] Satoko's words, however, are incompatible with her actual influence over Akiyuki. He never takes her words seriously. He has already heard a rumor that Noriko had given birth to Ryūzō's son. With no regard for Satoko's words or the rumor, Akiyuki began an affair with Noriko some time after returning from prison. Although Ryūzō denies the rumor, Mon assumes that seizing Noriko is "important"[99] to Ryūzō precisely because she is desired by Akiyuki. This implies that Satoko is again marked as "useless" by Ryūzō and Akiyuki and that, instead of Hideo, her position in the homosocial triangle with these two men has been replaced by Noriko.

The "uselessness" of Satoko's intervention to break the father and son's homosocial bond can be comprehended through Spivak's observation regarding the subaltern women's resistance in a masculinist society. Spivak observes: "once a woman performs an act of resistance without infrastructure that would make us recognize resistance, her resistance is in vain."[100] Lacking Spivak's infrastructure, Satoko is a woman whose resistance is in vain. This was perhaps inevitable given that, since birth, she has been excluded from

---

98. NKZ 6:213.

99. NKZ 6:71.

100. Spivak and Milevska 2006, 60.

conventional patriarchal society. Until the age of seven, Satoko lived in an orphanage as the illegitimate daughter of a prostitute. Once she was older, she herself became a prostitute, regarded by society as immoral and *kegare*. Even after leaving prostitution, Satoko remains a sexed subject in the enclosed community in which rumors about her promiscuous past and alleged incestuous relationship with her father circulate endlessly.

The infrastructure that Satoko needs in her attempt to make her voice audible is access to the language of the law authorized by a man in a position of supremacy. This need can be seen in Okiyo, who becomes a mendicant monk, a man, in a manner similar to Antigone. Like Okiyo and Antigone, Satoko attempts to appropriate divine law in her challenge against the law of the father and society. She does this by affiliating with the male founder of the local water cult. In addition to former prostitutes, the followers of the water cult include many aged outcaste women forced to move to other areas because of the dismantlement of their *hisabetsu buraku* homes. After becoming an assistant instructor in the cult, Satoko leads these women in a ritual ceremony of purification that requires them to drink large amounts of water. The scene quoted below in which Satoko talks to Yuki, a former prostitute who is also the eldest sister of Akiyuki's stepfather, demonstrates Satoko's assumption of the "divine" law.

Satoko explained that because Yuki had stocked the sediment of male poison through receiving the lustful ejaculation of innumerable men since being sold at the age of twelve by her mother because of their extreme poverty[101] ... and because she had also stored the dregs that accumulated throughout her own life of more than sixty years, her body was now a bag of poison. "Because the poison has damaged your eyes and changed your ears, you hear clear sounds as if they were a muddy noise, or a nightin-

---

101. Nakagami's depiction of the age at which Yuki was sold by her mother into prostitution varies. While it is fifteen in *Kareki nada*, it is suggested in *Chi no hate* that she was only fourteen or even twelve.

gale singing the Lotus Sutra or a cicada vibrating as someone
speaking evil about you, so your mind has become warped, and
you feel like saying bad things about others." Satoko continued in
a whisper, "Nobody is born as a bag of poison. As the Sun God
rises from the East to purify the dirty night with the morning
glow, so the sunshine lights up all creation to revive our innocence
just like a newborn baby. When the poison starts bubbling we
must find it immediately and pray to the Sun holding up our
hands, or we must drink water to purify ourselves."[102]

Satoko's fanatic commitment to the water cult can be understood as
her attempt to "remove pollution." By explaining the water cult
doctrine to Yuki, Satoko expresses her own view of *kegare* and the
fact that prostitutes, including herself, become "bags of poison"
because their bodies have received the "ejaculation of lust" from
countless men. Strictly speaking, Satoko inverts the common understanding of *kegare* as associated with women's bodily functions in
that, from her perspective, *kegare* originates from the *doku*, poison,
of lustful men who pass it on to prostitutes. This is a shift from the
hegemonic view, held by the male founder of the water cult, of
women themselves as innately *kegare*.

Although it is represented by the masculinist "divine" law, Satoko's explanation reveals her misandry and resistance against the
patriarchy that stigmatizes prostitutes as immoral. For her, *kegare* is
the masculinist patriarchal law that disguises male lust by objectifying woman. Because "Kyōdai shinjū" displays the sister's strict ob-
servance of the incest taboo, Satoko's identification with Okiyo signifies her being bound by the law of kinship and the community.
This is Satoko's paradox: she hates the masculinist law as *kegare* but
at the same time conspires with the law to humiliate prostitutes and
other taboo breakers as *kegare*. This paradox closely parallels Nakagami's view of "*hisabetsu sha* (people who are discriminated against)
as *sabetsu sha* (people who themselves discriminate)." Satoko's self-
contempt should be seen in contrast to Akiyuki's declaration that he

---

102. NKZ 6:85.

"can become anything," which is effectively a statement of his desire to become nothing, neither *hisabetsu sha* nor *sabetsu sha*.

After Ryūzō's suicide, Satoko vents her anger in front of Akiyuki, his coworkers, Mon, and her (Satoko's) own mother.

> "I bet he [Ryūzō] would have paid to sleep with me, that beast![103]
> ... While he cared for that daughter [Tomiko] by putting her in a
> treasure box so that nobody could touch her, because I was born
> from this simple, idiot prostitute, he had no hesitation in making
> this daughter pregnant. That fly shit wanted me to give birth to
> his child as if he was a stud horse and he really thought how won-
> derful it would be if my brother and I had children." Mon was
> choking with shock. The young men looked at Akiyuki who stood
> with a dark expression on his face. Kinoe [Satoko's mother] hung
> her head and tried to stem the tears that were streaming down her
> face with her hands. "I'll give birth to your child, my brother. I'll
> have sex with you as if it was my first time and I'll give birth to a
> child who is just like a chunk of poison."[104]

For Satoko, both Tomiko and Akiyuki's lover, Noriko, are typical *hakoiri musume* (literally, a daughter who is a treasure kept in a box)[105] whose sexuality is preserved without breaking the incest taboo. Such women are highly valued in terms of the "traffic in women" that is the social aim of exogamy, which, in Sedgwick's words, is "the use of women as changeable, perhaps symbolic, property" for the fundamental purpose of cementing male homosocial bonds. The passage further displays Satoko's anger at the parents who never inducted her into the patriarchal law as the infrastructure necessary to save her from breaking the incest taboo. In other words,

---

103. In this sentence, Satoko uses the verb *agaru* to describe her assumption of Ryūzō's intention to sleep with her. The term *agaru* implies a man buying a prostitute. For example, *girō ni agaru* (to go up the steps into the brothel). See "Agaru" in *Daijisen* 1995, 24.

104. NKZ 6:445–46.

105. *Daijisen* 1994, 2117–18.

her parents never acted to save Satoko from falling in love with Akiyuki. Nevertheless, this couple's incestuous love, to cite Butler's words again, that "can only be consummated by its obliteration" and is therefore "no consummation at all."

In fear of the fact that she committed incest, Satoko accepts the severe penance of being whipped by the cult founder. Following this, she often refers to herself as "clean" like a "virgin."[106] Her obsession with purity and virginity paradoxically marks her internalization of masculinist lust, its *kegare*. Akiyuki, who feels guilty for fueling his sister's fearful obsession with incest, speaks to Satoko in private as they are driving in a car together after Ryūzō's death:

> "Are you afraid of fucking me?" Akiyuki suddenly asked Satoko. Satoko gazed at Akiyuki. "I have nothing to be afraid of," he said. "I have seen a man die." "I have been watching you since our first meeting, my brother. I still remember you," Satoko replied as if she was singing. "That man who went to the other world never knew that my brother is as clean and pure as water. It is always women who are so polluted that flies come buzzing around." Feeling a sudden rush of indignation, Akiyuki slowed the car. "Do you think I am a man who has never been polluted?" he said. It occurred to Akiyuki that he himself had transformed entirely into Hamamura Ryūzō.[107]

Given her perspective of *kegare* as masculinist law, Satoko's designation of Akiyuki as "clean and pure as water" implies that for her he is a man who does not internalize masculinist law and is therefore able to break the taboos of incest and fratricide. Because she regards Akiyuki as "pure," Satoko retains her memory of his affection (*itoshisa*), even though this affection came during his incestuous transgression against her, a transgression that actually disguised his Oedipal/homosocial desire for the father. In this sense, the severe penance she undergoes actually serves to remove *kegare* not from

---

106. NKZ 6:212.
107. NKZ 6:446.

herself but from Akiyuki. We might thus read the sister's territorialization of the brother as an attempt, *imo*-like, to be dominant in their relationship. Like Antigone's adherence to the "divine" law and Okiyo's assumption of the sacred form of the *komusō*, Satoko's fanatic adherence to the water cult also operates to establish her "rivalry" toward and "superiority" over her half-brother.[108]

Akiyuki is aware of Satoko's feelings toward him and her fear of them violating the incest taboo. He feels resentment toward her penchant for purity, which displays her melancholy as a *hisabetsu sha* but at the same time demonstrates her discriminatory tendencies as a *sabetsu sha* against those, including Akiyuki, who are regarded by the society as *kegare*. By declaring, "I have nothing to be afraid of," Akiyuki agrees to Satoko's desire to have a child with him. At the same time, he knows that she is torn with fear about the narrative of incestuous love, which is impossible to realize except through its erasure. At the end of *Chi no hate*, Akiyuki leaves the area without telling anyone. Satoko sees his car "driving away at high speed as if it was an expression of [his] gentleness."[109] For Satoko, his departure conveys his affection and willingness to accept his sister as a whole. This includes her love for him and her fear.

Nakagami's strategy of having Satoko introduce the "Kyōdai shinjū" narrative into *Kareki nada* presents the sister's voice expressing her desire to territorialize her brother and defy the patriarchal social authority of her father. Ryūzō's misogynist view of Satoko as "useless," however, marks her subalternity in the male homosocial bond. Satoko's fanatic adherence to the water cult can be interpreted as the subaltern sister's vain attempt to gain a voice by internalizing the divine law of the cult leader, which she regards as superior to the law of human society. Her assumption of the cult's "religious" precepts as the infrastructure on which she will depend to have her voice heard represents her self-contempt as polluted and her insistence on the supremacy of purity. This insistence reveals her dis-

---

108. Butler 2000, 11.
109. NKZ 6:450.

crimination against others whom she herself stigmatizes as *kegare*. For Satoko, her brother's disappearance from the *roji* signifies a break in her attachment to "Kyōdai shinjū," which presents death as a realization of incestuous love. By depicting Akiyuki's departure, Nakagami represents the brother and sister's ultimate communication, that is, Akiyuki's understanding of the sister's voice—her fear of her love for him—and Satoko's perception of his departure as his expression of affection (*itoshisa*) for her.

CHAPTER 5

The Voices of Aged Buraku Women

The Perspective of the *Omina*

This chapter discusses Nakagami's representation of the old woman, or *oba*, from the Burakumin community in Kumano. In Nakagami's narratives, aged women from the outcaste community are often referred to as *oba*. Although *oba* can be explained simply as a local dialectic variation of *obasan* (middle-aged woman or aunt) or *obāsan* (the elderly woman or grandmother), I argue that this term demonstrates the writer's expression of the geopolitical and gender idiosyncrasies of aged Burakumin women from Japan's peripheral South.

I begin my discussion of Nakagami's perspective of the *oba* and her voice with brief reference to the writer's essay series "Monogatari no keifu" ("Genealogy of narratives," 1979–1985). This work presents Nakagami's view of the tradition of *monogatari* as a woman narrating, especially by *omina*, the old woman with the power to pass down community narratives to the younger generations. I examine *Sen'nen no yuraku* (*A thousand years of pleasure*, 1982) as a variant of *monogatari* that echoes with the voice of a Burakumin *omina*, Oryū no oba (Aunt Ryū). The second half of the chapter examines the voices of the two aged outcaste women, Yuki and Moyo, who feature in

225

the Akiyuki trilogy. The voices of these women express the fragile trace that remains after the death of Oryū no oba. The fact that, as we shall see, these two women's voices are rarely or never heard suggests the erasure of the *omina*'s subaltern narrative and the power of that narrative. By focusing on how these women have been traumatized by their experience of sex, I demonstrate that although they are *oba*, Yuki and Moyo can never become *omina* because the community never hears (listens to) their voices.

In "Monogatari no keifu," Nakagami explains that the primitive state of *monogatari* is oral and narrated by the old woman, *omina*, sometimes known as *ōna*.[1] I noted in the introduction that the word *monogatari* implies the oral tradition of people talking (*katari*) about things (*mono*) from generation to generation. As discussed previously, in a 1978 public lecture in Osaka, Nakagami notes that *mono* is "soul" and *katari* is "not only the activity of telling, but also the passing down of religious precepts and historical memories."[2] One essay in the series particularly demonstrates Nakagami's unique interpretation of the aged woman writer Enchi Fumiko (1905–1986) as *omina*. By reading Enchi's short story "Fuyu no tabi: Shisha to no taiwa" ("Winter journey: Dialogue with the dead," 1971), a narrative centered around a dialogue between "I" and a soul who seems to be the dead Mishima Yukio (1925–1970), Nakagami sees Enchi as an *omina* relating the tales of dead souls.[3] Nakagami's essay refers to the scene in which "I" meets the soul while searching for the Japanese script of a musical play titled *Le Martyre de Saint Sébastien* (1911).[4] Famous for the image in which he re-created the agony of the martyred saint, Mishima longed to be the tragic hero of the drama he had jointly translated.

---

1. NKZ 15:245.

2. Nakagami 1999c, 225.

3. NKZ 15:231–56.

4. *Le Martyre de Saint Sébastien* was translated from the French into Japanese in 1966 by Mishima and Ikeda Kōtarō. The French original was a five-act musical mystery play about St. Sebastian written in 1911 by Gabriele D'Annunzio (1863–1938) with music by Claude Debussy (1862–1918).

In his discussion, Nakagami extensively cites Enchi's narrative, written in 1971, the year after Mishima's sensational death. "I" is the narrator, and the "ghost" is apparently the spirit of the writer who took his own life:

["I" said to the ghost], my homeland is different to that of Saint Sebastian, but I nevertheless have a bond with the same homeland as you, so I often think of you even though you are no longer of this world.

"By homeland, do you mean Japan or some different place?"

"Well, even though there are many mixed-blood elements in you, I think our homeland is the theater."

I could see from his eyes that he agreed. ...

As I leaned back against the seat of the train which sped along the Tokaidō line, the blurred [media] image of his dead head flashed across my mind's eye and I also pictured the vivid form of Kumagai's wife, cradling the severed head of Atsumori (in reality her own son, Kojirō)—"bringing the severed head to her breast"—while my ears filled with the phantom sound of a *shamisen* accompaniment to the *jōruri* chant.[5] ...

For in my own strange imagination, the slash of his abdomen and severed head were forms of theater—not the work of Sophocles, Racine or the *noh* theater—these were the abdominal slash and the severed head of *kabuki*.

---

5. This passage is based on the narrative of "Kumagai jinya" ("The Kumagai camp"). This work premiered in 1751 as one of five acts in the *ningyo jōruri* play *Ichinotani futaba gunki* (*A tale of two young warriors in the battle of Ichinotani*). There is also a kabuki version of this narrative, which is based on *Heike monogatari* (*The Tale of Heike*, twelfth century). "Kumagai jinya" depicts the tragic encounter of the sixteen-year-old warrior Taira no Atsumori with his enemy, Kumagai Naozane, who was fighting for the Minamoto clan. Kumagai captures Atsumori, but he cannot kill the young warrior because Atsumori's mother had saved his life in the past. Out of battlefield necessity, Kumagai decapitates his own son, Kojirō, who is the same age as Atsumori. Kumagai's wife is shocked by and filled with grief at the death of her son. Kumagai, too, is deeply distressed by his deed and eventually enters the priesthood. For further detail, see *Ichinotani futaba gunki* 1968.

This [the *kabuki* theater], of course, had exercised influence over him for a much longer time than [the narrative of] Saint Sebastian.[6]

Regarding Enchi as an *omina* and referring to her early literary activity as a dramatist, Nakagami notes her unique interpretation of Mishima's suicide from her "theatrical perspective."[7] This perspective results in Enchi focusing on the dramatic elements of the suicide, such as the "slash of the abdomen" (*harakiri*) and the "severed head" (*kirikubi*), in contrast to the journalistic elements, such as the intrusion into the Self-Defence Force offices, the failure of the coup d'état, or Mishima as a leader of the Hitler Youth–like Tate no kai.[8]

Nakagami explains that Enchi's "theatrical perspective" regards Mishima's death as induced by theater, notably *kabuki*, in which bloody scenes of murder, *harakiri*, and decapitation are ubiquitous. Detached from "reality" by their shared theoretical perspective, Enchi and Mishima can envision the beauty of bloody death. However, Mishima broke the "rule" of theater by committing real death. Nakagami reads Enchi's indignation at the "reality" of Mishima's death in a scene in which "I" cites a famous line by Higuchi Ichiyō

---

6. This excerpt is cited in Enchi 1994, 115–16, and in Nakagami's "Monogatari no keifu" (NKZ 15:232–33).

7. NKZ 15:231–34.

8. Tate no kai (Shield Society, 1968–1971) was a private militia in Japan founded in response to the New Left movement. The group was led by Mishima and dedicated to traditional Japanese values, including the veneration of the emperor. Tate no kai members were mainly recruited from university students who belonged to Minzoku-ha (The Nationalist Group). Mishima and Tate no kai were granted the right to train with Japan's Self-Defence Force. On November 25, 1970, Mishima and four Tate no kai members briefly seized control of the Self-Defence Force headquarters and attempted to rally the soldiers to stage a coup to restore imperial rule. When this failed, Mishima and Morita Masakatsu (1945–1970), the Tate no kai's main student leader, committed suicide by *seppuku* (slashing the abdomen). For further details see Stokes 1975.

(1872–1896)—"I really am a woman" (*Makoto ni ware wa onna nari keru mono o*)[9]—to describe her sense of loss and bereavement upon hearing of the suicide. More important, for Nakagami, this citation confirms Enchi's place in a genealogy of female (*joryū*) writers who retained abundant knowledge about and insight into *monogatari* but were still marginalized from mainstream Japanese literature at the time of the publication of Enchi's narrative. By reading Enchi's narrative of the dead "soul," Nakagami observes the power of an *omina*'s narrative to reveal the violent nature of *monogatari*.

In terms of his view of *monogatari* as female narrating, Nakagami's notion of *omina* also resonates with the storytelling legends told by Shihi no omina (seventh–eighth century) and Hieda no Are (seventh–eighth century). The former was a woman servant of Empress Jitō (645–702). Their dialogue in the form of a thirty-one-syllable poem in *Man'yōshū* demonstrates the significance of the female storyteller in ancient times.[10] The latter is known for being instrumental in the compilation of *Kojiki*. Although the sex of Hieda no Are is uncertain, this figure is assumed by scholars such as Yanagita Kunio and Saigō Nobutsuna (1916–2008) to be a female shaman.[11] In Nakagami's words, *omina* was a *kii sutēshon* (key station) of knowledge and information and a "teller of *kotonoha* [words] and *kotodama* [word souls]" in the ancient community of Japan.[12]

---

9. This excerpt is cited in Enchi 1994, 119 and Nakagami's "Monogatari no keifu" (NKZ 15:232–33).

10. Below are the translated poems of Empress Jitō and Shihi no omina taken from Hideo Levy's translation of *The Ten Thousand Leaves* 1981, 151–52.

Poem given by the Empress to the old woman Shihi:

Lately I do not hear / the talk that Shihi forces on me, / though I tell her, "Stop," / and now I long for it.

Poem presented by the old woman Shihi in response:

Though I say, "I want to stop," / you command me, "Speak! Speak!" / So Shihi speaks, and then you say / I force it on you!

11. See Yanagita 1990, 288–304, and Saigō 1973, 9–56.

12. NKZ 15:245.

Nakagami argues that the source of *monogatari* is the *omina*'s marginalization, which I interpret as subalternity. He calls *omina* the "fictional mother" and the "inverted great mother."

> Through appropriating the perspective of the fictional mother, that is, the inverted great mother who is the marginalized mother, we can escape the Western model of binary opposites which have, without resistance, overrun the modern world. We can thereby discover the presence of decay which is, just like the twist of the Möbius strip, apparent as the other side of the sublimity of the life force. We can also see the power of the old woman who exists on the border, and beyond the border, of this world and the next ... and who thus renews this world.[13]

Nakagami's phrases "fictional mother" and "inverted great mother" are used in association with the phenomenon of aging, that is, the woman's infertility and her consequent "marginalized" status in the community. For Nakagami, communal practices like *ubasute* (abandoning the aged) and cannibalism are the root of religion and rituals—rituals that return the aged's power of the life to the whole community.[14] His depiction of the voice of the aged Buraku woman can be considered an application of the concept of *omina* and, through his literary representation, the return of her power to the Burakumin community. Although she points out that the "true" subaltern is "gender-unspecified," I noted in chapter 1 that Spivak suggests that the typical case of "the foreclosed native informant" is "the poorest woman of the South."[15] Drawing on this view, this chapter discusses Nakagami as a writer (the educated native informant) who tries to "represent" the voice of the foreclosed and gendered *oba*.

---

13. NKZ 15:249.
14. NKZ 15:248–49.
15. Spivak 1999, 6.

Voice of the Burakumin *Omina*

Sen'nen no yuraku, a collection of six linked stories, was serialized from 1980 to 1982 and published in book form in 1982. Although the stories in the book do not follow a set chronology, the narrative spans approximately thirty years, from Japanese imperial rule into the postwar era. Each narrative features a beautiful young man of the Nakamoto clan who was born into a segregated *roji* community. All of the six protagonists live excessively lustful or violent lives, involving activities such as theft, rape, murder, and substance abuse. Each dies an early death by his own hand or at the hand of another. Furthermore, each is either an illegitimate child or a child who, neglected by his own family, was raised collectively by the *roji* community. In this respect, a major role is played by the community midwife, an elderly woman known as Oryū no oba. Referring to the *oba* as "the data-bank of the *roji*," Asada notes that this illiterate midwife "remembers all the dates of the births and deaths of all the people" in her community.[16] Having brought each *roji* child into the world, Oryū no oba is depicted as a mother figure for the Nakamoto boys. Her role is encapsulated in Nakagami's observation that the *hisabetsu buraku* is "a maternal place."[17]

Oryū no oba was a bereaved mother whose three-year-old son died after "a bowl of tea gruel" accidentally spilled over his head.[18] From the perspective of the *ryōsai kenbo* (good wife, wise mother) and *fukoku kyōhei* (rich country, strong military) ideologies that dominated at the time,[19] Oryū no oba failed to raise her son to fight in the name of the emperor, and she was therefore not qualified to be a respectable mother. Her husband, Reijo, was a lay Buddhist priest known contemptuously as a *kebōzu* (hair priest). This term derived

---

16. Asada 1996, 29.

17. Nakagami and Abe 1995, 63.

18. Nakagami 1982, 2.

19. For further detail, see Koyama 1992.

from the fact that ordained priests shaved their heads but *kebōzu* did not. These men were further disparaged since, rather than having the wages of a temple priest, they continued working in their former occupations, which were often associated with impoverished rural work.[20] Previously a shoemaker, Reijo abandoned his trade to become a priest after the priest of the local Jōsenji Temple, who ministered compassionately to and sympathized with the plight of the *roji* community, was convicted of plotting to assassinate the emperor, "the very Son of Heaven."[21] In his narratives of the *roji*, Nakagami, who had a strong consciousness of the events of the 1910/11 High Treason incident, often alludes to the historical figure of local Jōsenji Temple priest Takagi Kenmyō (1864–1914), one of six defendants from Shingū sentenced to life in prison for his alleged role in the incident. Immediately after the incident he was excommunicated from Higashi Honganji, the head temple of the Jōdo shinshū school of Pure Land Buddhism. Takagi committed suicide in Akita Prison in 1914. The High Treason incident victims were politically tainted; in *Sen'nen no yuraku*, Oryū no oba, is also depicted as a figure marginalized by this taint.

Oryū no oba plays a key role in providing observations that weave the *Sen'nen no yuraku* text together and she has therefore been the subject of lengthy discussion in Nakagami criticism. As Karlsson points out, she is not the narrator, even though her consciousness orients significant sections of the novel.[22] In reading *Sen'nen no yuraku*, we should first note that the novel is written in third person with Oryū no oba's consciousness and recollections of the *roji* intermittently inserted throughout the text. The following is the opening sentence of "Hanzō no tori" (translated by Ian Hideo Levy as "Hanzo's Bird"), the first narrative in *Sen'nen no yuraku*.

---

20. For further detail, see Yanagita's essay "Kebōzu kō" ("An essay on kebōzu priests," 1915–1916) in Yanagita 1990, 11:419–546.

21. Nakagami 1982, 6.

22. Karlsson 2009, 162–64.

The sweet stifling fragrance of summer mallows had suddenly crept in from the back door with the first wisps of dawn, and Oryu, thinking the blossoms' smell would choke her, opened her eyes and, seeing the photograph of her husband Reijo looming faintly white in the darkness from where it had been placed on a stand next to the family altar, had a feeling that her marriage to Reijo, a man like a noble Buddha, must have been an impossible illusion.[23]

明け方になって急に家の裏口から夏芙蓉の甘いにおいが入り込んで来たので息苦しく、まるで花のにおいに息をとめられるように思ってオリュウノオバは眼をさまし、仏壇の横にしつらえた台に乗せた夫の礼如さんの額に入った写真が微かに白く闇の中に浮き上がっているのをみて、尊い仏様のような人だった礼如さんと夫婦だった事が有り得ない幻だったような気がした.[24]

Levy remarks that he almost felt "despair" when first confronted by this "one long sentence" in "a violent flow of Japanese language."[25] Once he had translated this "detailed" account of Oryū no oba's consciousness, he felt "as if I had been forced to write an English sentence in which I had to make an impossible illusion into flesh and blood." Levy explains that the text demonstrates how Oryū no oba's *katari* (narration) "deviates" from modern Japanese literary convention. For Levy, who is also a translator of *Man'yōshū*, the violent flow of the nonheterogeneous *katari* that feature in Nakagami's writing confirms the emergence from the long tradition of Japanese language of new possibilities in modern Japanese literature.[26]

Levy's view closely parallels Nakagami's statement in the "Ise" chapter of *Kishū*.

---

23. Levy's translation, Nakagami 1982, 1.
24. NKZ 5:11.
25. Levy 1995, 3.
26. Levy 1995, 4.

> In order to repudiate the emperor's realm through language, I will
> have to adopt another strange tongue, not the omnipresent re-
> corded Japanese language of the "leaves that are words" [*koto-
> noha*]. Perhaps I must turn to the spoken word [*katari no kotoba*]
> which repudiates being written by a writer.[27]

We have seen how Nakagami, convinced that imperial authority in
Japan rested on the "written word," found it paradoxical that as a
Burakumin novelist he was required to draw on the written word to
write against the hegemonic center. As Zimmerman notes, this
realization motivated Nakagami to take up "the challenge of searching for a new mode of representation."[28] Citing the foregoing
passage, Japanese literary critics such as Komori Yōichi and Satō
Yasutomo also read *Sen'nen no yuraku* as demonstrating the writer's
motive for literary production.[29] Satō notes Nakagami's reference to
Burakumin genealogy in Kumano, the country of darkness, as a
"negative unbroken line" (*fu no bansei ikkei*).[30] This critic further
argues that *Sen'nen no yuraku* can be read as "the *roji* version of the
Kojiki" in that Nakagami's narrative takes a stand against the canonical ancient text, a text that consolidates the binary opposition between the emperor as central and superior and Kumano people as
peripheral and inferior.[31] Drawing on Spivak's view, we might regard "*katari no kotoba* which repudiates being written by a writer" as
the voice of "the foreclosed native informant," or the *mukoku*, to use
Nakagami's word. In the following section I investigate Nakagami
as a writer who, while aware of this paradox, attempts to represent
the voice of the Burakumin *omina*, Oryū no oba, one of the most
stigmatized members of society during Japan's imperial project.

---

27. The first sentence of this excerpt from *Kishū* was translated by Eve Zimmerman; the remainder is my translation. See Zimmerman 2007, 156. For the
Japanese text, see NKZ 14:609–10.

28. Zimmerman 2007, 157.

29. Komori 1999, 397, and Satō Y. 2012, 98–99.

30. See Nakagami's statement in Nakagami, Yoshimoto, and Mikami 1990, 17.

31. Satō Y. 2012, 99.

As previously noted, early material such as "Misaki" and *Kareki nada* avoided the use of language that overtly discriminated against Buraku people. *Sen'nen no yuraku* (and also *Chi no hate*, written around the same time) demonstrates a determination by Nakagami to depict the *roji* overtly as a *hisabetsu buraku*. As a result of the Japanese aversion to impurity, the *roji* is the dwelling place of those who are socially segregated as *kegare*. Oryū no oba's voice consciousness, therefore, includes many historical elements of the lives of Shingū *hisabetsu buraku* residents and forms of mainstream discrimination against them. Recalling the passage that so challenged Levy, the following excerpt from Nakagami's original text reads like one "violent flow of language."

It was before an age that he could remember when because in spite of their best efforts, [*roji*] men could never get a proper job[;] some hardy ones worked dragging wood-sledges and some boys with nimble fingers pulled their own carts through the gate built at the crest of the *roji* hill and down to the castle town to find work repairing footwear [*geta* and *zōri*] in the gay quarters where samurai mansions once stood, while others stayed in the *roji* to tan leather using the fresh water from a lotus pond, and it was at the time when these men were always gambling, thieving and picking pockets, that this young man was taken away from the *roji* to live in another place by his conscientious parents who opened a grocery store in the castle town. He said that he now felt sad about the *roji* because it had changed so much since he last saw it as a child, but Oryū no oba retorted that there was no use in a man like him who was still so young being sentimental. Since she realized that he had no idea that the hill behind the *roji* was a boundary between the castle town and another place and that on the top of the hill there was a small shrine which people called *midō* [temple] and a fence and gate installed at the site of the shrine, Oryū no oba told the man that in the past the gate closed after sunset in order to shut out any traffic between the *roji* and the town, and that for the week from New Year's Day the gate would be locked shut in order to prevent the *roji* people coming into the town, and that if *roji* people entered the town [during that time] people would chase them and beat them with batons.[32]

In a study of the *dōwa* districts in Shingū, Wakamatsu and Mizuuchi note that there was once a gate and gatekeeper on Garyūzan "hill" and that outcaste people were "forced" to live in the "marshy area" toward the foot of the hill.[33] This passage demonstrates the high "visibility" of the social and spatial difference between Burakumin and non-Burakumin in Shingū society before urbanization and the obliteration of Garyūzan.

The passage also displays the remarkable contrast between Oryū no oba and the young man: that is, between the older generation who witnessed and experienced the severity of mainstream discrimination against *roji* people and the younger generation who are unaware of that humiliating history. There is also the difference between the woman who remains in the outcaste homeland and retains her subalternity and the man who relocates to another town to excise himself from the stigma of the *roji*. Citing this extract, Noguchi notes that the young man who "felt sad about the *roji* because it had changed so much since he last saw it as a child" overlaps with Nakagami, who felt intense pain at the obliteration of the *roji*.[34] In *Kumano shū*, published in 1984, Nakagami acknowledged his strong attachment to his birthplace by referring to himself as "a child of the *roji*."[35] After witnessing the reform of the area, the writer realized that "the *roji* is [now] unrelated to me."[36] By migrating to Tokyo, Nakagami lost any connection to the "reality" of the *roji*—that is, to the subalternity of its residents and the *buraku mondai* of the area. In this sense, the young man featured in the *Sen'nen no yuraku* extract shares many characteristics with the writer and with the writer's alter ego, Akiyuki.

---

32. NKZ 5:34.
33. Wakamatsu and Mizuuchi 2001, 57.
34. Noguchi 2001, 81.
35. NKZ 5:232.
36. NKZ 5:413.

As the *omina* of the *roji*, Oryū no oba relates the legends and memories of the community to the younger generation. At the same time, she is amazed at their indifference to the *roji* community's long history of "burning humiliation."[37] In Nakagami's Kumano saga, Oryū no oba is almost the only character who clearly expresses anger against the mainstream violence committed against *roji* men during New Year festivities and the Emancipation Edict riots.

> Nobody apologized to us for the things they did in the past. People might say "equality for all," but once there is any shortage or a disaster like the earthquake that happened some years ago they will come to kill us for sure. The Koreans who were suddenly killed without any reason after the earthquake were identified as new Japanese citizens [during the war]—that's their sense of "equality for all." ...
>
> Oryū no oba declares "Today's egalitarianism is doubtful—when something happens the town people of Shingū and the citizens of the land will attack to kill us." Reijo comforted her saying "Don't talk like that, life and death are all the same."[38]

Referring to mainstream violence against *roji* people in the castle town of Shingū and against Koreans after the Great Kantō Earthquake (1923), Oryū no oba highlights the falsehood of the "equality for all" slogan espoused by the 1871 Emancipation Edict and 1872 abolishment of the feudal class system whereby *eta* and *hinin* were renamed *shinheimin*. For her, the government policy of "egalitarianism" merely acts as a trigger for mainstream frustration and violence against the marginalized. As noted in the introduction, discrimination against the *shinheimin* became more brutal with the ratification of the Emancipation Edict. As a follower of the Buddha, Reijo admonishes his wife for her resentment, declaring that before the "egalitarianism" of birth and death given to all people by fate, there is no difference between the mainstream or others. From

---

37. NKZ 5:54.
38. NKZ 5:142–43.

the Buddhist viewpoint, the government policy of "equality for all" is morally correct. Reijo's uncritical acceptance of the hegemonic doctrine and his desire to avoid conflict by remaining silent recalls the cliché related to taboos around Buraku issues, *neta ko o okosu na* (don't wake a sleeping baby). In contrast to her husband, Oryū no oba raises her voice to criticize the paradox of the hegemonic ideology which, while espousing equality, overtly stigmatized the marginalized and thereby set them up as targets in the riots initiated by the frustrated mainstream against the dramatic social changes of the Meiji era.

In *Sen'nen no yuraku*, Nakagami presents not only taboos of discrimination but also the sexual taboos that define the patriarchal context. These taboos include female infidelity, a widow's sexual relations (in wartime Japan, particularly, a widow was expected to remain chaste in honor of her dead husband),[39] and homosexuality. However, he demonstrates the absurdity of these taboos which, in addition to being completely disregarded by many in the *roji*, are equally disregarded by those outside the *roji* who engage in illicit relations with *roji* dwellers to express sexual identities that have been suppressed by hegemonic norms.

Since Nakagami considers sex—along with violence and religion—to be one of three main elements that contributes to the social construction of discrimination, the writer presents various sexual contexts to depict systematic discrimination. "Hanzō no tori" features lustful sexual activities that involve the *roji* hero (hereafter Hanzo, following the spelling in the English translation), a widow who lives in the Ukishima area of Shingū, and a man from outside the *roji*. The following is a conversation between Hanzo and the man from outside after they have spent a sex-filled night with the widow.

"We're going in different directions," said Hanzo [to the man]. "I'm going to turn up the mountain road from the Ukishima

---

39. Kawaguchi 2007, 91–108.

brothel, then head down to the alley on the other side." The man looked astonished. "You're from Nagayama?" he asked, giving another name for the alley. "You're from Nagayama?" he repeated, interested that Hanzo was from the ghetto of outcastes, the jumble of cattle skinners and sandal repairers and basket weavers. With a sudden air of condescension, he told him, "You're a good-looking man."[40]

Traditionally, Nakagami's *roji*—Kasuga—was called Nagayama (long hill) by non-Kasuga people (both Burakumin and non-Burakumin) because the district was situated behind the long hill of Garyūzan. Although Kasuga was a common name for the area, the term *Nagayama* appeared in official registers until 1974. For local Shingū people, *Nagayama* carried a discriminative and derogatory connotation as a "synonym of *dōwa* districts."[41] Outsiders' disdain for the *roji* is frequently depicted in *Sen'nen no yuraku*. In addition to Shingū being a site of narratives of "treason" and discrimination, for Nakagami, it was a site of narratives about sex. A castle town during the Tokugawa era, Shingū was both a center of the lumber industry and a site frequented by Kumano pilgrims. Borrowing from a key term used by Nakagami and Karatani in their perspective of Shingū's society and culture, we can refer to Shingū as a place of *kōtsū* (intercourse)—both sexual and relating to travel and trade—between various kinds of people from different backgrounds.[42]

Nakagami's depiction of Ukishima as a place for promiscuity also implies the area's intertextuality with narratives about sex. In this area, there is a small floating island called Ukishima no mori (Floating island forest), which consists of a mass of floating aquatic plants, mud, and peat. The precinct near this island was registered as a red-

---

40. Nakagami 1982, 18.

41. Wakamatsu and Mizuuchi 2001, 57 and 92–93.

42. See Nakagami and Karatani's views of *kōtsū* in Nakagami and Karatani 1979, 7–105.

light district from 1912 to 1958.[43] The Ukishima no mori is the site of an *iruikon* (marriage between two different species, usually a human and an animal) legend about the coupling of beautiful young girl called Oino and a large male snake. "Jasei no in" (translated as "Lust of the White Serpent"), a story from *Ugetsu monogatari* (*Tales of Moonlight and Rain*, 1776), a collection of supernatural tales by canonical Tokugawa-era writer Ueda Akinari (1734–1809), can be read as a variant of the Ukishima legend. While Akinari's "Jasei no in" is set in Shingū, the writer nonetheless reverses the gender of the couple from the legend to tell the tale of an *iruikon* between a beautiful young man (Toyo'o) and a female snake. As read in his essay on Akinari in "Monogatari no keifu" and in the short story "Ukishima," Nakagami interprets "Jasei no in" as Akinari's critical view of the original legend: Akinari writes to challenge the supremacy of masculine virility by depicting a naive man at the mercy of female desire—a man who desperately tries to escape from an *iruikon* taboo.[44]

If Akinari's text contests the conventional narrative of the helpless woman and the dangerous male, "Hanzō no tori" can be read as Nakagami's critique of the Ukishima legend and Akinari's story. In Nakagami's interpretation, all three are equal participants in the acts of sexual excess depicted, so neither Hanzo, the widow, nor the man is constructed as a victim in their sexual activities. However, once the context of discrimination is introduced—when the man discriminates against Hanzo by labeling him as an outcaste— Hanzo cannot help feeling inferior. His response is to adopt mainstream discriminatory attitudes toward same-sex male eroticism. In response to the man's condescending comment about his looks, Hanzo thinks:

> He could see toying with women and being toyed with by them, but to have a man, and an outsider, toying with him because of

---

43. NKZ 15:177.
44. NKZ 15:177.

his good looks, just like a homosexual—no thanks. Hanzo spat on the road. He felt just like some pretty boy [*yasa otoko*] who had sold his body for the sake of his friend in the alley. His pride was hurt, and he kept spitting as he climbed the mountain path back to the alley.[45]

Here Nakagami depicts the disturbing paradox of the marginalized individual himself demonstrating a marginalizing response. Unlike the hero in "Jasei no in," Hanzo never escapes the attraction of female desire and brings disaster on himself by "toying with women and being toyed with by them." He eventually dies after being stabbed in the back by a furious man from outside the *roji*. This depiction contains yet another paradox: while he is a victim of violence, which apparently relates to discrimination, Hanzo brings about his death by his own violation of taboos. Violence, which Nakagami sees as one of three elements of discrimination, becomes "visible" through the narrative of the outcaste man who breaks patriarchal taboos in society.

Yasa otoko is a phrase used throughout the narrative in reference to the Nakamoto men. This term recalls the attributes of the male protagonist of "Jasei no in." Featuring the spoilt son of a wealthy Shingū fisherman, "Jasei no in" is traditionally read as an account of the ordeal of a *yasa otoko* who is desired by a female snake. The young man, Toyo'o, is introduced in Akinari's text as follows: "Toyo'o, the third child, was a handsome youth with a predilection for learning and cultural pursuits typical of life in Kyoto, the nation's capital. He had no desire or inclination to devote his time and efforts to the family occupation."[46] Although normative masculinity in the Tokugawa era incorporated a love for the arts, the defining element was the physical ferocity of the samurai. Thus, while lauding a man's good looks, the term *yasa otoko* had a negative connotation in that it critiqued the mild-mannered love of the arts that sig-

45. Nakagami 1982, 18.
46. Ueda 1972, 20.

nals a lack of vitality and hegemonic masculinity. In "Jasei no in," this masculinity is represented as *masurao gokoro* (manly heart). As Zimmerman notes, by gaining *masurao gokoro*, Toyo'o is able to reject the snake woman, who represents the "supernatural and the demonic," in favor of the "linear, patriarchal order of the nation."[47] In the end, Toyo'o manages to survive while the snake woman is disposed of by a Buddhist priest. Toyo'o's new wife died sometime after being attacked by the snake woman. In other words, Toyo'o's *masurao gokoro* eventually killed both women. Toyo'o recalls the male protagonist in "Rakudo" who attempts to express his "man's heart" (*otoko no kokoro*) by burning his wife and daughters. The Nakamoto boys who lack hegemonic masculinity, on the other hand, cannot survive for long.

In addition to intertextuality with the local legend and the Edo narrative, Nakagami alludes to the geopolitical and historical oppression of Kumano by the hegemonic center by depicting Oryū no oba's consciousness as a silenced voice from the South.

[Oryū no oba thinks] As some in the hamlet said, the Nakamoto blood perhaps came from the [exiled] clan defeated by the Minamotos in the Battle of Yashima[48] ... it was this stagnant blood that made them spend their days and nights on music and dance, never thinking of the need to work hard to survive, lacking the spirit to meet the challenge of those who opposed them, tiring easily of whatever they might have been doing, and, although so poor that they could not buy food, helplessly drawn to having fun, drinking and indulging in the fragrance of women's makeup.[49]

---

47. Zimmerman 2007, 189.

48. The Battle of Yashima (Yashima no tatakai) took place in 1185 between the Minamoto clan (Genji) and the Taira clan (Heike) at Yashima in Sanuki (the old name for the area around Kagawa prefecture). In fleeing the Minamoto, the Taira were once more defeated by troops led by Minamoto no Yoshitsune (1159–1189). The Battle of Yashima is the penultimate battle between these samurai families. The Taira clan eventually fell in 1185 at Dan'noura in the Shimonoseki Straits. See *Daijisen* 1995, 2659.

49. NKZ 5:42.

Although aware of the beauty of the Nakamoto men, Oryū no oba also assesses them as lacking "the spirit to meet the challenge of those who opposed them," that is, as lacking *masurao gokoro*. For Oryū no oba, this is not the sole reason it was "only Nakamoto men who died young or became sickly."[50]

> Knowing that it would be easier for the young men to understand [their] destiny [as descendants of a cursed clan], Oryū no oba could have told them that it was because seven or ten generations ago some immoral man had cut out a beast's stomach that held a fetus, or had driven away a man who asked for water, unaware that the man was an incarnation of the Buddha; but she also knew that nothing she might say could halt the gradual decay, one by one, of the Nakamoto boys, with their blood that was so sacred because so thoroughly impure.[51]

Oryū no oba's consciousness of the tragic destiny of the Nakamoto men is foregrounded through her references to the local oral communal folklore of ancient nobles in political exile (*kishu ryūritan*), of traveling entertainers, of bullies who refused to give aide to Kūkai (774–835), the famous itinerant priest, and of those who broke the Buddhist taboo against killing animals. In *Sen'nen no yuraku*, the main Burakumin characters are represented as embodiments of various paradoxes, including purity/impurity and center/periphery.[52] Although the Nakamoto men belong to the most beautiful

---

50. NKZ 5:42.

51. NKZ 5:42–43. I translated this excerpt except for the last line, "their blood that was so sacred because so thoroughly impure," which I borrowed from Eve Zimmerman's translation. See Zimmerman 1999a, 134.

52. Drawing on Rosalie Colie's *Paradoxica Epidemica: The Renaissance Tradition of Paradox* (1966), Zimmerman also discusses Nakagami's use of "the power of paradox" as the "ability" to "upset the categories by which we organise our world." See Zimmerman 1999a, 130–52. In his Ph.D. dissertation, Takayashiki Masahito examines Nakagami's act of writing as a demonstration of the paradox between self-identification and integration into the collective. See Takayashiki 2007, 42–48.

clan, idolized by women from their community, they are stigmatized by the wider society as polluted outcastes. This strong sense of
paradox is represented in Oryū no oba's view of the blood of the
Nakamoto men as "so sacred" because it is so thoroughly "impure."

Nakagami's depiction of Nakamoto blood provoked considerable controversy. Some writers, such as Burakumin activist Hijikata
Tetsu and scholar of Buraku studies, Noguchi Michihiko, who
greatly respect Nakagami's literary and critical prowess, raised questions about this aspect of the narrative. Hijikata observed: "Through
characterizing the protagonists as 'sacred because they are outcaste,'
Nakagami tried to jump over, rather than dismantle, the wall of
discrimination. I, however, strongly doubt that he could truly succeed in going beyond a wall like that."[53] Noguchi correspondingly
sees the paradox of Nakamoto blood as "unsuccessful" for depicting the Burakumin clan as "splendid beings" by "inverting"—
rather than "denouncing"—mainstream discrimination against the
Burakumin as *kegare*.[54] For Noguchi, Nakagami's *roji* in *Sen'nen no
yuraku* (and the follow-up serial *Kiseki*) are merely "mythical" sites.
Therefore, any narration by Oryū no oba concerning difficulties
faced by people of the *roji* must be highly "fictitious."[55] Noguchi's
interpretation closely parallels that of Etō Jun in his well-known
essay on *Sen'nen no yuraku*, "'Roji' to takai" ("The roji" and the other
world, 1983). Here, Etō argues that *Sen'nen no yuraku* is never a
shōsetsu, that is, a record of the facts of daily life as controlled by
moral principles and restricted by time and space.[56] Instead, it is a
monogatari of the *roji*, of "other-worldly Japan" that is "narrated"[57]
by the voice of the illiterate Oryū no oba and then "transcribed"

---

53. Hijikata 1992a.

54. Noguchi 2001, 91.

55. Noguchi 2001, 211.

56. Etō 1992, 263.

57. As discussed in the previous section, although her consciousness orients
significant sections of the text, *Sen'nen no yuraku* is not a story "narrated" by Oryū
no oba's voice. Etō's perspective of Oryū no oba as Nakagami's reproduction of
a voice from "other-worldly Japan" has been criticized by many, such as Yomota

and "articulated" by Nakagami as writer.[58] Although Etō greatly admires *Sen'nen no yuraku* as a groundbreaking work of contemporary Japanese literature, Noguchi regards the work as problematic in terms of its representation of the *hisabetsu buraku*.

To Noguchi, and apparently Hijikata, too, Nakagami's *roji* narratives are "insufficient" as literature, or more precisely as Buraku literature, which both critics expect to "cut sharply into the actual discriminatory practices against the Burakumin."[59] Hijikata lists Shimazaki Tōson, Noma Hiroshi, Inoue Mitsuharu, and Sumii Sue as the most laudable writers of Buraku literature.[60] These authors depict protagonists who witness or experience the harsh reality of persistent discrimination and thus become aware of the importance of the Buraku liberation movement. From this perspective, Nakagami's novels will disappoint readers searching for such heroes and the liberation from discrimination they putatively bring. Rather than denouncing *buraku mondai*, Nakagami's objective was to expose and invert the nature of discrimination. As a writer who voluntarily "became a Burakumin," Nakagami tried to convert the stigma of "discrimination" into identity "difference." In doing so, he focused on representing the voices of the voiceless and the oral folklore that expressed the traces of the hearts and souls of these voiceless.

We might consider Oryū no oba in terms of Spivak's suggestion that the typical case of "the foreclosed native informant" is "the poorest woman of the South" with her "imagined (im)possible perspective." Drawing on these ideas, I focus on Nakagami's depiction of the paradoxical and absurd voice of the Burakumin *omina*, Oryū no oba. By profiling the paradox of the Nakamoto men's beauty through Oryū no oba's perspective, Nakagami profiles the exclusionary nature of communities and what is often the exclusionary nature of social identification within communities. This is apparent

---

Inuhiko and Watanabe Naomi. See Nakagami and Yomota 1996, 283–85, and Watanabe 1996, 209.

58. Etō 1992, 282–91.

59. Noguchi 2001, 91.

60. Hijikata 1992a.

from his depiction of the Nakamoto clan's community monopoly on the repair of Japanese traditional sandals (*geta* and *zōri*). As seen in the case of Reijo, who was also a member of the Nakamoto clan, occupations related to footwear (such as shoemaker) were often undertaken by Burakumin. Since they worked with animal skins, these people were ostracized by mainstream society as *kegare*. However, Nakagami demonstrates that exclusionary practices existed even *within* the Burakumin community. In *Sen'nen no yuraku*, one of the six Nakamoto men, Shin'ichirō, is a footwear repairer. He is also a thief who asks to join the *roji* guild of footwear repairers to divert suspicion away from his illegal activities. Since the Nakamoto clan was one of the oldest in the community, in spite of his criminality Shin'ichirō is immediately given membership of the guild by senior members, who encourage him to "reform" by engaging in this traditional job.[61] As she narrates Shin'ichirō's easy entry into the guild, Oryū no oba comments on the attitude of longstanding *roji* residents who, while embracing a local criminal, try to exclude newcomers from the occupational monopolies they control. By depicting the tensions that arise through this kind of conflict, Nakagami provides insights into the discriminatory systems that operate in all communities, including the Buraku community.

Discrimination against the weaker pair of a binary, such as periphery or impurity, inevitably occurs in the establishment of social identification. The weaker pair is excluded from the privileged mainstream, which demands a consistent and exclusionary identification with the power components of the group. The Nakamoto men—who are both beautiful and impure, part of the *roji* center and the mainstream marginalized—present a paradox that contests this usual practice. This paradox cannot be represented through conventional narratorial practices, only through narration by a "silenced" voice. In this text, the silenced voice is that of the social pariah, Oryū no oba. Oppressed by the mainstream, the stigmatized voice must inevitably narrate paradoxically.

---

61. NKZ 5:151.

Voice of the Aged Former Prostitute

Although *Sen'nen no yuraku* and *Chi no hate* were written around the same time, the first piece includes the voice of the *omina*, Oryū no oba, who gathers the threads of *roji* legends related to the cursed beauty of outcaste men. *Chi no hate*, however, displays the world after the death of the Burakumin *omina*. The *roji* has disappeared, transformed into grassland through the capitalist project of urbanization. Because most *roji* residents have been evicted and forced to move to other places, there is no one to commemorate the second anniversary of Oryū no oba's death. The death of this community "mother" implies the end of the mythical "maternal place" of the *roji*.

In place of Oryū no oba, the data bank of the community, *Chi no hate* features women who are former prostitutes, such as Satoko and Yuki. These women replace Akiyuki's mother and sister, Fusa and Mie, who appear as central characters in the first two volumes of the Akiyuki trilogy. While Fusa and Mie are recognized as women from the *roji* community even after they leave the area, neither Satoko nor Yuki have such legitimacy. Satoko is regarded as a single outcaste woman who lives in the entertainment district without belonging to any community other than the water cult. Yuki is, strictly speaking, not a *roji* woman because she is the eldest sister of the Takehara clan, an outcaste family from outside the Kasuga *roji*. In the sense that she frequents the *roji* to circulate rumors, Yuki can nevertheless be seen as a member of the subaltern community. As noted, she is also a follower of the water cult, instructed by Satoko. While "Misaki," *Kareki nada*, and *Sen'nen no yuraku* display *roji* women whose voices endlessly reminisce about the memory of the dead men like Ikuo and his father from the Nakamoto clan,[62] *Chi no hate* presents the wandering former prostitutes whose voices are never

---

62. In *Sen'nen no yuraku*, Akiyuki's brother, Ikuo, who died at the age of twenty-four, is depicted in the genealogy of the Nakamoto clan because his father (Fusa's first husband, who also died young) is one of the sons of the clan. However, Ikuo only appears sparingly in the trilogy.

given a hearing by those with power within the outcaste community.[63] Focusing on Nakagami's depiction of these aged outcaste women, I consider Yuki as an *oba* who, unlike Oryū no oba, is never able to become *omina*, a narrator of *monogatari*.

Yuki is the eldest sister of Akiyuki's stepfather, Takehara Shigezō. In *Kareki nada* and *Chi no hate*, she appears as a lonely aged widow who is disliked by her family because of her fastidious gossipy nature and her indulgence in long monologues about her own tragic past. Because she continually boasts about the prosperity of the Takehara family, Yuki is the object of the scorn of the entire community. The eldest daughter of six siblings, Yuki lost her father when she was a child. This left her outcaste family living in abject poverty. When she was about fifteen, her mother sold her to a brothel in Ise. The site since ancient times of the principal Shinto shrine, Ise also had a thriving licensed quarter. Although in the Akiyuki trilogy Yuki is in her mid-sixties and called *oba* by the community, her male acquaintances, such as Ryūzō and Akiyuki, sometimes refer to her as *ine*, the meaning of which approximates "missy" or even "sister." In Nakagami's narrative, young Burakumin woman characters are often called *ine*. The use of this term for an older single woman like Yuki, however, has derogatory connotations such as those found in the English phrase "old maid." Yuki as an *ine* demonstrates the presence in the *roji* of the aged Buraku woman who once, because she was an eldest sister, was sent to work in the sex industry as a prostitute (*jorō*) to support her family. In his essay "Monogatari no keifu," Nakagami uses the *kanji* 姐 to identify the *ine* as a woman who has "reproductive ability,"[64] thus distinguishing her from *imo* (sister, young woman) or *oba* (aunt, aged woman). Hence, *ine* is a term particularly used for mature young women in Nakagami's nar-

---

63. Satoko apparently values herself as the younger sister (*imōto*) of Akiyuki, while Yuki constructs her identity as an eldest sister (*ane*) who sacrificed herself to support her family.

64. NKZ 15:247–49.

rative of the marginalized South.[65] Why, then, is this term used in reference to Yuki?

Key features in Nakagami's depiction of the *ine* include being a daughter from a fatherless outcaste family, being a loyal sister to her brothers, and being a migrant worker who supports her mother and siblings (often through sex work). Apart from Yuki, the character who most clearly displays these *ine* characteristics is the protagonist's eldest half-sister, Yoshiko. When she was fifteen, Yoshiko went as an adolescent migrant worker to a silk factory near Nagoya and took a job to support her fatherless family. Some years later, she married the heir of the silk mill. Through her marriage, Yoshiko became isolated from her family both physically and emotionally. The aging, single Yuki, on the other hand, has intensified her attachment to and sense of responsibility toward her blood family over the years.

It is significant that the eldest daughter in the fatherless Burakumin family often assumes the role of father and mother to her siblings. This can be seen in the passage below:

> By the time her first younger brother, the eldest son of the family, became financially independent as an engineering contractor and was able to come ransom her, Yuki had already spent the springtime of her life as a prostitute. She saw the marriage of each of her three younger brothers—the eldest son, the second son and the youngest son—and also of her two younger sisters. After being redeemed by her first younger brother, Yuki met a man who, though well aware of her prostitute past, fell in love with her. When they decided to marry, the war escalated. The man was drafted. The eldest and second sons were drafted, too. ... The

---

65. Although *ine* can simply be explained as a phonetic variation of *ane*, I argue that the difference between *ane* and *ine* is in fact a difference of standard language and local dialect. In other words, this term marks the previously discussed geopolitical binary oppositions of hegemonic North and peripheral South.

second son's wife ran off with a traveling entertainer leaving behind the baby, Fumiaki [Akiyuki's older stepbrother]. Yuki became Fumiaki's carer. She often worried that the wife's departure needed to be kept secret from the second son so that he did not do something reckless like rebel against the government or lose the desire to fight in the war. ...

After the war ended, the eldest son and the second son returned. Eventually, the second son met Fusa, who had five children. The following year, Yuki also started a so-called family. The man was ten years older than her and died five years later. She never became pregnant. She really thought that she was the only one who had been dogged by constant misfortune. As things returned to normal after the war and people emerged from poverty and forgot hunger, each of her three younger brothers and two sisters soon forgot how they had trampled on Yuki's life. She often thought how they had no idea who had helped make them what they were today. She felt that her five siblings, and their partners and even their mistresses, despised her because of her past life as a prostitute.[66]

The reference to her brothers as the first, second, and youngest "sons" implies Yuki's parental role in the family. When she accepts her weeping mother's request that she become a prostitute, Yuki becomes a substitute for the patriarch whose role is to support the family. This was also the moment when Yuki, the daughter, surpassed her aged mother as a mature woman in both economic and sexual potency. Internalising her mother's desire for the reconstruction of a patriarchal family (*ie*), Yuki supports her male siblings' coming of age by sacrificing her own chance to be a respectable wife and mother. Seen in this context, it is not necessarily surprising that those who do not have a role in the succession of the Takehara family, such as her two younger sisters and her dead husband, are seemingly less important for her than her brothers. Although she sees her past as miserable, Yuki feels proud of her contribution to the Take-

---

66. NKZ 3:267–68.

hara family and, because of her strong attachment to her blood kinship, she remains an *ine* even when her age marks her as an *oba*.

When we consider Yuki as a target of *kuchi berashi* (reducing the number of mouths a family needs to feed), her position as the eldest sister who displayed signs of maturity first among her siblings marks her misfortune. In this context, Yuki can be seen as one of many eldest Asian daughters despatched to work in the sex industry. These girls and young women feature in Matsui Yayori's 1985 report entitled "Ajia no baishun chitai o iku" (Visiting prostitution precincts in Asia) in which the author reports that, significantly, there are more eldest daughters than daughters of other sibling rank working as prostitutes in tourist destinations and military bases in Asian countries such as Thailand and the Philippines.[67] Yuki and these Asian prostitutes can be collectively regarded as the most subaltern daughters from the marginalised South.

As seen in the long passage cited above, Yuki's voice, expressed in the form of rambling memories and thoughts, are often presented as third person narration rather than depicted as an actual speaking voice that is heard and responded to by another person. This signifies that her voice is trapped in the framework of the patriarchal narrative which is internalised by both Yuki as a speaker and the people of the *roji* as listeners. Even though this demonstrates her assenting to convention, Yuki is thoroughly constricted by this convention so that her voice echoes in vain throughout a community that regards this aged single former prostitute as deviant. Nakagami's depiction of Yuki's voice can be divided into two main elements: rumors or information about others and the silenced voice that tries to speak its own story. The first implies her desire to be the narrator (*katarite* or *omina*) of the community, while the second demonstrates her *naibu*, inner landscape, which cannot help but regard itself as "trampled" and ultimately polluted.

In the following paragraphs, I will make a close reading of Yuki's tale about the rape of a twelve-year-old intellectually handi-

---

67. Matsui 2009, 215–28.

capped girl (*hakuchi*,[68] literally idiot) who lives in the *roji* with her grandmother. The intellectually handicapped girl is also a key character who demonstrates Nakagami's view of the gendered Buraku woman whose voice is silenced. The rape in question occurs when the "idiot" girl is sexually molested by Tōru, the son of the eldest Takehara son (Jin'ichirō) and his mistress. Tōru is therefore Yuki's nephew. He is also Akiyuki's cousin and co-worker in the business run by Akiyuki's stepfather. Akiyuki and Tōru have sympathised with each other since they were children because of their similarly awkward positions as illegitimate sons in the Takehara family. Akiyuki is furthermore the only person who actually saw Tōru and the girl together at the time that the rape is said to have been committed. Although Akiyuki keeps this secret, rumors soon circulate within the *roji* about Tōru's deed. When the girl's pregnancy becomes obvious, Yuki also knows that it was Tōru who molested the girl. In the *roji*, people begin to claim that the girl had supernatural powers, so that after she "was beaten by her grandmother she began to shine and float in the air, smashing the household Buddhist altar." Some tell the angry grandmother, who is trying to find the rapist, that "when Tōru went up to the hill, the idiot girl followed."[69]

When the pregnancy runs its course and a child is born, although she is aware of Tōru's guilt, Yuki's desire to protect the family name sees her shift blame to the outsider, Akiyuki.

> After a while, the idiot girl gave birth to a child as if it was the height of her humiliation. When the baby was sent to Tōru and his mother, even though Yuki knew that it was Tōru's baby, she felt deceived. ... She tried to believe that it was Akiyuki who had made Tōru responsible. ... Because Akiyuki had been brought to stay at Shigezō's house as Fusa's child, Yuki openly blamed him for the rape of the idiot girl who was as innocent as the gods and the Buddha—the girl might have had her first period, but to play

---

68. NKZ 6:292.
69. NKZ 6:292.

with a virgin vagina that was not ready to accept a man ... was beyond the pale of human behavior.[70]

Because Tōru is one of the sons of her family, Yuki seeks to make Akiyuki her scapegoat. In addition to having no blood relation to the family, he is also known as the killer of his stepbrother Hideo. During the three years of Akiyuki's imprisonment, and in spite of the fact that everyone in the community knows the truth, Yuki circulates her fabricated story. After Tōru suffers a nervous breakdown, Yuki becomes like a devoted mother, treating Tōru as an "idiot child," believing that otherwise she cannot remain in the community.[71] Yuki's sense of responsibility toward Tōru and her desire to excuse his deed demonstrates her position in her family, which is not only that of father and wife or mother, but also, recalling Antigone, the metaphorical wife of her brothers. Rather than their incompetent mothers, it is she who cares for her nephews (Fumiaki and Tōru). Like Antigone, Yuki can be seen as the family's sole devoted and obedient sister who has a metaphorical incestuous relationship with her brothers.

Yet as she talks about the pain experienced by the intellectually handicapped girl, Yuki comes to identify herself with the rape victim. Her identification reveals her desire to be "innocent" like "the gods and the Buddha," while nevertheless implying her self-contempt as *kegare*.

> As if she was delirious with fever, Yuki recalled the time when she first began to work as a prostitute and announced to all in the *roji* how painful it was for an immature vagina to have a penis inserted like a sharp piece of wood and how such a lacerated vagina would become swollen and inflamed. In the process she felt that the idiot girl who left the baby and vanished away with the grandmother was her other self.[72]

---

70. NKZ 6:292.
71. NKZ 6:292.
72. NKZ 6:292.

By speaking for the voiceless vanished girl, Yuki attempts—indulges herself—to use her voice to denounce the atrocity of the rape. In doing so, for the first time she is able to verbalize and express her experience of vaginal pain without the restrictions of the discourse of her duty toward the family. Referring to the internationally acclaimed play by Eve Ensler (b. 1953), *The Vagina Monologues* (premiered 1996), I argue that Yuki's monologue can be regarded as a Burakumin woman's "vagina monologue," that is, a voice of resistance against male violence.

The Vagina Monologues consists of a series of one-woman deliveries based on the playwright's interviews with more than two hundred women from a range of backgrounds including American, Jewish, East Asian, Bosnian, and Afghan. Each monologue addresses a feature of the feminine experience related to subjects such as love, sex, menstruation, rape, masturbation, birth, orgasm, and gynecological examination. Translated into forty-eight languages, *The Vagina Monologues* was largely received as an opportunity for women's voices to speak loudly, to be carefully heard, to be discussed and criticized, and to contribute to a worldwide movement of antiviolence and female empowerment.[73] Ensler explains that she

---

73. See Hammers 2006 and Flanders 2012. Ensler's work has not been without criticism. Her omission of history and the current US intervention in Afghanistan from her poem "Under the Burqa" (2003) has been interpreted as her complicity with the New Empire. Spivak's 1981 essay, "French Feminism in an International Frame," is useful when considering problems associated with Ensler's representation of the experiences of "Third World" women. In this essay, Spivak criticizes Julia Kristeva's work *About Chinese Women* (1977) as an "obsessively self-centred" representation of the histories and lives of Chinese women because it is constituted in terms of the Western female subject. In Spivak's view, Western thinkers often invoke the Other of the West, as Ensler does the woman from Afghanistan, as a way to question their own identity and ideology. See Spivak 1988c, 137. In other words, by invoking the question of the Other (Chinese women) in her analysis, Kristeva actually represents her concern about the theoretical oppression of women's corporeal experience in European culture. Although the language of *The Vagina Monologues* is intended to break "the barriers between self and other, subject and object, West and East, liberated and op-

was born into a middle-class family and received a high-quality education in the United States, and she was the victim of her father's violence. While she was forced to sacrifice her "emotional and psychological well-being," her economically secure circumstances, her education (which was paid for by her violent father), and the strong nation in which she was born gave her the ability to write and act out these women's voices.[74]

The vagina monologue delivered by Yuki, which tells of the ordeal of the voiceless raped girl, is disregarded and disdained by the women and men in her community. By showing the powerlessness of Yuki's voice, Nakagami demonstrates the impossibility of the voice of this gendered subject speaking to or being carefully heard by the mainstream. His depiction of Yuki's unheard monologue about her affiliation with the "idiot girl" articulates the aging woman's hidden desire to self-identify as "innocent" and the self-contempt that marks her inner landscape. This self-contempt reveals the power of the concept of *kegare*, which is internalized by the community as a commonsense idea that dismisses as polluted and thus humiliates the sexually violated woman. The older woman's tragedy is that she can only tell her story by "exploiting" the ordeal of the girl in this way. Ultimately Yuki appropriates the girl's story—which presumably she has never heard—rather than giving the girl a chance to speak. For Yuki, the girl is "innocent" and unable to tell her own story because her mental disability prevents her from understanding or internalizing the hegemonic concept of *kegare*.

Nakagami's depiction of Yuki illustrates that a "vagina mono-

---

pressed" (Shueller 2011, 17), the context of representation in the work paradoxically marks the writer/actor's subjectivity and hegemonic control over the women represented. In this way, *The Vagina Monologues* can be seen as a text that inevitably duplicates the imperialist attitudes of nineteenth-century bourgeois women toward "Third World" women. Nevertheless, Ensler's work constitutes an attempt to have women's voices heard.

74. Ensler 2006, xvi. As Shueller notes, Ensler's work can be seen as exemplifying Cixous's declaration, "Write your self. Your body must be heard." See Shueller 2011, 18, and Cixous 1980, 250.

logue" from the marginalized South can never replicate that from the North, which is valued as a "spellbinding, funny and almost unbearably moving"[75] work of art. It is, on the contrary, a fore-closed "delirious" utterance that can only faintly and momentarily be detected through a representation, such as that provided by Nakagami, of its impossibility to be heard. Drawing on Spivak's words again, Yuki's "resistance" to men by denouncing their rape of sexually immature girls can be seen as a woman's act of "resistance without [the necessary] infrastructure that would make us recognize [the act as] resistance." It is, therefore, "in vain."

Voice of the Aged Mute Woman

I discuss here a second example of a sexually stigmatized aging woman who appears in the last volume of the Akiyuki trilogy: the aged mute, Moyo no oba, who lost her power of speech as a young woman after being raped by *roji* men. As a resident of the outcaste community and a rape victim, she is a subject who experiences multiple layers of oppression within and outside the community. Naka-gami's depiction of Moyo no oba's disability again confirms Spivak's view of the impossibility of "the sexed subaltern subject" having a space in which to make her voice audible.

Although her background is unclear, Moyo no oba is apparently a *roji*-born daughter of the Oritake family.[76] She was once a beautiful young woman who worked as a live-in maid in the house of a wealthy man, Sakura. She became mute after being raped by Ryūzō, who worked for Sakura's lumber business, and his gambling companion, Yoshi. The rape was committed when these young men, on a rampage of terror, broke into the Sakura residence to rob and set fire to the place. Sometime after this dreadful experience, Moyo

---

75. This is an excerpt from the book review of *Variety* quoted in the back cover of *The Vagina Monologues*. See the back cover of Ensler 2001.

76. NKZ 6:121.

came to the *roji* community with a small boy, Ryōichi. (Later, they moved to a neighboring town.) When Mon asked whether Ryōichi was truly her son, Moyo no oba was evasive. Without revealing the identity of the men who attacked her, she "narrated" (*katatta*) the tale of the cruel deeds of two "wolf-like" men who broke into Sakura's house.[77] Although readers are not told how Mon hears and understands the story told by Moyo no oba, who does not speak, the account of the mute woman's "voiceless" *katari* is presented as follows.

> The two men spread gasoline to set the place on fire. After forcing Moyo to hand over everything of value, one of the men attacked her while the other went to the room where the master Sakura slept and emerged after a while, his body splattered with blood, holding an armful of valuable papers that he shoved into a large burlap sack and, as the buttocks of the other moved insistently up and down, he pushed down on those buttocks with his foot in its *jikatabi*, saying "fuck her harder, harder." As Moyo moaned with pain, the man gazed at her with his dark penetrating eyes. When she heard the crackling sound of fire close by and saw that the man had relinquished his hold on the burlap bag, unfastened his belt, pulled down his trousers, and kicked the other off her body, Moyo tried to scream but failed. She had lost her voice since then—although she saw everything they did and was terribly violated by them, Moyo was left alive because they thought this woman would never tell anyone.[78]

A brief exchange between Akiyuki and Sakura in *Chi no hate* indicates that Ryūzō and Yoshi probably kidnapped Moyo after the break-in and continued to rape her over a period of time. Moyo no oba's (mute) voice, like Yuki's "vagina monologue," is always presented as a third-person narrative. This is in contrast to the voice of one of her rapists, which is presented with quotation marks as a

---

77. NKZ 6:129.
78. NKZ 6:129.

speaking voice. Furthermore, the "foreclosed" voice of Moyo no oba is heard and understood only by Mon, another Buraku woman. Following the death of Oryū no oba, Mon assumes an *omina*-like quality to become the "key station" whose memory stores the knowledge of the fragmented *roji* community. Both Mon and Moyo no oba deviate from the patriarchal norm and from mainstream society in general.

Many people in the *roji* community believed that Moyo no oba lost her voice when cursed by "a long-nosed crow goblin" (*karasu tengu*) of local legend. They assumed that Ryōichi was an illegitimate child to whom Moyo secretly gave birth outside the *roji*. Yoshi, however, calls Ryōichi "the child of someone's mistress,"[79] insisting that the boy was abandoned by another party rather than being Moyo's child. In saying this, he excludes Ryōichi from the genealogy of *roji* men the former fanatically believes to be related to Genghis Khan.[80] Moyo no oba's stigmatization by *roji* people as a woman cursed by a devil-like "goblin," which evokes the discourse of the witch hunt, and Yoshi's exclusion of Ryōichi demonstrate how traditional *roji* residents marginalize the unmarried woman and the child whose father is unknown.

As noted, the *roji* is "a maternal place" in which the children, including illegitimate children or those who are neglected by their own families, are raised collectively by the community. It is only in the *roji*, apparently her birthplace, that Moyo can find refuge with her child. Even so, she tended to confine herself indoors as if avoiding the *roji*'s endless rumor and curious eyes.

> Every night in her house in the *roji*, Moyo no oba would chant a sutra. Because she seldom left the house, after chanting she would ask Ryōichi to tell her about things that happened outside. Although he wanted to confess that he had stolen mandarins from the lolly shop … stolen coins from the money basket of the shop … and then secretly gone to the cafeteria to have curry and rice,

---

79. NKZ 6:34.
80. NKZ 6:277–78.

Ryōichi instead told Moyo no oba that a baby with two bodies was born in the Tagami house situated beside the *roji* community well, and that a monster with a face that has no eyes, no nose and no mouth, appears each night in the house of the tinker nicknamed Pariki and begs for the eyes and nose, even ones made of tin, of a normal human. These were all stories that Ryōichi made up to hide what he actually did. In surprise, as if she sympathized with their pain, Moyo no oba made a sound from her throat without forming words, asking Ryōichi to tell her how the Siamese twins would stay and grow up in the *roji*, a place where lame and deformed humans gathered.[81]

Although he wanted to talk about his petty crimes, young Ryōichi would tell Moyo no oba his fabricated stories about "lame and deformed humans." This he did in response to the sounds in her throat which, although "never forming words,"[82] eagerly asked Ryōichi to tell more about *roji* misfits. Understanding Moyo no oba's "voice," Ryōichi narrated his fictions each night.

After Ryōichi tells her the Siamese twins had an operation to become "two humans who have half a body each from the chest down,"[83] Moyo no oba becomes even less inclined to go out. Shutting herself away in her house, she ponders the difference between people who must remain inside and people who are able to walk freely about.

While the lame and deformed humans created by Ryōichi lived in the darkness of the *roji*, those who were able to walk about in the sun were always the people who, in spite of the fact that they had might have had certain factors inside, appeared on the surface to have no stigma. These seemingly unblemished people enjoyed making love and gambling, as if indulging themselves in the pleasure of being born human.[84]

---

81. NKZ 6:317.
82. NKZ 6:317.
83. NKZ 6:318.
84. NKZ 6:318.

Through the presentation of contradictory images such as disabled and "normal," light and darkness, and outside and inside, this passage expresses Moyo no oba's recognition of the binaries within the outcaste community. Her understanding of the stigma lodged within people who saunter about freely asserting their desire can be read as the raped woman's insight into the perverted acts of the men (Ryūzō and Yoshi) who traumatized her and the *roji* people who consigned her to "the darkness." I assert that the mute Moyo no oba is inscribed with the most agonized *mukoku* (silenced voice) status in Nakagami's narratives.

Nakagami's representation of the mute woman's enthusiasm for the narratives of the *roji* in fact recalls the voice of Oryū no oba, which often narrated absurdities and supernatural stories. Given that Ryōichi presents himself to others as an orphan in the care of Moyo no oba, their relationship might be seen as similar to that of Oryū no oba and the Nakamoto boys. It is even possible that Ryōichi is Akiyuki's younger half-brother by Ryūzō. Ryōichi calls his childhood friend Akiyuki "captain." Both are "an illegitimate child of the *roji*" who do not have Nakamoto blood. When he realizes that Akiyuki has never met Moyo no oba (even though she once lived in the community), Ryōichi is amazed. After deciding to introduce Akiyuki to Moyo no oba, Ryōichi comments: "Even though everyone has known about you [Akiyuki] from your birth, you know nothing about us."

While Ryōichi looks for Moyo no oba in her "small and ramshackle house,"[85] Akiyuki sees her outside in her tiny vegetable garden.

> "Are you Moyo no oba of the Oritake?" As Akiyuki spoke, the woman stepped back for a split second with her eyes wide open in horror, pursed her lips and made a hoarse sound like the rustling noise of leaves. ... The sound was not a word, just a noise from her windpipe. When he realized this was because she was mute, Akiyuki halted awkwardly and looked at Ryōichi who was

---

85. NKZ 6:121.

walking toward them. ... "Moyo no oba," Ryōichi said to the woman who had hair like dry straw and who wore a dirt-stained summer dress which looked like a loose nightdress, "this is Akiyuki, a younger brother of the dead Ikuo, the child of Fusa and that man, Ryūzō." Ryōichi spoke as if telling Akiyuki that the oba's hearing was not impaired. When Ryōichi heard the noise that she gasped out, he gave a slight nod, laughed and said, "Captain, she thought you were an electrician." [Akiyuki replied,] "She can't speak very well, can she?" Ryōichi then explained, "She wasn't like that from birth. She lost her voice when she was young—are you sure that you really don't know her story?"[86]

Moyo no oba tells Akiyuki, with Ryōichi mediating, how she lost her voice.

[Moyo explained that] she became mute after drinking tea which had been poisoned by her lover's ex-girlfriend. Her story, however, then changed. One day, at dusk, she heard a flapping of wings from the hill, no trace of which remained today. She looked up. There were people with wings stealthily flying across the blue and dazzlingly clear sky, over a lone pine tree at the top of the hill. Knowing the local legend of goblins who flew far from Korea, China and India ... she knew at one glance that they were these long-nosed crow goblins [karasu tengu]. ... She was so surprised and wanted her neighbors to see them, but when she tried to call out a crow goblin flew down to Moyo and whispered—I'll make you silent for life. She tried to scream but her voice was already lost.[87]

Ryōichi interprets the sounds that come from Moyo no oba's throat, sounds that to Akiyuki are just like "the cry of a beast." He adds the explanation that "after that happened, the oba felt scared of the *roji* and she moved to live here."[88]

---

86. NKZ 6:121.
87. NKZ 6:122.
88. NKZ 6:122.

Moyo no oba tells her story probably only because she is desperate to hide her terror upon seeing Akiyuki, who resembles one of the "wolf-like" men of her traumatic memory. As a result, her storytelling lacks the *omina* quality necessary to narrate the tragic history of the *roji* to the community. Through her son's mediation, her "noise" informs Akiyuki, the ignorant young man from the *roji*, about the community's fear of alien people who come from elsewhere and the cruel way women like the Moyo no oba are oppressed. In other words, Moyo no oba's voice can only be represented as an *omina*'s voice through the son, Ryōichi, who has the ability to comprehend her. Ryōichi's presence as a son is the most significant difference between Moyo no oba and Yuki. Whereas Yuki's voice is simply ignored by community members, including her own family, who dismiss any desire she may have to become *omina*, the beast-like sounds that emerge from Moyo no oba's throat are heard as words and transformed into an audible voice by Ryōichi.

While investigating past atrocities committed by Ryūzō, Akiyuki asks Ryōichi to take him once more to meet Moyo no oba. Although feeling a strong brother-like (homosocial) bond with Akiyuki, Ryōichi firmly rejects this request, which he realizes will lead to an attempt by Akiyuki to force Moyo no oba to reveal her secret. As the pair visit Yoshi in the hospital ward, where the older man lies dying, Ryōichi says to Akiyuki, who has just lost Ryūzō:

> "I will never let you see the mute Moyo no oba no matter how hard you push or threaten me. I have sealed that secret as a secret. Do you remember how I told you the story of the half human? ... I would make myself into a half human by hopping on one foot, closing one eye and using only one hand—I stole things from the lolly shop, I followed the *roji*'s only priest, Reijo, to make fun of him because of the strange way he walked, and I fought boys from other places in the mountains—then I would tell these stories to Moyo no oba. She was always scared of Ryūzō and Yoshi. When they are dead, the half human will no longer be needed. There'll be no need for me to lie any longer."
>
> "You're trying to comfort me, aren't you?" replied Akiyuki;

Ryōichi looked at him with his dark blue eyes and muttered, "Yes, I am."[89]

In stark contrast to Ryūzō, who committed an enigmatic suicide without revealing his real intention to Akiyuki, Ryōichi states his feelings honestly. Ryōichi humiliated himself as a "half human" in response to his mother's silence and the insistence by Yoshi—possibly his father—that the young man was not a child of Moya no oba or indeed of himself. At the same time, this narrative of the half human rescued Ryōichi from the real story of a child born from an act that was so atrocious he may have regretted being born at all. From this perspective, we can read Moyo no oba's silence about her secret—arising from the terror of the rape—and Ryōichi's acceptance, in spite of the cost, of his mother's determination to keep this secret, as the ultimate exchange of love between a mother and son.

Ryōichi's refusal to allow Akiyuki to meet Moyo no oba a second time, and his subsequent explanation of the tale of the half human, can be interpreted as Nakagami's strategy for representing the silenced voice of the most oppressed subject of the South, the aged mute woman. Although it is Ryōichi who declares, "I have sealed that secret as a secret," he does this on behalf of his mother with full knowledge and understanding of the oppressive impact of the extreme sexual violence to which she was subjected. In other words, Nakagami provides an alternative representation of the silenced voice of the sexed woman. This strategy depicts the deep feeling between the old woman and the young man, who have decided never to identify themselves in public as mother and son. This decision has dire consequences for Ryōichi. Supporting his mother in sealing the secret of his birth is to give up access to a genealogy by which he could create an identity for himself within the *roji* community. In this sense, Ryōichi embodies the originless concept of nomadism. This is in stark contrast to his possible father, Yoshi, who is obsessed with a fictional *roji* genealogy deriving

---

89. NKZ 6:434.

from Genghis Khan. Karatani argues that "killing the father" signifies the imperative for the son "to overcome the older generation" so as "to continuously advance."[90] Ryōichi realizes this through his metaphoric "patricide." Akiyuki's acceptance of Ryōichi's statement as a form of comfort suggests an older brother hearing the voice of the younger urging him to break free from the father's oppression and "continuously advance."

In conclusion, Nakagami's view of *monogatari* as a tradition of narration by *omina* provides a strong base for investigating the depiction of *oba* in his narrative. In this chapter I reviewed the role of Oryū no oba in *Sen'nen no yuraku* and how her paradoxical perspective thoroughly contested hegemonic principles such as hierarchical binaries and social identification. I also examined the depiction of Yuki and Moyo no oba in the Akiyuki trilogy. As the voice of a Buraku *oba* who remains alive after the dismantlement of her community, Yuki's voice is depicted as one that, unlike *omina*'s voice, lacks any ability to narrate her view of the world. The representation of Yuki's denunciation of the masculinist exploitation of female sexuality demonstrates Spivak's view of the subaltern woman's resistance, which is inevitably in vain because she is "foreclosed" by the hegemonic society and thereby lacks access to any necessary infrastructure that would permit recognition of her resistance.

Nakagami's inscription of the mute voice of Moyo no oba, on the other hand, is realized through the relationship between a mother and son who, although they refrain from conventionally identifying themselves as such, are nonetheless bonded by a deep love and shared understanding of their subalternity. By depicting this form of kinship, Nakagami demonstrates, among other things, the possibility of being neither *hisabetsu sha* nor *sabetsu sha*, that is, of being a person who never subscribes to the exclusionist practice of identification that rationalizes discrimination against those who deviate from hegemonic norms. The narrative also demonstrates the high cost of taking such a stand.

---

90. Karatani 2006, 175.

Conclusion

This book has explored how Nakagami Kenji inscribed the voices of the *mukoku*—the voiceless—into his narratives. Nakagami was the first published postwar-born writer with a Burakumin background, and many of his narratives feature accounts of life in *hisabetsu buraku* communities in which Buraku people with widely differing experiences live their lives. As a group, these people remain marginalized in Japanese society, and their members can easily be rendered voiceless. I argue that Nakagami's literature is an attempt to address this issue and give voice to a range of individuals within this and other marginalized groups.

In spite of an emphasis in existing scholarship on the strong male characters that appear in Nakagami's corpus, many of the writer's *mukoku* Burakumin are women. Women characters have not been completely absent from commentary on Nakagami's material inside or outside of Japan. But attention has been limited in terms of the range of women found in Nakagami's texts and has often focused on the shaman-like qualities of Oryū no oba, an old woman from the *Sen'nen no yuraku* narrative collection. Alternately, characters like Akiyuki's half-sister, Satoko, have featured merely in terms of the relationship between the woman involved and the protagonist. I have sought to profile the women that I discuss in a way that highlights their subjectivity and even agency. These are attributes that are often unacknowledged in the communities within which these women reside.

Given that Nakagami's narratives largely depict the oppressed lives of women and men Burakumin from his Kishū Kumano homeland, I began my discussion by presenting the author's geopolitical perspective of Kumano as Japan's peripheral "South." As Derrida points out, Nakagami critiques peripherality as an ideology that rationalizes geopolitical binarism, namely, the domination of the marginalized "South" by the hegemonic center of the "North." Drawing on Gramsci's study of subaltern class in southern Italy and Marx's view of ideology as the "ideas of the ruling class," I articulated how the ideas of these thinkers, reinterpreted by scholars such as Spivak, Said, and Karatani, destabilize mainstream representations of social binaries to open the possibility of collapsing those binaries and recognizing the legitimacy of difference. This difference is what Nakagami sought to bring to the fore in his narratives.

The principal theoretical anchor of the book was Spivak's theory of representing the subaltern. This theory largely created the possibility for me to hear the voices of the women in Nakagami's work. I appropriated Spivak's idea of the subaltern (derived from Gramsci), which I argued can be used to understand Nakagami's representations of oppressed Burakumin and how these people have been marginalized by mainstream discourses in Japan. I argued that Spivak's ideas on geopolitics and the role of the intellectual (also derived from Gramsci), have a close parallel to Nakagami's geopolitical perspective and the ambivalence felt by the writer in terms of his position as an outcaste community member who simultaneously held a writer's privilege. Central to my discussion were Spivak's ideas on voice or, more important, voicelessness. In her essay "Can the Subaltern Speak?" and the collection *A Critique of Postcolonial Reason*, Spivak argues that the multiple workings of hegemonic ideologies such as colonialism, imperialism, and patriarchy prevent the subaltern from speaking to or being heard by mainstream society. Spivak warns that the discourse of "the intellectual" or even the "indigenous" representative—in other words, the "native informant"—can possibly close out—"foreclose"—marginalized people. The ultimate exemplar among these marginalized people, according to Spivak, is the poorest woman from the South. These ideas are closely connected to Spivak's notion of "infrastructure," which we might explain as a framework of social support. In a masculinist society, marginalized identities such as the poorest woman from the South are denied access to this infrastructure. This denial entrenches their voiceless state. These women are never granted the role of cultural or political representative for their communities for multiple reasons, such as gender (being a woman), age (not being young), and illiteracy (not being able to access the written word). Even when an intellectual believes they may have presented the voice of the subaltern, the subaltern's true voice is often muted by the hegemonic ideas on which the intellectual draws. I articulated this mechanism as the paradox of representing the silenced voice.

My discussion of Nakagami's short story "Rakudo," featured in chapter 2, demonstrates my approach to the writer's texts. While I examined Nakagami's representation of the voice of a violent young husband, I particularly profiled the silence of the wife. Complementing Spivak's framework with Mizuta's gender critique, I theorized the patriarch's violence against his wife as a typical modern Japanese literary representation of the "discourse of men." This is the masculinist construction of woman as possessing an innate maternal sexuality, about which the male fantasizes in his "private" realm or interiority. Spivak's view of the Hindu practice of sati was particularly useful when considering the protagonist's tyrannical dream of self-immolation with his family as an expression of an ill-tempered patriarch's penchant for the patriarchal dogma of female self-sacrifice and his desire for eternal family unity. Equally as powerful, "Rakudo" depicts the wife's definitive refusal of her husband's desire for her to be the "mother." Distraught when his wife appears as the Other, the husband commits severe violence against the woman who refuses to conform to his fantasy. After suffering this violence, the wife leaves her home with the couple's two young daughters, exposing the loss and emptiness that characterizes the man's inner landscape. While the husband's interiority is revealed, the wife conceals her inner self, even in the letter she sends to her husband after their separation. I articulated the wife's silence as her (un)voiced rejection of and defiance against male violence and patriarchal discourse.

I have noted that existing discussions of Satoko, a woman who features in the Akiyuki trilogy, often present her as little more than a passive prop for her incestuous half-brother, Akiyuki. Focusing in chapter 4 on the historical and cultural context of the sister (*imōto*) and its literary representation, however, I contested this trend by articulating Satoko as an exemplar of Spivak's "sexed subaltern subject" who has "no space" to speak in modern patriarchal society. Satoko's extreme devotion to the water cult, I argued, was the subaltern sister's attempt, like that of Antigone in the ancient Greek drama, to gain a voice by assuming the support of a divine law that is superior to the masculine law of human society. Although she appropriates the cult's "religious" precepts as infrastructure to voice herself, Satoko nonetheless reveals her contempt for herself as *kegare* (impurity) and her strong desire to be pure. While despising the masculinist law as *kegare*, she conspires with that law to humiliate those who are socially discriminated against as *kegare*. In his depiction of Satoko, Nakagami demonstrates the paradox that *hisabetsu sha* (people who are discriminated against) are also *sabetsu sha* (people who themselves discriminate).

Nakagami's narratives are significant for their profound representations of aged women, and chapter 5 discussed the writer's representation of the old women or *oba* from the Kumano Burakumin community. Nakagami's view of the *oba*'s voice was examined by reading his essay on *monogatari* as a tradition of narrating by the *omina*, the old woman with the power to tell stories of and for the community. Drawing on Nakagami's view of *omina* and on Spivak's discussion of the (foreclosed) native informant, I began by considering the voice of the *roji omina*, Oryū no oba, the acclaimed elderly woman featured in *Sen'nen no yuraku*. Nakagami depicts Oryū no oba's voice (or consciousness) as the source of the narration of the religious precepts that underpinned oral communal folklore and historical memories of the oppressed. The absurdity, amorality, and paradox heard in Oryū no oba's voice consistently contested hegemonic principles, including the hierarchical binaries that led to discrimination against Burakumin. Depicting these elements in the *omina*'s voice is one way Nakagami seeks to invalidate hegemonic mainstream thought that refuses the legitimacy of difference.[1]

Chapter 5 also discussed the voices of Yuki and Moyo, two aged outcaste women depicted in the Akiyuki trilogy. With the obliteration of the *roji*, these women had no space from which to become *omina* and narrate their view of the world. Drawing on Spivak, I read Yuki's monologue about the wounding of the immature vagina of the intellectually disabled girl as a representation of the "native" voice that can only speak by appropriating the experience of a subject as oppressed as herself. Yuki's voice is nonetheless completely disregarded by the mainstream. This erasure of the aged *oba*'s voice confirms Spivak's view that since the subaltern woman lacks access to the masculinist "infrastructure" that would authorize her voice, her resistance is inevitably in vain.

Moyo no oba, who became mute after being raped by *roji* men as a young woman, was examined as an exemplar of Nakagami's representation of the most oppressed woman from the subaltern South. Her speaking disability is a striking metonym for Spivak's claim of the impossibility of the sexed subaltern subject having a space to speak. I nevertheless theorized agency in her silence, which, I argued, expressed her "voice," or her desire, to protect her son from the agonizing reality of his origin as the child of a brutal rape. Perceiving his mother's position, the son interprets her "beast-like" voice to inform Akiyuki about the cruel nature of community which, while refusing to "hear" Moyo's silence, tries to force her to speak. By depicting the unconventional kinship between a mother

---

1. Although *Sen'nen no yuraku* portrays Oryū no oba as a marginalized and therefore transcendent figure who becomes the great mother of the community, by the time of *Chi no hate* and the effacement of the *roji*, the site of the *omina*'s narratives, Oryū no oba has died and her voice is no longer heard. The exception to this is *Kiseki* (*The miracle*, 1989), in which the narratives of the *Sen'nen no yuraku omina* feature merely as the hallucination of an aged alcoholic man who was committed to a psychiatric hospital after the effacement of the *roji*.

and son who mutually forgo identifying themselves in terms of this relationship, Nakagami represents the silenced voice that narrates deep mutual love and compassion. Limited though it is and in spite of her horrific experience, Moyo paradoxically has the infrastructure of her son's support, which enabled this mute woman to speak at least partially or, when she chose, to remain silent.

Nakagami's texts clearly feature a range of important male characters, and I sometimes focus on their activities. A key objective of this book was to profile several texts not widely discussed in Nakagami scholarship. In chapter 2 I discussed examples of Nakagami's early work critiquing the perspective of the late 1960s New Left. Examples included the author reading a verse by Osada Hiroshi and his engagement with the discourse of Yoshimoto Takaaki, also a spirited poet and theorist who had a strong influence on Japan's New Left. I also examined a number of early writings to investigate Nakagami's attempts to represent the inner voices of transgressive young men, including himself. I discussed the young writer's criticism of New Left representation of itself as a gathering of "romantic, collective and agonized" subjects. I also considered Yoshimoto Takaaki's 1960s theory of *taishū no genzō* (archetypal image of the masses) to provide insights into the collective *taishū* identity of Japanese society. The collective identity Yoshimoto proposed, however, was one that Nakagami saw as difference-erasing. Through juxtaposing his "uneducated" half-brother from the marginalized Kumano community with elite New Left activists from the urban *taishū* society, Nakagami clearly demonstrated the deep dichotomy between periphery and center, illiterate and literate. While feeling contempt for New Left writers, Nakagami was nonetheless aware that unlike his illiterate half-brother, he himself was one of that privileged group of young people who had a choice to commit themselves to literature and/or activism. For Nakagami, literacy was the most significant difference between himself and his half-brother—literally a difference of life or death.

In terms of presenting material that did not feature in previous scholarship, I note once more the significance of the 1976 narrative

"Rakudo." This text presents a transgressive man committing violence against his family as a means of expressing his voice and a wife whose voice is largely but not completely erased by his violence. In spite of what is arguably the critical importance of that text in demonstrating Nakagami's capacity to write the human condition in extremes, "Rakudo" has rarely been discussed inside or outside Japan.

In addition to introducing little-known Nakagami works, my discussion revisited works that a number of scholars have considered previously. The notion of the transgressive young man was apparent in Nakagami's discussion of the nineteen-year-old serial killer Nagayama Norio, as expressed in the widely analyzed essay "Hanzaisha Nagayama Norio kara no hōkoku." For Nakagami, Nagayama's voice was the self-expression of the illiterate offender who had no access to the act of writing. This realization created a turning point for Nakagami, who thereby found his own literary voice, one that did not resort to any exterior ideologies and that had the capacity to write the "bare" voices of transgressive youth afflicted by loss. This, I argued, is the foundation of Nakagami's autobiographical yet clearly fictional short stories and the fictional Akiyuki trilogy. Both depict the activities of violent young men.

Accordingly, I provided a rereading of the Akiyuki trilogy and *Sen'nen no yuraku*, two of Nakagami's most widely circulated and discussed narratives dealing with transgressive outcaste men. In doing so, I provided a new interpretation of aspects of both works, particularly the Akiyuki trilogy. Chapter 3 focused on the Akiyuki trilogy to analyze the author's depiction of the voice of a transgressive young man, Akiyuki, and his subaltern family and community located in a Kumano *roji*. While I reviewed "Misaki" and *Kareki nada*, the first two narratives of the trilogy, this was principally to provide a foundation for my reading of the final work, *Chi no hate shijō no toki*. The focus of my analysis of "Misaki" and *Kareki nada* was the violation of taboos, including Akiyuki committing incest with his half-sister and murdering his half-brother. I noted how these acts could be read as the son's patricidal challenge against the father. I articulated how the father and son's rivalrous relationship was marked by characteristics that were both Oedipal and homosexual. Drawing on the theory of *monogatari* by Hasumi and on Nakagami's own ideas about this genre of written expression, I discussed how Akiyuki's transgressive acts were generated by the powerful law of narrative that invokes the cyclic repetition of tragic events and by the rumors related to the matrilineal family that are endlessly circulated by members of the *roji* community.

Although Spivak was useful in this respect in terms of the subalternity of these male characters, I also examined Sedgwick on homosociality. It is clear that in spite of Nakagami's often sensitive and insightful representation of women's experiences, the textual space of his narratives is a very homosocial environment. Drawing on Sedgwick, I read the incestuous encounter between Akiyuki and Satoko, for example, as the brother's exploitation of his half-sister's sexuality in an Oedipal challenge that conceals the young man's "homosocial" desire to consolidate his bond with the father. The misogynistic view of Satoko as "useless" held by her father and brother clearly demonstrates her subalternity in the male homosocial bond.

The importance of folklore and oral tradition to Nakagami is well known, and in chapter 4 I investigated the use of "Kyōdai shinjū," a ballad from the Kasuga Burakumin precinct, in the writer's narration of the incest committed by Akiyuki against Satoko. By inscribing the "Kyōdai shinjū" narrative into the Akiyuki trilogy, Nakagami depicts Satoko's silenced voice as attempting to territorialize her brother and defy her father as an embodiment of patriarchal social authority. Nakagami understood "Kyōdai shinjū" as a narrative brought to his hometown by Burakumin women who worked as migrant factory girls (*jokō*) in the silk industry during the modern era. The writer reads the ballad as the hidden voice of these women and as an account of the oppressive social penalties imposed by the community on deviance. Through referring to Yanagita's study of *imo no chikara* (the power of woman), I interpreted the sister (*imōto*) in the ballad as the gendered subject silenced by modern patriarchal ideologies. My reading presented "Kyōdai shinjū" as the narrative of a sister's unspeakable love for her brother and her defiance against masculinist kinship/state law. Drawing on Judith Butler's analysis of *Antigone*, I argued that "Kyōdai shinjū" narrates the archetypal representation of the sister's death as a form of marriage to her brother. The ballad also articulates the penalty demanded by the hegemonic law for those who transgress. For Satoko, Akiyuki's departure from the *roji* was a sign for her to break her attachment to the "Kyōdai shinjū" narrative that fed her fear of death as the consequence of incestuous love. This suggests that the sexed sister's silenced voice was finally heard by her beloved brother, who in turn felt strong affection (*itoshisa*) for her.

In an argument on the theme of voicelessness, language paradoxically must play a major role. Chapter 1 considered Nakagami's sense of responsibility as a "person who has [the power of] language." This discussion focused on an excerpt from the nonfiction travel journal *Kishū*, in which the writer relates a meeting with Burakumin fishermen. In private conversation with a local fisherman's wife after that meeting, Nakagami became aware of the trinary hierarchy between himself as a writer with a power of language, the local Burakumin representatives who presented the "legitimate" community position that there was no discrimination against Burakumin fisherman, and the voiceless people who were absent from or whose voices were closed out of the meeting. Through "unlearning" his writerly privilege, Nakagami was able to have an informal conversation with this woman, who ambiguously narrated the unfair differences in port use charges between traditional and newcomer Burakumin fishermen. By writing these experiences, Nakagami became conscious of difference as structural discrimination generated by the various power relationships between a community and the outside and, importantly, within the members of a community itself.

The issue of language is intimately associated with discrimination, and unlike the first two volumes of the trilogy, *Chi no hate* unambiguously depicts both Akiyuki's background and the *roji* community as associated with the outcaste context through inscribing the text with derogatory Burakumin terms like *eta* and *yotsu*. These are terms related to the concept of *kegare*, which has justified discrimination against the Burakumin through various eras. *Chi no hate* stands apart from "Misaki" and *Kareki nada* because it was written after Nakagami's identification of himself as a novelist who chose to "become a Burakumin." With this in mind, I analyzed *Chi no hate* as Nakagami's representation of the voice of the Burakumin. Foregrounding the writer's claim that *hisabetsu sha* are also *sabetsu sha*, I argued that this claim was an expression of Nakagami's desire to become nothing, that is, to become neither *hisabetsu sha* nor *sabetsu sha*.

The works discussed here by no means cover the full range of Nakagami's literary production. As evident in *Nichirin no tsubasa* (*Wings of the sun*, 1984) and *Sanka* (*Paean*, 1990), a key theme of his narratives depicted from the mid-1980s to his death in 1992 is the representation of the diaspora-like drift of the Burakumin, whose homeland has been lost. He profiled people such as yakuza or sex workers who gather in various marginal spaces left behind or reproduced by capitalist expansion and urbanization projects. Following this model, *Keibetsu* (*Scorn*, 1992) depicts a young migrant woman striptease dancer who works in Kabuki chō, Tokyo. Referencing the statement made by Nakagami after the loss his homeland that "the *roji* is everywhere," Hideo Levy explains that the *Keibetsu* setting, Tokyo's largest and most notorious entertainment district, became for Nakagami one of many variations of the *roji*.[2] Marketed as a "novel of romantic love,"[3] *Keibetsu* was serialized in *Asahi shinbun* between February and October 1991 and published in book form in July 1992, just a month before the writer passed away at the age of forty-six. Over 600 pages in length, this is the only completed narrative among a number—including *Izoku* (*A different clan*), *Wani no*

2. See Levy's comment in an NHK documentary film titled *Sakka Nakagami Kenji no sekai* (*The world of the writer, Nakagami Kenji*, 1996).

3. NKZ 11:424.

seiiki (*Sanctuary of the crocodile*), *Neppū* (*Hot wind*), and *Ran no sūkō* (*The sublimity of the orchid*)—that were written concurrently throughout the early 1990s until the decline in Nakagami's health. There is currently no English-language discussion of these later works that explores Nakagami's representation of the unheard voice of the oppressed. Expanding the scope of the current study in this way would permit an investigation of Nakagami as a writer of the transnational community that emerged in Japan in the context of globalization and neoliberalism.

I conclude by once more drawing attention to the fact that referencing Spivak in my analysis has permitted me to read Nakagami in a way that reveals previously unrecognized aspects of his work. Without this theoretical base, it would not have been possible for me to profile the sexually stigmatized woman who appear in the writer's texts. By revisiting the voices of key male characters, I articulated how the masculinist practice and ideologies that underpin many of the writer's works often render women characters voiceless. These women variously narrate love, desire, and resistance in largely unheard dialogue among themselves and with the key men who have been the focus of much previous scholarship. While never denying the attention given in Nakagami's narratives to transgressive men, I see his works as also providing a distinctive representation of the silenced subaltern woman. It is easy to read *Hōsenka* (*Touch-me-not*, 1980), a work that profiles Akiyuki's mother as the protagonist, as a text that principally depicts the protagonist woman as an object of the gaze of the male characters and of her writer son, Nakagami. It is certainly not an incorrect reading to conclude that women in many of Nakagami's works can be devices that highlight the homosocial and patriarchal desire of powerful men. Yet Spivak's theoretical framework opens up the writer's texts in a way that permits an in-depth engagement with these women.

Nakagami's narratives reveal the paradoxical circumstances of oppressed women who, though they strongly desire to have their voices heard, lack the infrastructure necessary for this to happen in the highly masculinist communities in which they are located. Any

attempt to access this infrastructure generally results in harsh punishment. To assume the voice of the "divine" law in her challenge
against the human law of the father and society, Satoko must endure
the severe penance of the water cult, that is, she must physically
harm herself to purify her "polluted" body. Although supported by
her prosperous brothers after returning from the brothel, the aged
eldest sister and former prostitute Yuki never frees herself from the
stigma that is visited upon her by her siblings and neighbors as a
polluted former sex worker. Although Moyo's mute voice is understood by her secret son as a mother's protective love, she is eternally
silenced by the unspeakable memory of rape. These women characters demonstrate the many ways Nakagami tirelessly accepted the
ongoing paradoxical challenge to represent the silenced voice of society's Other. This Other was not confined merely to the transgressive men profiled in the first Nakagami "boom" but also included
the doubly oppressed women of Japan's subaltern community.

Bibliography

Akamatsu Keisuke. 1993. *Onna no rekishi to minzoku*. Tokyo: Akashi shoten.

Akiyama Shun. 1991. *Teihon: Naibu no ningen*. Tokyo: Ozawa shoten.

Akuzawa Mariko. 2016. "Changing Patterns of Discrimination in Japan: Rise of Hate Speech and Exclusivism on the Internet, and Challenges to Human Rights Education." *Taiwan Human Rights Journal* 3 (4): 37–50.

Amos, Timothy D. 2011. *Embodying Difference: The Making of Burakumin in Modern Japan*. Honolulu: University of Hawai'i Press.

Asada Akira. 1984. *Kozō to chikara: Kigō ron o koete*. Tokyo: Keisō shobō.

———. 1996. "Nakagami Kenji o saidōnyū suru." In *Gunzō Nihon no sakka 24: Nakagami Kenji*, edited by Karatani Kōjin, 22–34. Tokyo: Shōgakukan.

Asada Akira, Karatani Kōjin, Hasumi Shigehiko, and Miura Masashi. 2002. *Kindai nihon no hihyō*, vol. 2. Tokyo: Kōdansha bungei bunko.

Asada Akira, Okuizumi Hikaru, Karatani Kōjin, and Watanabe Naomi. 2000. "Sai/sabetsu, soshite monogatari no seisei." In *Nakagami Kenji to Kumano*, 216–59. Tokyo: Ōta shuppan.

Asano Urara. 2014. *Mo no ryōiki: Nakagami Kenji sakuhin kenkyū*. Tokyo: Kanrin shobō.

Ashcroft, Bill, Gareth Griffiths, and Helen Tiffin. 1989. *The Empire Writes Back: Theory and Practice in Post-Colonial Literatures*. London: Routledge.

———. 2007. *Post-Colonial Studies: The Key Concepts*. London: Routledge.

Austin, John Langshaw. 1962. *How to Do Things with Words: The William James Lectures Delivered at Harvard University in 1955*. Oxford: Clarendon Press.

Barthes, Roland. 1977. *Image-Music-Text*. Translated by Stephen Heath. New York: Hill and Wang.

Bauman, Zygmunt. 2001. *Community: Seeking Safety in an Insecure World*. Cambridge: Polity.

Bhabha, Homi K. 2012. *The Location of Culture*. London: Taylor and Francis.

Bondy, Christopher. 2015. *Voice, Silence, and Self: Negotiations of Buraku Identity in Contemporary Japan*. Cambridge, MA: Harvard University Asia Center.

Buraku mondai, jinken jiten. 2001. Osaka: Buraku kaihō jinken kenkyūjo.

Buraku mondai jiten. 2000. Osaka: Kaihō shuppansha.

Busia, Abena P. A. 1989. "Silencing Sycorax: On African Colonial Discourse and the Unvoiced Female." *Cultural Critique* 14: 81–104.

Butler, Judith. 1990. *Gender Trouble: Feminism and the Subversion of Identity*. New York: Routledge.

———. 2000. *Antigone's Claim: Kinship between Life and Death*. New York: Columbia University Press.

Cixous, Hélène. 1980. "The Laugh of the Medusa." In *New French Feminism*, edited by Elaine Marks and Isabelle de Courtivron. New York: Schocken.

Cornyetz, Nina. 1999. *Dangerous Women, Deadly Words: Phallic Fantasy and Modernity in Three Japanese Writers*. Stanford, CA: Stanford University Press.

———. 2010. "Peninsular Cartography: Topology in Nakagami Kenji's Kishū." In *Perversion and Modern Japan: Psychoanalysis, Literature, Culture*, edited by Nina Cornyetz and Keith Vincent, 125–44. London: Routledge.

Derrida, Jacques. 1976. *Of Grammatology*. Translated by Gayatri Chakravorty Spivak. Baltimore: Johns Hopkins University Press.

———. 1982. "Différance." In *Margins of Philosophy*, translated by Alan Bass, 3–27. Chicago: University of Chicago Press.

Daijisen. 1995. Tokyo: Shōgakukan.

Deleuze, Gilles, and Félix Guattari. 2004. *A Thousand Plateaus*. Translated by Brian Massumi. New York: Continuum.

Eagleton, Terry. 1999. "Review of Gayatri Chakravorty Spivak, A Critique of Postcolonial Reason: Toward a History of the Vanishing Present." *London Review of Books* 21 (10): 3–6.

Enchi Fumiko. 1994. "Fuyu no tabi: Shisha to no taiwa." In *Nihon gensō bungaku shūsei: Enchi Fumiko*, 112–41. Tokyo: Tosho kankōkai.

Ensler, Eve. 2001. *The Vagina Monologues*. New York: Villard.

————. 2006. *Insecure at Last: Losing It in Our Security-Obsessed World*. New York: Random House.

Etō Jun. 1995. *Seijuku to sōshitsu: 'Haha' no hōkai*. Tokyo: Kōdansha bungei bunko.

————. 1992. "'Roji' to takai: Koe to moji to buntai." In Nakagami Kenji, *Sen'nen no yuraku*, 252-91. Tokyo: Kawade bunko.

————. 1996. "Bungei jihyō: Showa 52 nen 2 gatsu." In *Gunzō Nihon no sakka 24: Nakagami Kenji*, edited by Karatani Kōjin, 142–45. Tokyo: Shōgakukan.

ETV tokushū Nagayama Norio hyakujikan no kokuhaku: Fūin sareta seishin kantei no shinjitsu. 2012. Documentary film broadcasted by NHK. Produced by Masuda Hideki.

ETV tokushū Roji no koe chichi no koe: Nakagami Kenji o sagashite. 2016. Documentary film broadcasted by NHK. Filmed by Okada Tōru.

Faulkner, William. 1991. *Absalom, Absalom!* New York: Vintage.

————. 2003. "Remarks on Absalom, Absalom!" In *William Faulkner's Absalom, Absalom!: A Casebook*, edited by Fred Hobson, 283–90. New York: Oxford University Press.

Ferry, Luc, and Alain Renaut. 1990. *French Philosophy of the Sixties: An Essay on Antihumanism*. Translated by Mary Schnackenberg Cattani. Amherst: University of Massachusetts Press.

Flanders, Laura. 2012. "Eve Ensler Rising." *The Nation*, November 26, 2012, 11–17.

Foucault, Michel, and Gilles Deleuze. 1977. "Intellectuals and Power: A Conversation between Michel Foucault and Gilles Deleuze." Translated by Donald F. Bouchard and Sherry Simon. In *Language, Counter Memory, Practice: Selected Essays and Interviews*, edited by Donald F. Bouchard, 205–17. Oxford: Basil Blackwell.

Fowler, Edward. 1988. *The Rhetoric of Confession: Shishōsetsu in Early Twentieth-Century Japanese Fiction*. Berkeley: University of California Press.

————. 2000. "The Buraku in Modern Japanese Literature: Texts and Contexts." *Journal of Japanese Studies* 26 (1) (Winter): 1–39.

Freud, Sigmund. 1976. "The Dissolution of the Oedipus Complex." Translated by James Strachey. In *On Sexuality*, edited by Angela Richards, 7: 313–22. Harmondsworth: Penguin.

Gramsci, Antonio. 1971. *Selections from the Prison Notebooks*. Edited by Quintin Hoare and Geoffrey Nowell Smith. Translated by Quintin Hoare. London: Lawrence and Wishart.

———. *The Antonio Gramsci Reader*. 2000. Edited by David Forgacs. Translated by Quintin Hoare. New York: New York University Press.

Guha, Ranajit. 1982. *Subaltern Studies: Writinga on South Asian History and Society*, vol. 1. Oxford: Oxford University Press.

Hammers, Michele L. 2006. "Talking about 'Down There:' The Politics of Publicizing the Female Body through *The Vagina Monologues*." *Women's Studies in Communication* 26 (2): 220–43.

Haniya Yutaka. 1998–2001. *Haniya Yutaka zenshū*. 19 vols. Tokyo: Kōdansha.

Hartley, Barbara. 2003. "The Mother as Artifice and Desire in Enchi Fumiko, Ariyoshi Sawako and Tanizaki Jun'ichirō." PhD diss., University of Queensland.

———. 2013. "The High Treason Incident, Ōishi Seinosuke and the Shingū Group." In *Japan and the High Treason Incident*, edited by Masako Gavin and Ben Middleton, 159–71. London: Routledge.

Hasumi Shigehiko. 1984. *Shōsetsu ron = Hihyō ron*. Tokyo: Seidosha.

———. 1985. *Monogatari hihan josetsu*. Tokyo: Chūō kōronsha.

———. 1994. *Shōsetsu kara tōku hanare te*. Tokyo: Chūō kōronsha.

Hasumi Shigehiko, Watanabe Naomi, Asada Akira, and Karatani Kōjin. 1994. "Nakagami Kenji o megutte: Sōkeisei to ekurichūru." *Hihyō kūkan* 12: 18–45.

Hatanaka Toshiyuki. 2004. *Mibun, sabetsu, aidentiti: 'Buraku shi' wa bohyō to naru ka*. Kyoto: Kamogawa shuppan.

Hayashi Tatsuo. 1940. "Imo no chikara." *Asahi shinbun*, December 19.

Hijikata Tetsu. 1992a. "Buraku mondai to bungaku o kangaeru." *Asahi shinbun*, October 7.

———. 1992b. "Dōhyō: Nakagami Kenji o itamu." *Buraku kaihō* (October): 58–59.

Hirano Hidehisa. 1982. "'Roji' no motsu imi: Nakagami Kenji ron." In *Bungaku no naka no hisabetsu buraku zō: Sengo hen*, edited by Umezawa Toshihiko, Hirano Hidehisa, and Yamagishi Takashi, 269–85. Tokyo: Akashi shoten.

Ichinotani futaba gunki. 1968. *Nihon koten bungaku taikei*, vol. 99, edited by Yūda Yoshio. Tokyo: Iwanami shoten.

Iguchi Tokio. 2004. *Kiki to tōsō: Ōe Kenzaburō to Nakagami Kenji.* Tokyo: Sakuhinsha.

Iida, Yumiko. 2002. *Rethinking Identity in Modern Japan.* London: Routledge.

Inoue Kiyoshi. 1969. *Buraku no rekishi to kaihō riron.* Tokyo: Tabata shoten.

Irigaray, Luce. 1985. *Speculum of the Other Woman.* Translated by Gillian Gill. Ithaca, NY: Cornell University Press.

Ishikawa Kazuo. 1977. *Ishikawa Kazuo gokuchū nikki.* Tokyo: San'ichi shobō.

Ishikawa, Machiko. 2011. "Nakagami Kenji's 'Writing Back to the Centre' through the Subaltern Narrative: Reading the Hidden Outcaste Voice in 'Misaki' and *Kareki nada.*" *New Voices* 5: 1–24.

———. 2012. "Keibetsu: 1991 nen ni egakareta onna no monogatari." *Kumano daigaku bunshū Go-oh* 9: 151–70.

Jacobs, Carol. 1996. "Dusting Antigone." *MLN* 3 (5): 890–917.

Kadooka Nobuhiko. 2016. *Fushigi na buraku mondai.* Tokyo: Chikuma shobō.

Kang Okcho. 1999. "Shoki Gramsci no shisō to Italia nanbu shugi." *Jōkyō* 10 (3): 127–44.

Karatani Kōjin. 1996. *Marukusu sono kanōsei no chūshin.* Tokyo: Kōdansha gakujutsu bunko.

———. 2000. "Hajime ni." In *Nakagami Kenji to Kumano,* 4–7. Tokyo: Ōta shuppan.

———. 2004. *Teihon Karatani Kōjin shū 5: Rekishi to hanpuku.* Tokyo: Iwanami shoten.

———. 2006. *Sakaguchi Ango to Nakagami Kenji.* Tokyo: Kōdansha bungei bunko.

———. 2012a. *History and Repetition,* edited by Seiji M. Lippit. New York: Columbia University Press.

———. 2012b. "Nakagami Kenji no shi." In *Bessatsu Taiyō: Nakagami Kenji,* edited by Takazawa Shūji, 4–5. Tokyo: Heibonsha.

Karatani Kōjin and Kawamura Jirō. 1996. "Nakagami Kenji: Jidai to bungaku." In *Gunzo Nihon no sakka 24: Nakagami Kenji,* edited by Karatani Kōjin, 149–67. Tokyo: Shōgakukan.

Karatani Kōjin, Eve Zimmerman, Suga Hidemi, Yomota Inuhiko, and Watanabe Naomi. 2000. "Sen'nen no bungaku: Nakagami Kenji to Kumano." In *Nakagami Kenji to Kumano,* 175–215. Tokyo: Ōta shuppan.

Karlsson, Mats. 2001. *The Kumano Saga of Nakagami Kenji*. Edsbruk: Aka-demitryck AB.

———. 2009. "Review of Eve Zimmerman's 'Out of the Alleyway: Naka-gami Kenji and the Poetics of Outcaste Fiction'." *Japanese Studies* 29 (1) (May): 162–64.

———. 2014. "Ōbei ni okeru Nakagami Kenji hihyō gaikan." In *Naka-gami Kenji shū: Geppō*, 5:2–13. Tokyo: Inscript.

Kashima Shigeru. 2009. *Yoshimoto Takaaki 1968*. Tokyo: Heibonsha shin-sho.

Katayama Kazuo. 2010. "Shūdan Shūshokusha no kōdo keizai seichō." *Ningen jōhōgaku kenkyū* 15: 11–28.

Kawaguchi Emiko. 2007. "'Mibōjin' no tōjō. Meiji, Taishō ki no mibōjin zō." *Nihon joshi daigaku: Ningen shakai kenkyū kiyō* 13: 91–108.

Kawamoto Yoshikazu. 2000. "Taiko no oto: Nakagami Kenji to buraku mondai." *Buraku kaihō* (November): 60–71.

Kawamura Minato. 1983. "Nakagami Kenji 'Chi no hate shijō no toki': sekai no fukusō." *Bungei* (July): 200–209.

Keibetsu. 2011. Directed by Hiroki Ryūichi. Kadokawa Pictures.

Kobayashi Toshiaki. 2009. *Chichi to ko no shisō: Nihon no kindai o yomi toku*. Tokyo: Chikuma shinsho.

Kōjien. 1983. 3rd ed., edited by Shinmura Izuru. Tokyo: Iwanami shoten.

Kojiki. 1968. Translated by Donald L. Philippi. Tokyo: University of Tokyo Press.

Kojima Nobuo. 1988. *Hōyō kazoku*. Tokyo: Kōdansha bungei bunko.

Komashaku Kimi. 1987. *Natsume Sōseki to iu hito: Wagahai wa wagahai de aru*. Tokyo: Shisō no kagaku sha.

Komori Yōichi. 1999. *Shōsetsu to hihyō*. Tokyo: Seori shobō.

Koyama Shizuko. 1992. *Ryōsai kenbo to iu kihan*. Tokyo: Keisō shobō.

Kurata Yōko. 2010. *Kataru rōjo katarareru rōjo: Nihon kingendai bungaku ni miru onna no oi*. Tokyo: Gagugei shorin.

Kurihara Miwako. 2008. *Tarō ga koi o suru koro made ni wa*. Tokyo: Gentōsha.

Kurokawa Midori. 1999. *Ika to dōka no aida: Hisabetsu buraku ninshiki no kiseki*. Aoki shoten.

———. 2011. *Kindai Buraku shi: Meiji kara gendai made*. Tokyo: Heibonsha.

———. 2016. *Tsukurareta "jinshu": Buraku sabetsu to reishizumu*. Tokyo: Yūshisha.

Landry, Donna, and Gerald M. MacLean. 1996. "Reading Spivak." In *The*

Spivak Reader, edited by Donna Landry and Gerald M. MacLean, 1–14. New York: Routledge.

Long, Margherita. 2006. "Nakagami and the Denial of Lineage: On Maternity, Abjection, and the Japanese Outcast Class." *Differences: A Journal of Feminist Cultural Studies* 17 (2): 1–32.

Loomba, Ania. 1998. *Colonialism/Postcolonialism*. London: Routledge.

Levy, Ian Hideo. 1995. "Nihon go no sukēru ni fureta toki." In *Nakagami Kenji zenshu: Geppō*, edited by Karatani Kōjin, Asada Akira, Yomota Inuhiko, and Watanabe Naomi, 5: 3–4. Tokyo: Shūeisha.

Maruya Saiichi. 1989. "Tanizaki Jun'ichirō shō senpyō." *Chūō kōron* 11 (1989): 388–90.

Marx, Karl. 1963. *The Eighteenth Brumaire of Louis Bonaparte*. New York: International Publishers.

Marx, Karl, and Frederick Engels. 1970. "The German Ideology." In *The German Ideology*, translated by W. Lough, 33–120. New York: International Publishers.

Matsui Yayori. 2009. "Ajia no baishun chitai o iku." In *Shinpen Nihon no feminizumu 6: Sexuality*, 215–28. Tokyo: Iwanami shoten.

Matsuura Rieko. 1995. "Taisetsu na dansei sakka." In *Nakagami Kenji zenshū: Geppō*, edited by Karatani Kōjin, Asada Akira, Yomota Inuhiko, and Watanabe Naomi, 7: 4–5. Tokyo: Shūeisha.

McCormack, Noah. 2002. "Buraku Emigration in the Meiji Era: Other Ways to Become 'Japanese.'" *East Asian History* 23: 87–108.

McKnight, Anne. 1999. "Crypticism, or Nakagami Kenji's Transplanted Faulkner: Plants, Saga and Sabetsu." *Faulkner Journal of Japan* 1, http://www.faulknerjapan.com/journal/No1/anne.htm (accessed March 19, 2019).

———. 2011. *Nakagami, Japan: Buraku and the Writing of Ethnicity*. Minneapolis: University of Minnesota Press.

Mizuta Noriko. 1993. *Monogatari to han monogatari no fūkei: Bungaku to josei no sōzōryoku*. Tokyo: Tabata shoten.

Mizuta Lippit, Noriko. 1980. *Reality and Fiction in Modern Japanese Literature*. Armonk, NY: M. E. Sharpe.

Monnet, Livia. 1996a. "Ghostly Women, Displaced Femininities and Male Family Romances: Violence, Gender and Sexuality in Two Texts by Nakagami Kenji: Part 1." *Japan Forum* 8 (1): 13–34.

———. 1996b. "Ghostly Women, Displaced Femininities and Male Family Romances: Violence, Gender and Sexuality in Two Texts by Naka-gami Kenji: Part 2." *Japan Forum* 8 (2): 221–39.

Morikawa Tatsuya. 1968. *Haniya Yutaka ron.* Tokyo: Shinbisha.

Morris, Mark. 1996. "Gossip and History; Nakagami, Faulkner, García Márquez." *Japan Forum* 8 (1): 13–34.

Morris, Mark. 1999. "The Untouchables." Review of *The Cape and Other Stories from the Japanese Ghetto*, by Kenji Nakagami. *New York Times*, October 24.

Moriyasu Toshiji. 2003. *Nakagami Kenji ron: Kumano, roji, gensō.* Osaka: Kaihō shuppansha.

Morton, Stephen. 2003. *Gayatri Chakravorty Spivak.* London: Routledge.

Mouffe, Chantal. 1979. "Hegemony and Ideology in Gramsci." In *Gramsci and Marxist Theory*, edited by Chantal Mouffe, 168–204. New York: Routledge.

Mulvey, Laura. 1975. "Visual Pleasure and Narrative Cinema." *Screen* 16 (3): 6–18.

Nagashima Takayoshi. 1996. "Shūrokubun kaisetsu." In *Gunzō Nihon no sakka 24: Nakagami Kenji*, 299–306. Tokyo: Shōgakukan.

Nagayama Norio. 1990. *Kibashi.* Tokyo: Kawade Bunko.

Nakagami Kenji. 1982. *Hanzo's Bird.* Translated by Ian Hideo Levy. Tokyo: Nihon Hon'yakuka Yōsei Center.

———. 1991. "Keibetsu no rensai o oete." *Asahi shinbun*, October 22.

———. 1995–1996. *Nakagami Kenji zenshū* (NKZ), edited by Karatani Kōjin, Asada Akira, Yomota Inuhiko, and Watanabe Naomi. 15 vols. Tokyo: Shūeisha.

———. 1998. "Monogatari/han-monogatari o meguru 150 satsu." In *Hyōden: Nakagami Kenji*, edited by Takazawa Shūji, 243–52. Tokyo: Shūeisha.

———. 1999a. "Watashi wa 'nihonjin' nanoka." In *Nakagami Kenji hatsugen shūsei*, edited by Karatani Kōjin and Suga Hidemi, 6: 337–45. Tokyo: Daisan bunmeisha.

———. 1999b. "The Cape." Translated by Eve Zimmerman. In *The Cape and Other Stories from the Japanese Ghetto*, 1–91. Berkeley, CA: Stone Bridge Press.

———. 1999c. "Monogatari no teikei." In *Nakagami Kenji hatsugen shūsei*, edited by Karatani Kōjin and Suga Hidemi, 6: 223–39. Tokyo: Daisan bunmeisha.

————. 2000. "Ō no shussei no nazo." In *Nakagami Kenji to Kumano*, edited by Karatani Kōjin and Watanabe Naomi, 58–75. Tokyo: Ōta shuppan.

————. 2004. "Gendai shosetsu no hōhō." *Kumano shi* 5: 3–61.

————. 2012. "Kakuzai no sedai no fukō." In *Bessatsu Taiyō: Nakagami Kenji*, edited by Takazawa Shūji, 174–75. Tokyo: Heibonsha.

Nakagami Kenji and Abe Kin'ya. 1995. "Chūsei yōroppa, hisabetsumin, Kumano." In *Nakagami Kenji hatsugen shūsei*, edited by Karatani Kōjin and Suga Hidemi, 2: 45–65. Tokyo: Daisan bunmeisha.

Nakagami Kenji and Jacques Derrida. 1996. "Kegare to iu koto." In *Nakagami Kenji hatsugen shūsei*, edited by Karatani Kōjin and Suga Hidemi, 3: 9–35. Tokyo: Daisan bunmeisha.

Nakagami Kenji and Hasumi Shigehiko. 1980. "Seido to shite no monogatari." In *Nakagami Kenji zenhatsugen*, 2: 175–212. Tokyo: Shūeisha.

Nakagami Kenji and Karatani Kōjin. 1979. *Kobayashi Hideo o koete*. Tokyo: Kawade shobō shinsha.

————. 1997. "Roji no shōshitsu to ryūbō." In *Nakagami Kenji hatsugen shūsei*, edited by Karatani Kōjin and Suga Hidemi, 4: 316–52. Tokyo: Daisan bunmeisha.

————. 2011. "Bungaku no genzai o tou." In *Karatani Kōjin Nakagami Kenji zentaiwa*, 7–51. Tokyo: Kōdansha.

Nakagami Kenji and Kojima Nobuo. 1995. "Chi to fūdo no kongen o terasu: 'Chi no hate shijō no toki' o megutte." In *Nakagami Kenji hatsugen shūsei*, edited by Karatani Kōjin and Suga Hidemi, 1: 255–67. Tokyo: Daisan bunmeisha.

Nakagami Kenji and Minakami Tsutomu. 1980. "Fūdo to shutsuji no uta." In *Nakagami Kenji zenhatsugen*, 2: 163–74. Tokyo: Shūeisha.

Nakagami Kenji, Minakami Tsutomu, and Yasuoka Shōtarō. 1999. "Ningen no 'ne' ni fumikomu." In *Nakagami Kenji hatsugen shūsei*, edited by Karatani Kōjin and Suga Hidemi, 6: 77–120. Tokyo: Daisan bunmeisha.

Nakagami Kenji and Murakami Haruki. 1985. "Shigoto no genba kara." *Kokubungaku* 30 (3): 6–30.

Nakagami Kenji, Noma Hiroshi, and Yasuoka Shōtarō. 1999. "Shimin ni hisomu sabetsu shinri." In *Nakagami Kenji hatsugen shūsei*, edited by Karatani Kōjin and Suga Hidemi, 6: 9–61. Tokyo: Daisan bunmeisha.

Nakagami Kenji and Ōe Kenzaburō. 1980. "Tayōka suru gendai bungaku." In *Nakagami Kenji zenhatsugen*, 2: 475–513. Tokyo: Shūeisha.

Nakagami Kenji and Ogawa Kunio. 1981. "Yami no chikara: Dionisosu o motomete." In *Nakagami Kenji zenhatsugen*, 1: 39–66. Tokyo: Shūeisha.

Nakagami Kenji and Usha Subraminian. 1993. "Interview: Usha Subraminian." In *America, America*, 208–24. Tokyo: Kadokawa shoten.

Nakagami Kenji and Takahashi Toshio. 1996. "Roji to shinwa teki sekai no kōgaku." In *Nakagami Kenji hatsugen shūsei*, edited by Karatani Kōjin and Suga Hidemi, 5: 87–106. Tokyo: Daisan bunmeisha.

Nakahami Kenji and Tanigawa Gan. 1995. "Taishō kōdōtai to roji no ronri: mu no zōkei o megutte." In *Nakagami Kenji hatsugen shūsei*, edited by Karatani Kōjin and Suga Hidemi, 2: 9–44. Tokyo: Daisan bunmeisha.

Nakagami, Kenji and Tomioka Takao. 1996. "Hatsunetsu suru Ajia." In *Nakagami Kenji hatsugen shūsei*, edited by Karatani Kōjin and Suga Hidemi, 5: 230–35. Tokyo: Daisan bunmeisha.

Nakagami Kenji and Yasuoka Shōtarō. 1980. "Sakaguchi Ango to gendai." In *Nakagami Kenji zenhatsugen*, 2: 349–65. Tokyo: Shūeisha.

Nakagami Kenji and Yomota Inuhiko. 1996. "Tensei, monogatari, tennō: Mishima Yukio o megutte." In *Nakagami Kenji hatsugen shūsei*, edited by Karatani Kōjin and Suga Hidemi, 2: 265–309. Tokyo: Daisan bunmeisha.

Nakagami Kenji and Yoshimoto Takaaki. 2005. "Bungaku to genzai." In *Nakagami Kenji mishūroku tairon shūsei*, edited by Takazawa Shūji, 48–81. Tokyo: Sakuhinsha.

Nakagami Kenji, Yoshimoto Takaaki, and Mikami Osamu. 1990. *Kaitai sareru basho*. Tokyo: Shūeisha.

Nakagami Nori. 2017. *Tengu no kairo*. Tokyo: Chikuma shobō.

Nakazawa Shin'ichi. 1995. "Ongaku ga kaku." In *Nakagami Kenji zenshū: Geppō*, edited by Karatani Kōjin, Asada Akira, Yomota Inuhiko, and Watanabe Naomi, 5: 1–2. Tokyo: Shūeisha.

Neary, Ian. 2009. "Burakumin in Contemporary Japan." In *Japan's Minorities: The Illusion of Homogeneity*, edited by Michael Weiner, 59–83. New York: Routledge.

———. 2010. *The Buraku Issue in Modern Japan: The Career of Matsumoto Jiichirō*. London: Routledge.

Noguchi Michihiko. 2000. *Buraku mondai no paradaimu tenkan*. Tokyo: Akashi shoten.

———. 2001. "Nakagami Kenji no roji to buraku mondai." *Kaihō kenkyū Shiga* 11: 75–93.

Noma Hiroshi. 1971. *Seinen no wa.* Tokyo: Kawade shobō shinsha.

Ōe Kenzaburō. 1994. *Man'en gan'nen no futtobōru.* Tokyo: Kōdansha bungei bunko.

Oguma Eiji. 2005. *"Minshu" to "aikoku": Sengo nihon no nashonarizumu to kōkyōsei.* Tokyo: Shin'yōsha.

Okada Tōru. 2017. "Roji no koe chichi no koe: Nakagami Kenji o saga-shite." Unpublished lecture presented at Cultural Typhoon 2017, Waseda University, Tokyo, June 25.

Okeya Hideaki. 1985. "Kyozetsu no nashonarizumu." In *Yoshimoto Takaaki o "yomu,"* 74–90. Tokyo: Gendai kikaku shitsu.

Okuribito. 2008. Directed by Takita Yōjirō. Shōchiku.

Ono Yoshie. 1985. "Nakagami Kenji, Murakami Haruki: Futatsu no jazu, futatsu no amerika." *Kokubungaku* 30 (3): 79–87.

Orikuchi Shinobu. 2017. *Nihon bungaku no hassei josetsu.* Tokyo: Kadokawa.

Osada Hiroshi. 1965. *Warera shinsen na tabibito: Shishū.* Tokyo: Shichōsha.

Osaki, Tomohiro. 2016. "New Law to Fight Bias against 'Burakumin' Seen Falling Short." *Japan Times,* December 19.

Ōtsuka Eiji. 2011. *Imōto no unmei: Moeru kindai bungakusha tachi.* Tokyo: Shichōsha.

Philippi, Donald L. 1977. "Appendix A: Additional Notes." In *Kojiki,* 397–425. Tokyo: University of Tokyo Press.

Price, John. 1972. "A History of the Outcaste. Untouchability in Japan." In *Japan's Invisible Race: Caste in Culture and Personality,* edited by George De Vos and Hiroshi Wagatsuma, 6–30. Berkeley, CA: University of California Press.

Sakka Nakagami Kenji no sekai. 1966. Documentary film broadcasted by NHK.

Said, Edward W. 1988. "Foreword." In *Selected Subaltern Studies,* edited by Ranajit Guha and Gayatri Chakravorty Spivak, v–x. Oxford: Oxford University Press.

———. 1995. *Orientalism.* New York: Penguin Books.

———. 1996. *Representations of the Intellectual: The 1993 Reith Lectures.* New York: Vintage Books.

Saigō Nobutsuna. 1973. *Kojiki kenyū.* Tokyo: Miraisha.

Saitō Minako. 2009. "Feminizumu bungaku hihyō o 'yomu/manabu/kaku' tame ni." In *Shinpen Nihon no feminizumu 11: Feminizumu bungaku hihyō,* 1–30. Tokyo: Iwanami shoten.

Saitō Naoko. 2017. *Kekkon sabetsu no shakaigaku.* Tokyo: Keisō shobō.

Sanford, James H. 1977. "Shakuhachi Zen: The Fukeshu and Komuso." *Monumenta Nipponica* 32 (4): 411–40.

Sartre, Jean-Paul. 1948. *Existentialism and Humanism.* Translated by Philip Mairet. North Yorkshire: Methuen.

Satō Haruo. 1958. *Wanpaku jidai.* Tokyo: Keirinsha bunko.

Satō Yasutomo. 2012. "Sen'nen no yuraku." In *Bessatsu Taiyō: Nakagami Kenji*, edited by Takazawa Shūji, 98–99. Tokyo: Heibonsha.

Sayama: Mienai tejō o hazusu made. 2013. Directed by Kim Sungwoong. Eiga Sayama seisaku iinkai.

Sedgwick, Eve Kosofsky. 1990. *Epistemology of the Closet.* New York: Columbia University Press.

———. 1992. *Between Men: English Literature and Male Homosocial Desire.* New York: Columbia University Press.

Seki Reiko. 2009. "Ane no chikara—Higuchi Ichiyō yori." In *Shinpen Nihon no feminizumu 11: Feminizumu bungaku hihyō*, 109–15. Tokyo: Iwanami shoten.

Sen'nen no yuraku. 2012. Directed by Wakamatsu Kōji. Wakamatsu Production.

Sengo 70 nen Nippon no shōzō: Prologue. 2015. Documentary film broadcasted by NHK.

Sim, Stuart. 2002. "Postmodernism and Philosophy." In *The Routledge Companion to Postmodernism*, edited by Stuart Sim, 3–14. London: Routledge.

Shueller, Malini Johar. 2011. "Cross-Cultural Identification, Neoliberal Feminism, and Afghan Women." https://www.colorado.edu/genders archive1998-2013/2011/04/01/cross-cultural-identification-neo liberal-feminism-and-afghan-women (accessed March 19, 2019).

Someya Masahiro. 2009. "Mai hōmu no yuku e: Jūtaku ga urenai riyū." *Asahi shinbun*, October 9.

Sōmuchō. 1995. *Heisei gonendo dōwa chiku jittai haaku to chōsa kekka no gaiyō.* Tokyo: Sōmuchōkan kanbō chiiki kaizen taisakushitsu.

Sophocles. *Sophocles' Antigone.* 2000. Translated by Marianne McDonald. London: Nick Hern Books.

———. *Sophocles, Volume II. Antigone. The Women of Trachis. Philoctetes. Oedipus at Colonus.* 1994. Translated by Hugh Lloyd-Jones. Cambridge, MA: Harvard University Press.

————. *The Antigone of Sophocles in Greek and English*. 1894. Translated by Richard C. Jebb. Boston: Ginn.

Spivak, Gayatri Chakravorty. 1976. "Translator's Preface." In Jacques Derrida, *Of Grammatology*, 11–87. Baltimore, MD: Johns Hopkins University Press.

————. 1988a. "Can the Subaltern Speak?" In *Marxism and the Interpretation of Culture*, edited by Cary Nelson and Lawrence Grossberg, 271–313. Campaign: University of Illinois Press.

————. 1988b. "Subaltern Studies: Deconstructing Historiography." In *Selected Subaltern Studies*, edited by Ranajit Guha and Gayatri Chakravorty Spivak, 21–24. Oxford: Oxford University Press.

————. 1988c. *In Other Worlds: Essays in Cultural Politics*. New York: Routledge.

————. 1990. *The Post-Colonial Critic: Interviews, Strategies, Dialogues*. Edited by Sarah Harasym. New York: Routledge.

————. 1999. *A Critique of Postcolonial Reason: Toward a History of the Vanishing Present*. Cambridge, MA: Harvard University Press.

————. 2000. "Translation as Culture." *Parallax* 6 (1): 13–24.

Spivak, Gayatri Chakravorty, and Alfred Arteaga. 1996. "Bonding in Difference, Interview with Alfred Arteaga (1993–94)." In *The Spivak Reader*, edited by Donna Landry and Gerald M. MacLean, 15–28. New York: Routledge.

Spivak, Gayatri Chakravorty, and Suzana Milevska. 2006. "Resistance that Cannot Be Recognized as Such." In Gayatri Chakravorty Spivak, *Conversations with Gayatri Chakravorty Spivak*, 57–86. Calcutta: Seagull Books.

Spivak, Gayatri Chakravorty, Kazuko Takemura, and Fumie Ōhashi. 2008. "A Conversation with Gayatri Chakravorty Spivak: Spivak Colloquium at Ochanomizu University." *F-Gens Jānaru* 10: 122–37.

Stokes, Henry Scott. 1975. *The Life and Death of Yukio Mishima*. London: Peter Owen.

Strinati, Dominic. 1995. *An Introduction to Theories of Popular Culture*. New York: Routledge.

Suga Hidemi. 1999. *Puchiburu kyūshinshugi hihyō sengen: 90 nendai bungaku kaidoku*. Tokyo: Yotsuya raundo.

————. 2000. "Kaisetsu: Chichi goroshi no gyakusetsu." In Nakagami Kenji, *Chi no hate shijō no toki*, 663–69. Tokyo: Shōgakkan bunko.

————. 2003. *Kakumei teki na, amari ni mo kakumei teki na: 1968 nen no kakumei shiron.* Tokyo: Sakuhinsha.

Sugayama Shinji. 2000. "Genzai ni ikiru shūdan shūshoku." *UP* 332: 34–38.

Sugimoto, Yoshio. 2014. *An Introduction to Japanese Society.* Cambridge: Cambridge University Press.

Sumii Sue. 1993. *Hashi no nai kawa.* 7 vols. Tokyo: Shinchō bunko.

Suzuki, Tomi. 1996. *Narrating the Self: Fictions of Japanese Modernity.* Stanford, CA: Stanford University Press.

Tainaka Ichirō. 1977. "'Kōsei saiban yōkyū' to itteiru ga, 'kaidō' no 'Sayama tōsō' no hatan to gaiaku." *Shinbun Akahata,* December.

Takayama Fumihiko. 2007. *Erekutora: Nakagami Kenji no shōgai.* Tokyo: Bungei shunjū.

Takayashiki, Masahito. 2007. "Autonomy In Modern Japanese Literature." PhD diss., University of Sydney.

Takazawa Shūji. 1998. *Hyōden: Nakagami Kenji.* Tokyo: Shūeisha.

————. 2002. *Nakagami Kenji Jiten: ronkō to shuzai nichiroku.* Tokyo: Kōbunsha 21.

Takeuchi Rizō and Takayanagi Mitsutoshi. 1994. *Kadokawa nihon shi jiten.* Tokyo: Kadokawa Shoten.

Tansman, Alan. 1998. "History, Repetition, and Freedom in the Narratives of Nakagami Kenji." *Journal of Japanese Studies* 24 (2): 257–88.

Tamai Aoi. 2006. "'Iyo no Matsuyama kyōdai shinjū' zatsuroku." *Shinshin* 2 (March): 2–21.

Tamanoi, Mariko Asano. 1998. *Under the Shadow of Nationalism: Politics and Poetics of Rural Japanese Women.* Honolulu: University of Hawai'i Press.

Tanigawa Gan. 1985. "Shomin: Yoshimoto Takaaki." In *Yoshimoto Takaaki o "yomu,"* 29–42. Tokyo: Gendai kikaku shitsu.

Teraki Nobuaki. 1991. "Kii koku Saika gun ni okeru ichi kawata Buraku no seiritsu: Saika ikkō ikki to no kanren no kentō." *Buraku kaihō kenkyū* 81 (August): 54–81.

————. 1998. "The Buraku Question." *Buraku Liberation News* 104 (September), http://www.blhrri.org/old/blhrri_e/news/new104/new10402.htm (accessed March 19, 2019).

Teramoto Satoru. 1992. "Suiheisha jidai no omoide." *Buraku kaihō* (May): 94–106.

Thelle, Anne Helen. 2010. *Negotiating Identity: Nakagami Kenji's Kiseki and the Power of the Tale.* Munich: Iudicium.

The Ten Thousand Leaves: A Translation of the Man'yōshū, Japan's Premier Anthology of Classical Poetry. 1981. Translated by Ian Hideo Levy. Princeton, NJ: Princeton University Press.

Tipton, Elise K. 2008. *Modern Japan: A Social and Political History.* London: Taylor and Francis.

"Tochi sabetsu chōsa o kisei: 10.1 Osaka fu de kaisei jōrei ga sekō." 2011. *Kaihō shinbun.* November 7.

Tomioka Taeko, Ueno Chizuko, and Ogura Chikako. 1992. *Danryū bungaku ron.* Tokyo: Chikuma shobō.

Tomonaga Kenzō. 2005. "Buraku chimei sōkan jiken hakkaku kara genzai e no kiseki: Sabetsu teppai ni muke, gutaiteki na jōken o tsumiageru." *Sōzō* 14: 4–5.

Tomotsune, Tsutomu. 2003. "Nakagami Kenji and the Buraku Issue in Postwar Japan." *Inter-Asia Cultural Studies* 4 (2): 220–31.

Tomotsune Tsutomu. 2010. *Datsu kōseiteki hanran: Yoshimoto Takaaki, Nakagami Kenji, Jia Zhangke.* Tokyo: Ibunsha.

Tsuchida Ryūhei. 2005. "Kōdo seichō to shūdan shūshoku: chūsotsusha shūshoku kōzō no bunseki." *Tōhoku kōeki bunka daigaku sōgō kenkyū ronshū.* Bessatsu (Extra Issue): 117–52.

Tsujimoto Masanori. 1999. *Kegare ishiki to buraku sabetsu o kangaeru.* Osaka: Kaihō shuppansha.

Tsujimoto Yūichi. 1999. "Nakagami bungaku ni okeru Ise, Matsuzaka no isō." In *Iseshima to kindai bungaku,* edited by Hamakawa Katsuhiko and Handa Yoshinaga. Osaka: Izumi shoin.

Uchida Ryūshi. 2009. "Buraku mondai ni mukiau wakamono tachi." *Buraku kaihō* 618: 12–59.

———. 2011a. "Buraku mondai ni mukiau wakamono tachi." *Buraku kaihō* 639: 12–59.

———. 2011b. "Toshigata Buraku ni okeru rōdō seikatsu to aidentitī: 2009 nen Sumiyoshi chiiki rōdō jittai chōsa kara." *Buraku kaihō* 641: 78–86.

———. 2011c. "Buraku mondai ni mukiau wakamono tachi." *Buraku kaihō* 648: 12–47.

———. 2014. *Buraku mondai ni mukiau wakamono tachi.* Osaka: Kaihō shuppansha.

Ueda Akinari. 1972. *Tales of Moonlight and Rain: Japanese Gothic Tales.* Translated by Kenji Hamada. New York: Columbia University Press.

Uehara Yoshihiro. 2017. *Nihon no roji o tabisuru.* Tokyo: Bunshun bunko.

Ueno Chizuko. 2006. "Nakagami Kenji to 'kemono' ganbō." In *Onna to iu kairaku*, 18–20. Tokyo: Keisō shobō.

―――. 2013. *"Onna" no shisō: Watashi tachi wa anata o wasurenai*. Tokyo: Shūeisha International.

Uesugi Satoshi. 2010. *Korede nattoku! Buraku no rekishi: Zoku watashi no daigaku kōza*. Osaka: Kaihō shuppansha.

Uramoto Yoshifumi. 2011. *Renzoku tairyō sabetsu hagaki jiken: Higaisha to shite no hokori o kaketa tatakai*. Osaka: Kaihō shuppansha.

Wakamatsu Tsukasa and Mizuuchi Toshio. 2001. "Wakayama ken Shingū shi ni okeru dōwa chiku no hen'yō to Nakagami Kenji." *Ōsaka shiritsu daigaku: Jinken mondai kenkyū* 1: 55–93.

Watanabe Naomi. 1994. *Nihon kindai bungaku to "sabetsu."* Tokyo: Ōta shuppan.

―――. 1996. *Nakagami Kenji ron: Itoshisa ni tsuite*. Tokyo: Kawade shobō.

―――. 1999. *Fukei bungaku ron josetsu*. Tokyo: Ōta shuppan.

Yamamoto Kōji. 2009. *Kegare to ōharae*. Osaka: Kaihō shuppansha.

Yanagita Kunio. 1990. *Yanagita Kunio zenshū*. 32 vols. Tokyo: Chikuma bunko.

Yang Sok-il. 1995. *Yami no sōzōryoku*. Osaka: Kaihō shuppansha.

Yokochi Samuel, Yoshiko. 2008. "The Marvellous in the Real Image of Burakumin in Nakagami Kenji's Kumano Saga." In *Transcultural Japan: At the Borderland of Race, Gender and Identity*, edited by David Blake Willis and Stephen Murphy-Shigemitsu, 181–96. London: Routledge.

Yomota Inuhiko. 1996. *Kishu to tensei: Nakagami Kenji*. Tokyo: Shinchōsha.

Yoshimoto Takaaki. 1974. *Yoshimoto Takaaki zen chosakushū*, edited by Kawakami Haruo. 15 vols. Tokyo: Keishō shobō.

Zimmerman, Eve. 1999a. "In the Trap of Words: Nakagami Kenji and the Making of Degenerate Fictions." In *Ōe and Beyond: Fiction in Contemporary Japan*, edited by Stephan Snyder and Philip Gabriel, 130–52. Honolulu: University of Hawai'i Press.

―――. 1999b. "Translator's Preface." In *The Cape and Other Stories from the Japanese Ghetto*, ix–xiii. Berkeley, CA: Stone Bridge Press.

―――. 2007. *Out of the Alleyway: Nakagami Kenji and the Poetic of Outcaste Fiction*. Cambridge, MA: Harvard University Press.

Index

CPSIA information can be obtained
at www.ICGtesting.com
Printed in the USA
LVHW090039210220
647520LV00001B/6/J